THE RELIGION OF TIBET

THE RELIGION OF TIBET

BY

SIR CHARLES BELL

GYAN

ISBN : 978-81-212-1702-6(HB)

First Published, 1931

Published, 2018

Published by

Gyan Publishing House
5, Ansari Road
Daryaganj, New Delhi-110002
Phone: 011-47034999, 9811692060
www.gyanbooks.com
E-mail: books@gyanbooks.com

Printed at: G. Print Process, Delhi.

THE PAN-CHEN RIM-PO-CHE (THE TA-SHI LAMA)

This portrait, painted by a leading Tibetan artist, was presented to the author by the PAN-CHEN RIM-PO-CHE, *who himself wrote the above gold letters (His Holiness's name and titles), and affixed his seal*

PREFACE

THIS book attempts to describe firstly, how Buddhism, in a late and strange form, came to Tibet and was there developed to suit the needs of an exceptional country and people; and secondly, how, for several centuries and down to the present day, it dominates the Tibetan nation. About three-fourths of the material set out in these pages is new; i.e. valuable books and manuscripts given me by the Dalai Lama, the Pan-chen Rim-po-che (Ta-shi Lama), and others, as well as conversations with leading Tibetans in Lhasa and elsewhere. So many are interested in Buddhism, and so little is known of the inner workings of its Tibetan adaptation, that the subject may perhaps prove acceptable to a circle of readers.

I write Tibetan names and other words as they are pronounced in the central province round Lhasa. Tibetan spelling does not represent the modern pronunciation in any part of Tibet. But for a few of the names, &c.—the more important ones—I have entered the spelling in Tibetan script in the footnotes. There are several competing systems of transliteration into the roman character, but none are quite satisfactory, and students of things Tibetan may therefore prefer to have these words in Tibetan itself.

The illustrations, except one, are my own. This one, the frontispiece, I owe to His Holiness the Pan-chen Lama himself. My indebtedness in other fields is, I hope, made clear in the text.

C. B.

CONTENTS

PART ONE: HOW IT CAME

PART TWO: HOW IT RULES

LIST OF ILLUSTRATIONS

LIST OF MAPS

NOTE

THE Tibetan words romanized in this book should be pronounced as in English, subject to the following limitations and exceptions:

a when ending a word or syllable, as the *a* in *father*, e.g. *tsa-tsa*. Otherwise, as *u* in *rub*, e.g. *Cham*, pronounced like the English word *chum*.

e when ending a word or syllable, as *é* in French, e.g. *Rim-po-che*, *Drepung*. Otherwise, as in English, e.g. *Den-sa* as in English word *den*.

ö as *eu* in French *peu*.

u as *oo* in *root*.

ü as *u* in French *sur*.

ai as *eye*.

ny as the initial sound in *nuisance*.

ng and *ts* as in English. They are frequently used in Tibetan to begin words. Say *coming in*, eliminating the first four letters *comi*. Similarly, *weights*, eliminating *weigh*.

Hyphens have been inserted in Tibetan words throughout the book to show where syllables end.

Chu. A river.

Dzong. A fort, the head-quarters of a Tibetan district. In it resides the *Dzong-pön* with his staff.

Dzong-pön, i.e. 'Governor of Fort'. The Tibetan official in charge of the fort and district. In ordinary districts one holds sole charge; in important districts two exercise joint control.

Ku-sho. Honorific form of address applied to the aristocracy and especially to officials.

La. A mountain pass.

Lama. Europeans and Indians apply this word indiscriminately to all monks or priests, but Tibetans themselves reserve it for two classes of priests:

(*a*) Incarnations of deities or of those who in their past lives have attained to Buddhahood.

(*b*) Those who by their great knowledge and religious devotion, e.g. long meditation in caves, have raised themselves far above the mass of priests. One of this latter class is known as a 'Self-made Lama'.

Tsang-po. A large river.

Tso or *Nor*. A lake. *Tso* is the Tibetan, *Nor* the Mongol word.

PART ONE

HOW IT CAME

I

A HIDDEN LAND

As far as any nation can do so, Tibet lives alone. To the east tumbled mountain ranges and the deep gorges of some of the world's largest rivers fence off the lowlands of China. Those who would go from the south or west must needs push their way through the mass of the Himalaya, highest of all mountain ranges on the earth. To the north, still more severe, the arctic wastes of the great Northern Plateau—hundreds of miles across and more than a thousand miles in length—freeze out the strangers from more hospitable lands. Within these bounds dwells Tibet—dwells and broods in the heart of old Asia.

It has indeed been a hidden land. The Chinese pilgrims who crossed the continent and made their records of India during the fifth and the seventh centuries of the Christian era found no way through Tibet. The great Mongol invasions of the thirteenth century touched the Blue Lake (Koko Nor) in the north-eastern corner and some of the eastern districts, but penetrated no farther, though Tibet was their neighbour and their conquests in Hungary, Russia, Finland, and India were thousands of miles away. And Marco Polo in his wide wanderings explored Asiatic countries far and near, but did not penetrate Tibet.

Lying between twenty-seven and thirty-seven degrees north of the equator, at an altitude, mostly, of ten to twenty thousand feet above the level of the sea, the country is very cold, with a hot sun during three or four months in the summer. The wind, from eleven in the forenoon till after sunset, is violent and unceasing except during the warm season. From July to September the monsoon rain-clouds drench the plains of India. They dash themselves against the wall of the Himalaya; it is but a trickle, however, that surmounts the great range and goes forward into the Tibetan uplands. The annual rainfall is usually less than ten inches in the year; frequently no rain or snow falls for six months. The cold, clear air is as dry as the air of the desert.

So here we have a land, larger than France, Germany, Great Britain, Spain, and Italy combined, dry, cold, and comparatively infertile. Wide, treeless plains and broad, stony valleys are ringed round by mountains, yellow and grey, which divide district from district, and yet weld it all into one great homogeneous whole. It is a land of peasants, traders, brigands, beggars, but, most of all, a land of nomads driving their flocks and herds from one scanty pasturage to another.

No doubt Tibet used to spill over from time to time into neighbouring territories, but it is many centuries since this movement has come to an end. A diminishing population feels no need to annex other lands, or to emigrate into them. And neighbouring peoples have overflowed into it hardly at all. The Chinese, indeed, have done so a little on the eastern and north-eastern borders, where the uplands dip down gradually into the low hills of western China and the grass plains of Mongolia. But on its southern frontier the abrupt fall of the Himalaya has prevented any infiltration by the masses of the teeming Indian plains. Here, too, in past ages people of Tibetan stock have, bit by bit, come down and remained in northern and north-eastern India, but not for the last thousand years. Down below, the population may be five hundred to the square mile; up above barely five. But the crowded dweller in the tropics has no wish to live in the arctic solitudes beyond the mountain barrier, a hundred miles away.

Shut off thus from the rest of the world, the Tibetans have remained a homogeneous people. A Tibetan or a Mongol—for the two are closely related—is at once distinguishable from a Chinese; from an Indian he is utterly distinct. But the high mountain ranges that divide and

Tibet behind the Himalayan barrier

subdivide Tibet, coupled with the differences of elevation, climate, and rainfall, prevent full homogeneity, and so we find minor differences in the racial types. In the spoken language the dialects differ greatly, but the written language is everywhere the same.

Originally they were a race of nomads, and they are still very largely so. On the easier mountain slopes, and still more on the great plains which those mountains enclose, you will see the patient shepherds and their black, long-haired dogs, as large as those of the Newfoundland breed, watching their sheep and long-haired goats, their yaks, and other cattle. The nomad's mode of life makes him hardy: his diet is scanty; he does not waste much of his food. Man, indeed, cannot live entirely on the meat and milk products with which his flocks and herds provide him. Grain the Tibetan must have, and even vegetables, but his barley flour, as well as his turnips and radishes—green vegetables are not for him—he must bring from a distance and use sparingly. And, though now a large proportion of the people are peasants, the nomadic instincts still remain. Families are small. Mothers often nurse their children till two or three years old; venereal disease is common and many children die young.

A nomadic people wanders, and if its land is too small for it, may irrupt into the softer agricultural communities on its border, and raid or conquer these. But it does not progress much in the material culture which the more settled communities seek and obtain.

No; its thoughts turn to religion. The wide, open spaces of the earth, deserts and semi-deserts, are the homes of religion. Judaism, Christianity, and Islam all trace their vigorous development to the life of the desert. Buddhism, of the type that has been formed in Tibet and Mongolia, flourishes characteristically in their great expanses, which, though not absolute desert, come near to being so. The dry, cold, pure air stimulates his intellect, but isolation from the cities of men and from other nations deprives the Tibetan of subjects on which to feed his brain. So his mind turns inwards and spends itself on religious contemplation, helped still farther by the monotony of his life and the awe-inspiring scale on which Nature works around him. And, though he be a farmer, he may still often lead the nomad's life to supplement the meagre produce of his farm. There is all the difference in the world between the devout, religious outlook of Tibet and the philosophic materialism of agricultural China.

The faith of the nomad is simple, strong, austere. And so it is with the Tibetan. Pilgrimages are numerous and varied; some unremittingly austere, others more comfortable; yet others tinged with the commercial instinct, which is one of the dominant traits in the Tibetan character. Pilgrimages to Lhasa, the Holy City, exalt the prestige of the Grand Lama—known to some as Dalai Lama, to others as The Precious Protector, The Inmost One, and so on—and consolidate his influence over Tibet, Mongolia, and some of the tribes in China and Russia.

Another full entry in the character sheet of nomads tells of raiding and plunder. Long ago Pliny noted that the Arabs were addicted both to robbery and to trade. And the same holds good of some Tibetan tribes, in many ways religious, whose members may trade abroad peacefully for part of the year and devote themselves to brigandage nearer home for the rest—an orderly arrangement.

Even monks will go on marauding expeditions. The large monastery of Cha-trin in south-eastern Tibet had on its roll many monks who did so, and not once or twice but habitually. And when I was in Lhasa, in 1920, the Dalai Lama and others told me of a Mongol priest who had collected a band of adventurous spirits in the Mongol-Tibetan borderland and was looting all who passed through. 'Mongols', as the Dalai Lama told me, 'are now hardly able to come to Lhasa by the overland routes, and this causes me loss because the Mongols have great faith in me.' In fact, the offerings of devout Mongols bring welcome increase to the Lama's revenues.

This brigand-priest was talking of coming to Lhasa

Members of a robber tribe bringing salt for sale

Se-ra Monastery. High above it are rooms for meditation

Abbots of the Se-ra Monastery

to prostrate himself in worship before the Head of the Faith whose pilgrims he was plundering. But he wished to bring five hundred of his rough band with him. The Lama and his Government were quite willing that he should come, provided that he limited his escort to twenty, a manageable number. Religious devotion—and no doubt offerings—being the objective, there was no question of prohibition or punishment.

As with the Arabs from of old, so with the Tibetans. Many are devoted to robbery, all to trade, while religion overshadows everything. But the gentle teaching of the Buddha has had on the Tibetan a softening influence, such as is not to be found in the teaching of Muhammad.

Since the World War men and women everywhere ask each other, whether some way—somehow—cannot be found to avoid war in future. And the usual reply is that there must be a change of heart among the warring nations. A shrug and a smile; why ask for the impossible? And yet the impossible happened in Tibet, as the influence of Buddhism grew there. Previously they had organized war, raiding and conquering China, Turkistan, India, and Burma. Then it ceased. It was the new religion that made the change of heart that brought the new peace. Buddhism forbids the taking of life. And the Tibetans believe in their religion.

There is with these qualities a natural instinct for orderliness which is strongly marked in Tibet and from which, as we have seen, not even the brigands are altogether exempt. In the religious life this trait has helped Tibet to build up and maintain a complete system of hierarchical government, organized and equipped in every detail.

Yes; religion is the strongest of all influences in the minds of these people.

II

THE OLD FAITH

BEFORE Buddhism came to Tibet, the religion of the people, known to themselves as Pōn[1], appears to have been a form of Shamanism or Nature worship. It is over a thousand years since Buddhism established itself, and it is therefore difficult to give direct evidence as to the form which Shamanism assumed in Tibet. The Tibetan histories pay but little attention to the pre-Buddhist period, regarding it as unworthy of serious attention. Such few references as there are show a belief in spirits of earth and sky, spirits good and bad, the worshipping of the former, and the propitiation of the latter. Magical tambourines were among the necessary equipment of a professor or priest of this religion, enabling him to travel in the sky.

In the official Chinese histories of the fifth and sixth centuries of our era, that is at a time when the Pōnist religion was still in full power, are to be found descriptions of the religious rites of the Tibetans, including human sacrifice.

"The officers (Tibetan) are assembled once every year for the lesser oath of fealty. They sacrifice sheep, dogs, and monkeys, first breaking their legs and then killing them afterwards, exposing the intestines, and cutting them into pieces. The sorcerers having been summoned, they call on the gods of heaven and earth, of the mountains and rivers, of the sun, moon, stars, and planets, saying: "Should your hearts become changed, and your thoughts disloyal, the gods will see clearly and make you like these sheep and dogs." Every three years there is a grand ceremony, during which all are assembled in the night on a raised altar, on which are spread savoury meats. The victims sacrificed are men, horses, oxen, and asses, and

1 བོན་ Rhymes with *turn*.

prayers are offered up in this form: "Do you all, with one heart and united strength, cherish our native country. The god of heaven and the spirit of the earth will both know your thoughts, and if you break this oath, they will cause your bodies to be cut into pieces like unto these victims." '[1]

Of indirect evidence there is a good deal. The Mongols and the Tibetans being in such close affinity, physically and mentally, with each other, we can safely assume that then, as now, their religious beliefs were closely intertwined. And it is less than four hundred years since Sö-nam Gya-tso, the third Dalai Lama, converted the Mongols from their Shamanism to the Tibetan form of Buddhism. We have the records of early European travellers, who knew the Mongols before this conversion occurred. These show pictures of the scene which must, however, be received with caution, owing to the natural bias of those travellers towards the Christian religion.

A similar form of religion was formerly followed by the different tribes of Turkish stock, by the Finns and the Lapps and the peoples who dwelt in the north of Asia on the borders of the Arctic Circle. The Manchus also, and the Indians of North America, who, with the above may all be reckoned in the great Tatar or Mongolian branch of the human race, once held to the same religious system. The pressure of the newer religions, Buddhism, Muhammadanism, and Christianity, has greatly modified the old Shamanism, but it is still possible to recognize it, raising its head, and itself modifying the later religions.

So, too, has it been in Tibet. Buddhism has fought the Pönist beliefs throughout its thousand-year occupation of the Tibetan tablelands. It is fighting them still, as I have myself witnessed. But, while fighting, it has often compromised, so that now we have a mixture of the two. Therefore in Tibetan Buddhism itself we can in some measure understand what the beliefs of Pön were.

And yet there is difficulty. For the Buddhism that came

[1] *Journal of the Royal Asiatic Society*, 1880, p. 441.

to Tibet was full of Tantrik rites, and many of the departures from the original Buddhism are due to these. No doubt it was found that these Tantrik spells and charms were more akin to, and therefore exercised greater influence over, these nature-worshippers than did the cold logic of the Buddha's teaching. Nature works on an awe-inspiring scale among the massive mountain ranges and the wide plains of Tibet. Philosophical disquisitions failed to soothe or satisfy the primitive shepherds and herdsmen in their solitudes. Spirits were everywhere, some good but many evil, in trees, under rocks, in rivers and lakes, in the sky, in the middle air, under the earth. They must be propitiated by visible means and strong. Is a pass to be crossed? The spirits of the place must be worshipped with an offering of a stone, a rag, a branch, &c. Is a journey to be made? A soothsayer must be consulted to see whether it will turn out well. Is fortune consistently unkind? A sorcerer, or sorceress, will arrange good luck instead of bad. For the crops rain must be brought, and hail averted.

Thus divination, expelling the devils who bring sickness and other ills, propitiation of various spirits, sacrifices of animals, and even of human beings, were among the fundamentals of the old Pönist faith. There were no monasteries or nunneries, no monks or nuns, no temples or chapels, though nowadays these are so numerous as to dominate every inhabited Tibetan district. Those of us who have lived in the eastern Himalaya know something of the religious rites of the Lepchas, Limbus, and other aborigines, that cling to those towering mountain sides with their torrential rain and teeming vegetation. It is probable that in those rites we have to this day a survival of the Pönist religion but little changed from its life in Tibet two thousand years ago. And farther east the Lolo, Lissu, and Moso tribes still rule their lives mainly along the old Pönist lines.

The Tibetan histories affirm[1] that the early kings of

[1] *Journal of the Asiatic Society of Bengal*, No. III, 1881, pp. 215, 216.

Tibet from about 300 B.C. to A.D. 400 extended the Pönist religion. As the first recorded king was an Indian, the fifth son of the king of Kosala, it may be that some Brahmanical influences came in. But probably this was slight, for the connexion with India was not maintained during those reigns. Many followers of Pön in Tibet to-day tell one that Pön came originally from Shang-shung, a district said by some to be about one hundred miles north of Lhasa, and by others in western Tibet. It certainly flourishes greatly at the present day in Gya-de and Kong-po, two provinces near the Shang-shung district north of Lhasa. It was largely through aiding Pönist districts against the lamas that the Chinese were enabled to extend their influence in Tibet.

The most famous Tibetan epic or saga is that of Ke-sar,[1] king of the Ling country, a tract of country which my Tibetan acquaintances described as inhabited by agriculturists and situated in eastern Tibet or western China, preferably the former. One of the main episodes tells how the King of Hor, the great grazing area of north-central Tibet, carried off Ke-sar's wife. It relates the war that followed and Ke-sar's victory. The people of Hor were then—as indeed they are still—simple-minded herdsmen and shepherds, dwelling in the wild: those of Ling were more sophisticated, dwellers in villages and towns.

Ke-sar lived before the introduction of Buddhism into Tibet, or at any rate before its establishment, and the epic accordingly shows the country as it was under the Pönist faith. Those parts of the story which I have seen or heard are often in metre and deal with fighting, hunting, and competing deeds of prowess. Though there are occasional copies in manuscript, it is chiefly conveyed through recitation, and among those who recite it in central Tibet, one must assign the predominance to eastern Tibetans and the herdsmen of the northern uplands. Both men and women

1 ཀེ་སར་

recite, and some can recite for ten days without repeating themselves. Tibetans used to tell me that it is very popular, 'because it tells of war and fighting, the language is forcible and in a tuneful metre, and the epic is very old'.

A woman recited a small part of it to me. 'My father', she told me, 'used to recite the story, keeping the book, which was a large one, open before him. Many people used to come and hear him, including the officials and the landed gentry. Monks came also from their monasteries, because the language is sweet, but they did not stay so long as the others. I was only nine years old when I began to listen. "Stay and hear it", said my father, "it will be useful to you afterwards". So I know much of it by heart, and can recite for several days without repeating.'

She began by reading an account of the birth of Ke-sar.

The people of Ling had no king. So a deputation went to the top of a high mountain and prayed to the king of the gods to send them one. The king of the gods came down in the form of a vulture. They captured and bound him and released him only when he promised to send as king his son a boy of three years old. The latter accordingly came down from the country of the gods, but, as he had hair all over his body, the people did not recognize him as their king. So he returned to god-land. His father asked him why he had returned. He replied that he had been down and danced for three days before the people, but they did not recognize him as their king. 'Still I promised them: so you must go,' his father answered.

After some more of this I said, 'Let us have a recitation, as this part will evidently keep us some time.' 'It would keep us four days,' she replied, and went on to recite the part where Ke-sar, who had taken birth in the land as the son of a poor woman, competes for the hand of a princess. The competitors are told that he who kills the bird which is as large as a yak, has a breast of gold and wings of silver, will marry the princess. His aunt, now in the country of the gods, comes down and tells him what to do. He thus succeeds at the last moment in killing the bird and winning the royal bride.

Yaks carrying earthen pots and sacks of flour

Lepcha women and Tibetan men

This woman recited the epic with a good deal of gesture and with evident pleasure. It was clear that she took a real interest in it and in the personality of Ke-sar.

I will quote a small portion from one of the manuscript copies to show the kind of life and events depicted. A soldier from Ling has captured a spy from Hor, and sings as follows:

The time has arrived and I must sing a song.
He says that there is no one like him in Tibet.
I will show him an example to-day.
As the hawk picks up the Hor chickens on the road,
As an old man catches a flea,
I will hold them between my thumb and forefinger.
If you are powerful, come to me now.
If you kindle a fire, it will burn you.

. . . . .

Oh! ye three brothers, known as the foxes!
Have you any courage? If so, arise!
Oh! thou Sky-god of the White Tent tribe!
If thou possessest power, display miracles!
If the army of one hundred thousand men
Of Hor are brave, let them come forth.
The swords of other men are made of iron;
We do not need swords; our right hands are enough.
We will split the body in the middle, and cut the side into pieces.
Other men use clubs made of wood;
We require no wood; our thumbs and forefingers are enough.
We can destroy by rubbing thrice with our fingers.

. . . .

The blood of the liver will escape from the mouth.
Though we do not injure the skin,
We will take out all the entrails through the mouth.
The man will still be alive, though his heart will come to his mouth.

. . . .

If a skull-drum is to be sounded, it should be shaken like this.[1]
If a *dor-je* is to be held in the hand, this is the proper way.[2]

[1] Lifting up the spy and shaking him.

[2] Holding the spy very tightly, as the *dor-je* (thunderbolt-sceptre) should be held by a Buddhist priest.

If a drum is to be used, this is the way to beat it.[1]
If a rope is to be pulled, it should be pulled like this.
If a skin is to be tanned, it should be tanned like this.
This body with eyes and head
Will be made into a hat for the king of the White Tent tribe.[2]
I offer the heart to the war god of the white people of Ling.

. . . .

Oh! Yellow Hor, wait and listen to me.

Speaking thus, he rained blows upon the man and held his head down, so that he became unconscious and the bones came out of his mouth. He threw the man's right hand with the thumb ring to Me-ru-tse the Butcher. He threw the left leg with the boot to Top-chen. He threw the lungs, liver, and intestines to She-chen. He waved the skin and head over the White Tents of Hor three times. Then he tied them to one side of his body and slowly returned to Ling. When he arrived at the fort of the men of Ling, the heroes praised and comforted him.[3]

There are a few Buddhist references in the above, e.g. to the skull-drum and the *dor-je*. According to my friend, the 'Peak Secretary' (i.e. one of the Dalai Lama's Secretaries, each of whom is known by this title), Ke-sar lived during the reign of To-to-ri Nyen-tsen, in the fourth century of the Christian era. This was near the time when Buddhism was attempting its first entry into Tibet. But the general atmosphere is that of Pön, a race fond of war and of the chase, hardy, daring, savage, boastful, unfeeling. The gentle doctrines of the Buddha had as yet scarcely touched Tibet. Never could they be expected to shatter such a deep-set combination. It is, indeed, remarkable that during these thousand years they have softened the national temperament so far.

According to the head of the Lhe-ding family in Lhasa, 'There are three divisions of the Ke-sar epic, namely, the Hor-ling, the Jang-ling, and the Gya-ling. The last-

[1] Beating him.

[2] The other two tribes are the 'Black Tents' and the 'Yellow Tents'.

[3] The above translation was made for me by Mr. David Macdonald of Yatung, Tibet, from a manuscript copy of the Ke-sar Drung (folio 156) lent to me by Ku-sho Pa-lhe-se [illegible] 'asa.

named is rare. The reciters invoke the heroes of the story, who are believed to enter the bodies of the reciters and tell of their prowess. The epic is chiefly about war.'

After Buddhism was established, the Tibetan histories hardly even mention, much less describe, the wars that occurred; the interest centres on religious happenings. But King Ke-sar is, and will remain, a national hero, for the virile quality of that age still appeals to the Tibetan heart. Tibet, Mongolia, and China, each claims Ke-sar as of its own race. Certainly the temples dedicated to Ke-sar in Lhasa and elsewhere are known to all as 'Chinese Temples' (*Gya-mi Lha-kang*). Mr. Wisdom, however—as the Peak Secretary is named—would have it that 'Ke-sar, though he was the king of Mang-kam in eastern Tibet, is worshipped by the Chinese, because he went to China and drove out the female devils who used to eat human beings and infest western China at that time. That is why his temples in Tibet are popularly called Chinese Temples'.

The Pönist religion prevailed in Tibet without a rival till Buddhism came, first in the sixth century A.D. and more strongly in the seventh and eighth. Nowadays the chief god of Pön is termed 'Kün-tu Zang-po' ('All Good'), and its chief priest Shen-rap Mi-po, also deified, who stands towards Pön in somewhat the same relationship as the Buddha or Padma Sambhava stands towards Tibetan Buddhism. In fact, they now possess gods, demons, and saints, generally resembling those of Tibetan Buddhism, but with different names, these having been imported through Buddhist influence. Pönist monasteries are scattered throughout modern Tibet, but the original Pön knew not a monastery. They, too, are Buddhist innovations.

If one seeks for the nearest approach to the old Pönist faith, he will find it among the aboriginal tribes of the eastern Himalaya and western China; and among Tibetan tribes, such as the people of Po in south-eastern Tibet, who live in close contact with these aborigines or in similar surroundings. The unadulterated Pön, or that which stands nearest to it at the present day, is known in Tibet as 'Black Pön'; the modern compromise with Buddhism as 'White Pön'.

Priests of the Black Pön are greatly dreaded throughout Tibet, and so the central government in the Holy City has set its hand against them. As far as it can do so, it prohibits them from exercising the black art to the injury of others. Some twenty or thirty years ago the Supreme Council stirred the Governors of districts in eastern Tibet to action. Pönist priests, who had harmed villagers seriously by their sorceries, were seized and thrown into the tempestuous rivers of that land.

Still the White Pön, sometimes blacker, sometimes whiter, holds its ground tenaciously throughout most of Tibet, side by side with the Buddhist priesthood. It flourishes in many of the grazing uplands that lie between Lhasa and the Northern Plains (*Chang Tang*), in Gya-de and in Kong-po, throughout eastern Tibet, and especially in the south-eastern districts. In the Upper Chumbi Valley there are four monasteries devoted to Pön. I went over one of these at 'The Knee Ridge' (*Pü-mo Gang*), a branch of one in the province of Kong-po. The officiating priest first showed me a painting resembling Pal-den Lha-mo, the Buddhist goddess who guards Tibet in general, and the Tibetan Government in particular.

'We call her,' he says, 'Pal-den Si-sum Gye-mo, "The Glorious Queen of the Three Worlds". She is the Chief of all deities and the Head of all the worlds. It is she of whom your late Queen was an Incarnation.[1] In her mild aspect[2] she is the Saviour of all mankind. She is more powerful than any of the other deities. No; she cannot be said to be more powerful than the Buddhas, but she is the Mother of all the Buddhas, Kün-tu Zang-po being the Father. Without a mother there can be no son. Her name in her mild aspect is "The Great Mother of Mercy and

[1] This is said also of Pal-den Lha-mo.

[2] In Tibetan Buddhism deities are believed to have mild (*zhi-wa*) and fierce (*trak-po*) aspects, and to vary their actions accordingly.

Love".[1] She rules the whole world, including China, Tibet, Shang-shung, and Li.'

'Where is Li? Some have said that it is Nepal. Is that so?'

'It is beyond western Tibet[2] according to the books. We have not been there. It is not Nepal.

'There are nine Vehicles in Pön, namely, four doors and five repositories. This monastery belongs to "The White 'A' Vehicle", which is the eighth Vehicle, and includes the mystic portion of the doctrine. We practise also the ninth Vehicle, called "The Vehicle than which there is none higher".

'Our religion comes from Shang-shung. The Buddhist religion was imported afterwards from Bodh Gaya in India. The Buddhists pray "Om Ma-ni Pe-me Hun", but we pray "Om Ma-tre Mu-ye Sa-le Du". This is Shang-shung language, and we cannot explain the literal meaning of the words. The secondary meaning is complicated; each syllable has its own meaning.' Here the chief priest pointed out certain deities as represented by the different syllables of the above formula.

I noticed that the images and pictures in the monastery appeared to be similar to those in the Buddhist monasteries, but bore different names; e.g. one resembling Gotama Buddha was called 'Teacher Shen-rap'. The large central image in the chapel was one of Padma Sambhava[3]. Of him the chief priest says, 'The Buddhists say that he was self-produced from a lotus. That is untrue. Everybody has a father and a mother; even the Buddha had. Padma Sambhava was actually born in Shang-shung. He was the younger of two sons.'

The books in the monastery appeared also to be Buddhist. But the titles were different and the contents were altered to some extent to suit Pön. I had, however, time to ask only a few questions about them. The chief

[1] ཡུམ་ཆེན་ཐུགས་རྗེ་བྱམས་པ་ [2] སྟོད་

[3] The native of Udyana (to the north-west of India) who more than any one else introduced early Buddhism into Tibet.

priest appeared to take pride in explaining that Pön was nearly the same as Buddhism, while keen to point out what he described as the errors of Buddhism.

This instance alone, with its kindly deities and teachers and prayers, with its promise of mercy and love, is sufficient to show how far Pön has travelled since the savage days of Ke-sar. Such is the effect of Buddhism on Pön.

At the same time one saw—as indeed one was always seeing—something of the manner in which Pön had impregnated Buddhism before admitting it into the fastnesses of Tibet. For this Pönist monastery had a dispute with a Buddhist Doctor of Divinity[1] from Lhasa, the head and centre of Tibetan Buddhism. Its grievance was that the Doctor had imported into the neighbourhood an oracle,[2] more in accordance with the old Pönist practices and entirely opposed to the teaching of Gotama, the Buddha. And thereby the learned and astute Doctor had drawn a large number of the dwellers in this valley from the Pönist monastery to himself. The dispute had been referred to the Dalai Lama, and the Pönists wished me to use my influence with the Dalai Lama in their favour. It need hardly be recorded that I avoided putting my head into such a hornet's nest.

Is it not true indeed, of every great religion, that it must compromise with its predecessor? Hinduism took freely from the forms of Shamanism that it encountered. Many converts to Muhammadanism in India follow some of the religious practices of their Hindu co-villagers. Buddhism compromised with Hinduism in India, and has taken both from Hinduism and Pön in Tibet. Christianity has adopted many of the pagan rites embodied in the Roman and Celtic beliefs. No religion has thoroughly ousted its predecessor; the shepherd, the villager, the man in the street, could not—in the mass—stand that.

I have suggested above that it is in the aborigines of the

[1] *Ge-she* (དགེ་བཤེས་).

[2] *Chö-je* (ཆོས་རྗེ་).

The Chief Wizard Physician to a former Ruler of Sikkim

eastern Himalaya, rather than in the Buddhists of Tibet, that we can still find some resemblance to the old Pön of two thousand years ago. In Sikkim, for instance, a small Tibetan State now a British Protectorate, to the north of Bengal, the king and most of the leaders are Tibetan and Buddhist, but they are greatly influenced by the older faith. One of the large landed proprietors, whose brother lay seriously ill, employed simultaneously to attend him not only a Tibetan physician, and a Tibetan lama, but also a Lepcha sorcerer, skilled in Pönist ritual.

A Tibetan priest, Shap-trung, fully educated in the religion and literature of his country, a favourite disciple of a high and learned Incarnation, lived for several years in Darjeeling. Now Darjeeling was originally a part of Sikkim, and is still peopled by tribes whose religious beliefs are strongly tinged with Pön. Shap-trung had advised a friend against running counter to the Pönist spirits of the Lepchas. This friend wished to take an Excise post in Darjeeling, where a part of his duty would be to prevent the distillation of liquor in the private houses of the Lepchas. 'You will interfere with these people and with their gods,' the priest warned him. But the desire for money prevailed. He took the post and died soon afterwards. 'These Lepcha spirits', confessed Shap-trung, 'are more potent than our Buddhist spirits.'

A king of Sikkim had died. Not only had he exercised the kingship; he was also a priest, and ranked high in the priesthood. He died a young man, full of vigour, part of which he had devoted to the reform of the Pönist elements in the religion, which he sought to lead into the Way which the Buddha followed. His subjects shook their heads and prophesied calamity.

The low Sikkim valleys are infested with fever germs not less virulent than the worst in India itself. Travelling constantly in these during the unhealthy months, the young reformer contracted malaria of a dangerous type. When illness supervened, he consulted his English doctor, but, unknown to the latter, dosed himself simultaneously with English medicines of his own selection, and sometimes also with Tibetan drugs, the three kinds together. But his people viewed the cause of death differently. Why did he arouse the wrath of the Tiger Spirit? One in close touch with events gave me the story.

'The king had angered the spirits by his new ideas. One evening he was returning to his palace, and, as he drew near, his two greyhounds, which were with him, darted away together as if at some intruder. They charged and retreated, then charged and retreated again, though nobody was visible. The king felt chilly. His attendants told him that the Tiger Spirit must have come and touched him, for, though they could not see him, the dogs had done so. He was advised to have the necessary religious services performed, but his new ideas, according to which he believed that the propitiation of spirits was opposed to true Buddhism, made him refuse. And so the attack of the Tiger Spirit prevailed, and the king died.

'After his death, as is usual in such cases, the mark of the tiger's claw appeared on his body. In his case it was on the left shoulder, a place where it can be cured by due propitiatory rites. If the claw mark is over the heart, nothing will avail: the victim is doomed.'

The above is not the account of a Pönist. It was related by a highly placed Buddhist of Sikkim, and reflects his own unquestioned belief. Most of the leading Sikkimese families, originally of Tibetan descent and nominally Buddhist, keep in their gardens—hidden away—shrines to 'the Sikkim gods'. These are in addition to the orthodox Buddhist images. The reason adduced by a leading member of the State Council to a friend of mine, who lived among the people and knew them well, was simple and conclusive: 'We had better not leave them out; *they are very very old.*'

III

GOTAMA, THE BUDDHA

ALTHOUGH Tibet still clings to many beliefs and practices in her old Shamanistic faith, yet few nations have been influenced more profoundly by the words and the life of the great Teacher, who lived during the sixth century before Christ. Gotama, the Buddha, was one of the warrior, not of the priestly, class. His country was that of the Shakyas, a small republic in which his father was a leading man.[1]

This State lay north of Benares, along what is now the frontier between Nepal and India; the capital, the Buddha's birthplace, being within the present Nepalese frontier. Probably then as now the tract was inhabited by people of Tatar, i.e. Mongoloid, descent, as well as by Aryans; and the former may well have been more numerous in those days when the Tatar pressure on northern India was greater. It seems, therefore, natural that Buddhism should have entered so deeply into the souls of the Tatar nations; it is, indeed, possible that the Buddha himself had Tatar blood in his veins. The word 'Shakya' has itself a Tibetan ring about it. We know, too, that the Buddha set aside the framework of Brahmanical theology and sacrifice, replacing it by one more akin to that of Confucius, who was almost his contemporary.

A web of romance and miracle has been woven round the young man's early home life. His father tried to keep the sadness of life from him. But this proved impossible. One day he met a beggar bowed down with age; on another day a man with a raging fever, on another a dead man borne on a bier. His fourth experience was an ascetic, calm and dignified, and here he recognized an inward peace, a hope of escape from the evils of this world.

This account comes from later records, but one of the early books portrays his feelings as a young man. In this,

[1] *Hinduism and Buddhism*, by Sir Charles Eliot (Arnold), vol. i, p. xxii.

after describing the comfort of his home life, the Buddha goes on to say that he reflected how people feel repulsion at the sight of old age, sickness, and death. 'But is this right? I also,' he thought, 'am subject to decay, and am not free from the power of old age, sickness, and death. Is it right that I should feel horror, repulsion, and disgust when I see another in such a plight? And when I reflected thus, my disciples, all the joy of life, which there is in life, died within me.'[1]

And so, at the age of twenty-nine, the young noble left the pleasures of home, family, and friends behind, and wandered to other lands, a religious mendicant, eating such coarse food as might be put into his little begging-bowl. He went out to seek the riddle of existence, and sought it first, as Indians so often did and do, in a life of stern asceticism. This lasted for six years, till he was at death's door. But the Truth lay not this way. He recalled then how in his earlier youth he had sat in the shade of a rose-apple tree, and entered into the stage of contemplation known as the first rapture. So he took food to recover his strength, and passed through successive stages of contemplation, till at last he came to understand how suffering arises, and the path that leads to its cessation. He knew now that he was free, that he would be reborn no more. He became the Buddha, the Enlightened One.

The last scene was enacted, as tradition tells us, seated under a pipal tree (*Ficus religiosa*), seven miles from Gaya, a town in what is now the province of Bihar in northern India. This, the Bodhi tree, or rather its lineal descendant —for the present tree is quite young—is still to be seen, situated amid peaceful surroundings near the temple at Bodh Gaya. It is the ambition of every Tibetan to make a pilgrimage to Bodh Gaya, and there he will meet Buddhists from Burma, Ceylon, Japan, and other countries. In fact, one seldom visits it, at any rate during the cool season of the year, without meeting reverent Buddhists

[1] Anguttara Nikaya, iii. 35. See Eliot's *Hinduism and Buddhism*, vol. i, p. 134.

Temple at Bodh Gaya

Early Buddhist cave near Gaya

from distant lands, come to see where the foundation of their faith was laid.

And now, having found the Way, the Enlightened One must show it to mankind. This he does in the Deer Park at Benares a few weeks later, preaching his sermon to the five recluses who had lost their faith in him when he abandoned the ascetic life. He begins by saying that those who wish to follow religion must follow the Middle Way, avoiding self-indulgence on the one side and self-mortification on the other.

'There is a Middle Way, O recluses,' he says 'avoiding these two extremes.' . . . 'And which is that Middle Way? Verily it is the Noble Eightfold Path. That is to say:

Right Views (free from superstition or delusion),
Right Aspirations (high, and worthy of the intelligent, earnest man),
Right Speech (kindly, open, truthful),
Right Conduct (peaceful, honest, pure),
Right Livelihood (bringing hurt or danger to no living thing),
Right Effort (in self-training and in self-control),
Right Mindfulness (the active, watchful mind),
Right Rapture (in deep meditation on the realities of life).'[1]

He then enunciates the four Noble Truths, which may be summarized as suffering, the cause of suffering, the suppression of suffering, and the method of effecting that suppression. The cause of suffering is Thirst, 'the craving for the gratification of the passions, or the craving for a future life, or the craving for success in this present life.' And the way which leads to the suppression of this suffering is the Noble Eightfold Path.

The recluses were convinced, and became the Buddha's first disciples. A short sermon, indeed, but one which still mirrors the ideals held by hundreds of millions in the world to-day, two thousand five hundred years after it was preached.

[1] *Buddhism*, by T. W. Rhys Davids (Putnam), p. 137.

It will be noticed that this is a religion of conduct, not of belief; faith alone is not sufficient. By their fruits ye shall know them. And we have here a religion that is intellectual, rather than emotional. The cause of suffering is desire: this desire is due to ignorance. Love is the root of the Christian tree; Wisdom of the Buddhist, with Love as its first offshoot. All cannot gain the knowledge, but all can strive along the Eightfold Path, and so gain the knowledge and the wisdom in a future life.

The law which decides what each rebirth will be, in accordance with a belief held in India before the Buddha's day, is known in India as *karma*, a word meaning *action*. Every event is due, or partly due, to previous causes, and is itself the cause, or partial cause, of future events. So what is done in this life all helps to shape what happens in the next. As to the Buddha's doctrine that there is no self, no ego, and as to what passes at death, I forbear to discuss: it is the root teaching in its simple form that I am trying to express here, for it is that which has influenced the ordinary Tibetan in his, or her, daily life.

The thirst for the things of life, as stated above, causes rebirth after rebirth. The nature of this craving is explained in the Chain of Causation, of which we need only say that ignorance is the first cause, leading on through consciousness, contact, sensation, craving, and other links to birth and death. By ignorance appears to be meant ignorance of the true nature of the world and the true interests of mankind, that brings about the suffering which we see and feel. We were born into the world because of our ignorance in our last birth, and because of the desire for re-existence which was in us when we died.[1] The Buddha says that, if a monk possessed of the necessary good qualities desires to be born in his next life as a noble, or in one of the many heavens, 'then those predispositions and mental conditions, if repeated, conduce to rebirth' in the place he desires. Of one man we are told that when he was dying the spirits of the wood came round his death-

[1] *Hinduism and Buddhism*, by Eliot, vol. i, p. 211.

bed and bade him wish to be an emperor in his next life.[1] Exactly the same view holds in Tibet. During the last year of my time there it was generally held in Lhasa that during my previous life I was a Tibetan lama, who prayed on his death-bed that he might be reborn in some powerful country, so as to be able to help Tibet.[2] A few years before I came to Lhasa one of the highest Tibetan lamas had prayed after the same fashion.

Having followed the Perfect Path, the Buddhist eventually attains the status of an Arhat, that is, the perfected man. This was the aim of the Buddha; it is the central theme of the early Buddhist writings. It may also be called Nirvana, a word used more by Western writers than by Buddhists themselves. We cannot expect to define it, for the Buddha himself refused to do so. It is called deathless, endless, changeless; it implies happiness, but it is even beyond happiness. It is not annihilation, but rather the cessation of a process, like a wave that sinks in the sea. The water remains, the motion remains, but it exists no longer as a wave. As to any theory whether one who has attained nirvana after death exists or does not exist, the Buddha stigmatizes such as 'a jungle, a desert, a puppet show, a writhing, an entanglement, causing sorrow, anger, wrangling, and agony. It does not conduce to distaste for the world, to absence of passion, to the cessation of evil, to peace, to knowledge, to perfect enlightenment, to nirvana'. Nirvana is no more definable than the Christian Heaven.

It would take a long time to describe in detail the inner implications of these doctrines and rules, and the reader, too, might find the description wearisome. But two charges against Buddhism must be noticed.

It is said to be pessimistic. It does, indeed, dwell much on suffering, but it does so in order to explain the way of deliverance from suffering. It goes farther than Christianity in this respect, for it preaches that man, unaided, can effect his own deliverance. There is no pessimism here.

[1] Idem, vol. i, p. 210.

[2] See my *Tibet, Past and Present* (Oxford University Press), p. 205.

Again, Buddhism is often said to be selfish; that each works merely for his own salvation. But it is not so. As in Christianity so in Buddhism, unselfishness is a basis of the moral life. Says the Buddha, 'All good works whatever are not worth one-sixteenth part of the love, which sets free the heart. Love, which sets free the heart, comprises them.'[1] But knowledge, or wisdom, is of at least equal, perhaps greater, importance, for ignorance is the first cause of evil. In any case faith alone cannot save, and here we find Buddhism differing both from Brahmanism and from Christianity. And so we can understand that it is an intellectual rather than an emotional religion, and that it is very tolerant.

The Buddha's attitude to women has been criticized. It is true that he admitted women to his Order only after repeated refusals, and declared that, as a result of their admission, 'the pure religion' would stand fast for only five hundred instead of a thousand years. But his reason for this may have lain in the social system then prevailing in India, for he admitted that they were capable of attaining nirvana. And the solid fact remains that in Buddhist countries women hold a remarkably good position. Burma, Ceylon, Tibet exhibit the same picture. Politically and socially, Tibet is in the condition of Christian Europe in the Middle Ages, but the Tibetan woman's level is, and long has been, consistently higher than what Europe could then show.

Gotama was thirty-five years old when he attained Enlightenment, and so became the Buddha. Wandering over a part of northern India—now comprised in Bihar and the United Provinces—he preached for some forty-five years, dying in his eightieth year, a strong contrast when considered in conjunction with Christ's ministry on earth. Moving from place to place, preaching to the people, but still more instructing his own disciples, building up and strengthening the Order, and deciding each difficulty as it arose, the days passed by. We seem to

[1] *Itivuttaka*, iii. 7.

A Tibetan lady with her maid-servant

A lama of the old sect introduced by Padma Sambhava. His long hair shows that he is not celibate

The monastery of Sam-ye

see a picture of one who was tolerant but authoritative, a born leader with a compelling personal charm of his own.

His teaching did not, as did Christ's, arouse violent opposition, though it differed so greatly from the varying Hindu doctrines of the time. He did not denounce the Brahmans as a class; indeed, he was singularly gentle and tolerant. When he converted a general, who had been a Jain, he permitted him to continue to give food as before to the Jain monks who came to him. He sat by the sacred fire of a Brahman and discoursed, but did not denounce the worship which the Brahman carried on. In Tibet to the present day no feature of Buddhism is more strongly marked than its wide toleration.

The long life of the Buddhist religion is due partly to the lofty teaching of the Eightfold Path, and perhaps still more to the religious Order which Gotama founded. This Order came naturally as an adjunct to the social conditions then existing in India, for it was usual there for a religious man to give up the world and become a wandering mendicant. Later on, large monasteries were founded; in Tibet also in due course they were founded, and endure in great strength to the present day. There might indeed be dissension between Hindus and the early Buddhists, but apparently little, if any persecution; very different from the picture of the Christian Church. And on the whole the sects in Tibetan Buddhism work together more harmoniously than the Christian sects in England to-day.

In the teaching of the Buddha, as in that of Christ, there is no interference in politics, no seeking of temporal authority. But a fundamental difference between the two is found in the attitude towards prayer and sacrifice. The Buddha admits neither. It follows, therefore, that there is no forgiving of sins.

My old friend, the late king of Bhutan, who combined the new and the old with striking success, sent some of his young men to a Church of Scotland school in Kalimpong —a district formerly belonging to Bhutan and now lying to the south-west of that country—to receive education on

Western lines. A Singhalese Buddhist, writing to the Bhutanese Foreign Secretary, took strong objection to Buddhists being trained by 'those who believe in the abominable doctrine of the forgiveness of sins'.

Among laymen the Buddha prescribed abstinence from the five sins of taking life, drinking intoxicants, lying, stealing, and unchastity. And they were to strive for pleasant speech, kindness, temperance, consideration for others, and affection.

Such was the teaching of the Buddha. It became the dominant religion of India during the rule of Asoka in the third century B.C., and was still dominant during the reign of Kanishka in the first century A.D. Later on, it became corrupt, and was pushed out by Hinduism, and the violence of Muslim invaders. It remained longest in Bengal, and also in Bihar where Ikhtiyar-ud-Din Muhammad finally destroyed its power in 1193 by seizing the capital and massacring the Buddhist monks in their monasteries.

IV

BUDDHISM COMES TO TIBET

THESE doctrines of the Buddha appealed, as we have already seen, to the intellect rather than to the emotions of mankind. But, even in India, religious thought moves on continually. New ideas develop, new schools are formed. It is difficult to keep emotionalism out of religion, for it appeals to emotion more easily than to cold reason. And to such changes Buddhism, with its wide tolerance, was especially susceptible.

It would be going too far to say that the early Buddhism was completely free of deities, miracles, &c. The mass of the people at any rate could not go as far as that. But they were reduced to a minimum. The deities, who figure in the early Buddhist books, are mere supernumeraries; they are not an essential part of the life or teaching of the Buddha.

The great Emperor, Asoka, in the third century B.C., made Buddhism the predominant religion in India, and so it continued for four or five hundred years. But as the centuries rolled on, new doctrines, new schools developed in Buddhism as in Hinduism. Each religion influenced the other. In Buddhism two leading schools arose, the Mahayana, or Great Vehicle, and the Hinayana or Little Vehicle. The latter clung more nearly to the older teaching. The Mahayana brought in deities, superhuman beings, ritual, and personal devotion; it was more popular. Chief among these superhuman beings were the Bodhisattvas, those who had almost obtained Buddhahood. It was taught that men should try to become Bodhisattvas on their way to perfect Buddhahood. Bodhisattvas were worshipped, and faith was inculcated, two fundamental departures from the teaching of the Buddha, who did not recognize worship and did not insist on faith.

Mythology grew up round the Buddha. The belief soon arose that other Buddhas had illuminated the world from time to time before Gotama came. Later on, heavenly Buddhas were recognized. They were known as Jinas, and five of them were pre-eminent, among whom the Buddha of Measureless Light (*Ö-pa-me*)[1] is the best known in Tibet. Deities arose, and among these none was more important than the Lord of Mercy, who, under the name of *Chen-re-zi*[2], became in due course the patron deity of Tibet. And hardly less important was the goddess, known to Tibet as *Dröl-ma*, the Deliverer. Others were the Lord of Speech (*Jam-pe-yang*) and, somewhat later, the Holder of the Thunderbolt (*Dor-je Chang*).[3] *Chen-re-zi*, *Jam-pe-yang*, and *Dor-je Chang* form nowadays in Tibet a Trinity of all-powerful deities.

The sanctity of the Buddhist Canon was more and more emphasized, so that many of the texts were regarded as themselves sufficient for salvation. The sacred literature was worshipped. To certain words or formulae were attributed an inherent power; they became potent spells.

Gotama had refused discussion as to how the human race originated and whither it was moving. Questions of this kind he declared to be unprofitable, as being unanswerable by the human mind, and harmful to spiritual progress. But throughout its history India has ever been wont to delve into these dim mysteries. So the restrictions of the Founder were soon disregarded.

We need not here thread the maze of the varied schools and metaphysical discussions, the theory as to the three bodies of the Buddhas, the doctrine of voidness, the thesis as to the unreality of the external world, including—in a sense—the Buddhas themselves. Among the new teachers Nagarjuna, in the second century A.D., was conspicuous.

The gist of the Mahayanic teaching was as follows:

(1) A belief in Bodhisattvas.

(2) A code of ethics which teaches that everybody must do good in the interest of humanity as a whole, and make

[1] འོད་དཔག་མེད་ [2] སྤྱན་རས་གཟིགས་

[3] In order to minimize Oriental names as far as possible I omit the Indian names for these.

over to others all the karma that he may acquire by his virtues.

(3) A doctrine that Buddhas are supernatural beings.

(4) Various schools of metaphysics.

(5) A canon composed in Sanskrit.

(6) Worship of images. Elaborate ritual. Reliance on formulae and charms.

(7) A doctrine that salvation can be gained by having faith in a Buddha, and calling on his name.[1]

How greatly this religion differed from the teaching of the Founder! The doctrine of salvation by faith instead of by works, the belief in supernatural beings, the reliance on images, ritual, and charms, and the abstruse metaphysical discussions, all these were fundamental departures from the life as lived, from the word as spoken, by the Buddha himself. But they were popular; they appealed to the emotions of the many rather than to the intellect of the few.

From time to time high spirits take up the burden of a human life, and set the highest ethical standards, the purest code of moral conduct before the world around them. But who can follow these leaders? Who can live Christ's Sermon on the Mount, or tread the Eightfold Path of the Buddha? To quote only two of the difficulties in the Way, both these teachers praised poverty and celibacy. Not many will follow the first, and if all followed the second, they would end the human race. To hold fully the teaching of the Buddha or Christ is hardly possible except in a cloistered life: the former—appealing, as it did, so strongly to the intellect—called also for keen brains and a long, willing education.

The mass of humanity dwell in the murky valleys far below these moral and intellectual summits. So the Teacher's successors have to lower the standards, if the religion is to spread. And, in lowering these, they must permit some of the very practices, which the Teacher has forbidden.

From the second century of the Christian era, Hinduism

[1] See Eliot's *Hinduism and Buddhism*, vol. ii, p. 6.

increased steadily at the expense of Buddhism. But the invaders, who came to India from the north-west, favoured the Buddhists rather than the Hindus, whose caste restrictions prevented them from mixing freely with foreigners. When Buddhism came to Tibet later on, this north-western territory became one of the strongest links between the religion in Tibet and India.

Large monasteries and universities flourished, and a fuller dependence was placed on monastic discipline than on the old individual devotion to the Eightfold Path. Among the greatest were Nalanda, near Gaya, and Vikramashila, on the north bank of the Ganges, both of which were destined to send teachers and scriptures to Tibet. In the monasteries images were bathed ceremonially. Silk scarves were thrown at them, and omens deduced from the way the scarves fell, as is done in Tibet to this day. Even in the monasteries the doctrines resembled Hinduism rather than the teaching of the Buddha. The pliancy of Buddhism facilitated its conquests in China, Japan, and Tibet, but quickened its decline in India itself.

About the seventh century Tantrism became rife in northern India. Its essence was magic. Those who held to a prescribed ritual could gain salvation by magical methods. He who followed this line sought out a teacher, received initiation from him, and then repaired to a lonely place, and meditated with so strong a concentration as to suppress all thought. This done, he pronounced certain magical formulae, which, like the seed of a plant, grew up into the image of the Bodhisattva, whom he had come to worship. Eventually he himself took the form of the Bodhisattva and became one with him. Self-hypnotism of this and other kinds has often played a large part in Indian religions. Most teachers gained visions of gods and goddesses, and the same claim is made for Tibetan teachers and their disciples in their own country several centuries later.

Tantrism was a mixture of Mahayanism on the one side, and the aboriginal beliefs, the old nature-worship of India, on the other, the latter often coloured by the

Hinduism in which they were set. But the movement went farther still. A Bodhisattva might be represented as accompanied by a female deity, having achieved nirvana because he was united to this goddess. Accordingly, the belief was professed that nirvana, the highest spiritual sphere, was to be gained by sexual union, and this doctrine was followed by many Tantrik adepts.[1]

We have now descended into the depths to which Indian Buddhism had sunk, when it crossed the Himalayan range into the cold plateaux of Tibet. Tradition affirms that during the fourth century A.D. a chest containing Buddhist sacred books and a golden *chaitya* fell from the sky on the roof of the Tibetan king's palace. The king, who was sixty years old, worshipped these heavenly gifts, and therefore lived to the age of a hundred and twenty. It was revealed to him in a dream that his fifth successor would know the meaning of the sacred writings. We are at once in an atmosphere of magic, and in that atmosphere Tibet remains even now. But the Blue Treasury of Records,[2] perhaps the most trustworthy of all Tibetan histories, says that this account originated with a Pönist named 'Rejoicing in the Sky' and was just a Pönist story. 'In actual fact', the Blue Treasury continues, 'a Pandit, Lo-sem-tso, and a Translator, Li-te-se, brought the books. But the king, being illiterate, could not understand their purport, and therefore the Pandit and the Translator returned. This appears to be the pure truth.

. . . . .

'During the time of To-to-ri the religion was first met with. Those religious books were brought, and that was all. There was no writing or reading or explaining. It was during Song-tsen Gam-po's time that Tön-mi Sam-bo-ta was dispatched to India, and there from a teacher learnt well both the writing and the speech. . . . The king also

[1] Eliot, *Hinduism and Buddhism*, vol. ii, pp. 121–6.

[2] Tep-ter Ngön-po (དེབ་ཐེར་སྔོན་པོ). This, and the other histories on which I rely, are described in the chapter, 'Sources', at the end of the book.

devoted a long time to learning the letters. . . . The king himself acted as the head of the religion.'[1]

Song-tsen Gam-po ascended the throne in A.D. 642 when thirteen years of age, and established Lhasa as the capital. Where the Potala palace now stands was known as Red Hill, and here he built a fort, a wall-painting of which—far smaller than the present building—may be seen to this day in one of its ante-chambers. He conquered territories in China and India, and took as his two chief wives a princess from China and a princess from Nepal. These, being Buddhists, were the cause of his conversion to Buddhism. He preached various texts, inculcated the worship of different gods and goddesses, founded hermitages, and built monasteries. But Buddhism is a religion of peace, and Song-tsen was by nature a fighter. Moreover, Pönist opposition was strong. 'At that time,' we are told, 'the subjects began to revile the king. The king heard, and therefore enacted the religious law for the observance of the ten virtuous acts. Accordingly, he was known by the name of Song-tsen Gam-po[2] (i.e. "The Straight, Strong, Deep").' The Chronicle adds that 'he established all the Tibetan people in a state of virtuous life',[3] but we may well question this generous assertion. The Blue Treasury is probably on firmer ground when it asseverates, 'He founded a body of priesthood where a few priests were ordained as a beginning. In other respects he gave a strong religious impulse to the whole of Tibet.'

No doubt he established the foundation. His name is to this day a household word; indeed, he is revered as an Incarnation of Chen-re-zi, the Lord of Mercy, the patron deity of Tibet. Tibetan artists love to depict him turning the Wheel of Religion, with Chen-re-zi's spiritual guide, the Buddha of Boundless Light, on his head. He wears the 'flag-clothes', the white silk robes permitted only to the greatest kings.

[1] Tep-ter Ngön-po, vol. i, fol. 20.   [2] སྲོང་བཙན་སྒམ་པོ་

[3] Pu-tön (བུ་སྟོན་) Rim-po-che's Chö-jung, fol. 111.

Rough painting of Chen-re-zi, in the eleven-headed form, on a rock in Lhasa

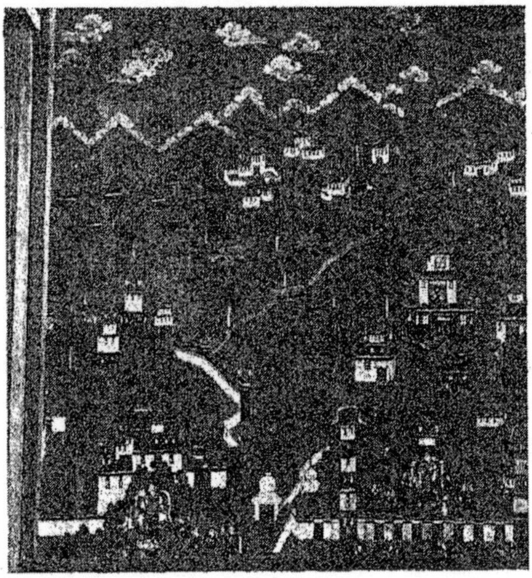

'A wall painting (of the original buildings) may be seen in one of its ante-chambers'

His great-great-grandson, Tri-de Tsuk-ten, is said to have resumed the work of furthering Buddhism by having some of the texts (*sutra*) translated, as well as works on astrology and medicine.[1] He invited Buddhist monks from Ladakh and from China. 'But he did not succeed in making any Tibetan don a monk's robe.' So it is clear that Buddhism had not yet established much of a foothold in Tibet. He was, however, more successful in strengthening his military control by building a large number of forts.[2] This doubtless was more in his line.

The new religion, in fact, did not push forward till a hundred years after the death of the King Straight-Strong-Deep. Tibet was now under the rule of Ti-song De-tsen,[3] whose mother was Chinese. He had a powerful minister, named Ma-zhang, who opposed Buddhism. 'The king, though a believer could not do anything, as the minister was too powerful.'[4] A Tibetan official, who was in favour of Buddhism, brought many sacred volumes from China, but feared to produce them. And when, becoming bolder, he founded two monasteries in the district that he was governing, he was dismissed. Undaunted, he went to Nepal, and met an Indian abbot, Shanti Rakshita. Meanwhile, as we are told, Gö Tri-zang, one of the Buddhist ministers, conspired with the king and the other Buddhist ministers. One of the latter said, 'The minister Ma-zhang has great power in his hand, but he is black-hearted regarding the religion. Therefore our endeavour to propagate Buddhist tenets will not be crowned with success.' To this Gö Tri-zang replied, 'I can devise a method, but the king and the Buddhist ministers should aid me in my attempt.' Pu-tön continues, 'Thus the king and the ministers conspired secretly. Gö Tri-zang devised secret means by which they buried Ma-zhang alive in a grave and covered the mouth of the grave with a large boulder.'[5] 'This,' says the Blue Treasury, 'facilitated the

[1] Pu-tön Rim-po-che, fol. 112.

[2] Tep-ter Ngön-po, vol. i, fol. 20.

[3] ཁྲི་སྲོང་ལྡེ་བཙན

[4] Tep-ter Ngön-po, vol. i, fol. 21.

[5] Pu-tön Rim-po-che, fol. 113.

bringing of Shanti Rakshita into Tibet.'[1] We are far away now from the gentle proselytizing of the Buddha and his disciples. The Tibetans were virile but hard, and it is perhaps appropriate that on their conversion to Buddhism they should have selected the Lord of Mercy as their patron.

The Abbot preached a sermon, not on the lines of the Buddha's first sermon, but 'on the ten pious acts and the eighteen hells, at which the local deities took umbrage. They raised a thunderstorm; the palace on Red Hill was struck by lightning.'[2] Crops were washed away, and disease fell on men and cattle. 'In consequence of those ominous occurrences the subjects rebelled against the king, saying that it was owing to the introduction of Buddhism that such inauspicious events were taking place. Accordingly, Shanti Rakshita was sent to Nepal for a while.[3]

Later on, he was, with some difficulty, induced to return. But his teaching, which was more in accordance with the early Buddhist teaching could not gain acceptance in Tibet. Accordingly, he advised the king to send for 'the great Tantrik teacher Padma Sambhava, who has great might and powers of magic. He alone can clear the Tibetan soil of the evil spirits'. For, as he said, 'Until we subdue the evil spirits, it is impossible to preach Buddhism. Moreover,' he was acute enough to observe, 'it was due to their malignancy that your forefathers died young.'[4] Buddhism could not cope with the nature-worship, the mystery and magic of old Tibet, a nation of fighters and raiders, reared in a cold, hard climate.

Tibet would say that Europe's reaction to Christian teaching has been somewhat similar. A Tibetan once quoted to me from the New Testament:

'Love your enemies, do good to them that hate you, bless them that curse you, pray for them that despitefully use you. . . . To him that smiteth thee on the one cheek offer also the other; and from him that taketh away thy cloke withhold not thy coat also.'

[1] Tep-ter Ngön-po, vol. i, fol. 21.
[2] Idem.
[3] Pu-tön Rim-po-che, fol. 113.
[4] Idem.

He did not understand how a nation could believe in such teaching and yet be constantly at war, not loving its enemies, but hitting back hard, even killing them, and forcibly subduing other nations to its will: not encouraging the robber or thief, but punishing him severely.

It is interesting to notice that the Tibetan king invited his teacher from India, not from China. The reason may be found in the fact that Tibet was at this time—the eighth century A.D.—one of the chief military powers in Asia, governing parts of Central Asia and China. The latter paid tribute to Tibet, and when a later Chinese emperor refused to pay, the Tibetans captured and sacked the Chinese capital. Relations with China being strained, Tibet may have looked to India, the first home of Buddhism, rather than to China, though the latter was more akin to it. Such a course was all the easier because the eighth century was a period when a peculiarly corrupt form of Buddhism was uppermost in India. It was a form that could harmonize and compromise with the demonolatry of the Tibetan masses.

The home of Padma Sambhava, whose name means 'The Lotus Born', was in the hill country, now known as Swat, that lies between Kashmir and Afghanistan. The inhabitants were Mahayanists, but especially devoted to the magic and exorcism that distinguishes Tantrik ritual. He had studied in Bengal, which was then a centre of Tantrism. This evidently was more acceptable to the Tibetan people, for we find that he succeeded in his mission. 'By his occult magical powers he subdued all the spirits and demons and bound them under a solemn oath to abstain in future from doing harm to men or to Buddhism.'[1] He then founded (A.D. 749) the first large monastery to be built in Tibet. For the site he chose Sam-ye, thirty miles south-east of Lhasa, and fashioned the construction after the model of Odantapuri in northern India. To this day it is one of the most important monasteries in Tibet.

[1] Pu-tön Rim-po-che, fol. 114.

The *Feast of Pleasure* tells us that 'In this year of the Fire Female Sheep there were four fundamental divisions[1] of Buddhists in India. The king considered that the Sarvastivadin would be the best of all for Tibet. So twelve monks of that school were invited from India, and Shanti Rakshita worked as their Abbot.'

We are further told that 'seven intelligent Tibetan youths were now for the first time admitted into the monkish order, in order to make the experiment whether in Tibet men could embrace the religious life as a profession or not.'[2] Pu-tön adds that 'all the images were made after models of Tibetan men and women.'

It is interesting to notice that, although Tantrism, with all its wizardry, might be expected to appeal to the Tibetan mind, yet the Sarvastivadin sect, which made less use of this, was chosen. It flourished at the time in Kashmir and Central Asia. Perhaps it was favoured by the upper and more intellectual classes, while those sects, that were impregnated with Tantrism, appealed to the masses of the people. It was from the latter, as time went on, that the Tibetan priesthood were mainly recruited, and therefore Tantrik teaching has always had a great hold over the country.

By Tibetans the 'Lotus Born' is known as the 'Precious Teacher', or simply as the 'Teacher'. His images and pictures represent him as having a somewhat angry face, and as accompanied by two wives, thus differing in two important attributes from the world's idea of monkhood. He could evidently succeed better without celibacy or saintly calm. Comparatively few Tibetans can ever have seen the lotus plant blooming in the tropical luxuriance of the Indian plains. Yet it has become one of the main examples and emblems of Tibetan Buddhism; the theme of a wise saying, the throne of a deity or saint, in painting and sculpture.

The Blue Treasury lays down that from the time of To-

[1] རྩ་བའི་སྡེ་

[2] Fol. 38, and Pu-tön, fol. 114.

to-ri Buddhism did exist in Tibet, but only to the extent of worshipping books and relics. In the time of Song-tsen Gam-po, Tantrism was first introduced. Song-tsen founded the worship of Chen-re-zi, the Great Compassionate one, which 'has become so popular that even children repeat the six-syllabled formula' (Om Ma-ni Pe-me Hum). But in Ti-song's reign Tantrism, which evidently worked in harmony with the purer doctrines of the Sarvastivadins, forged ahead; women, as well as men, obtained miraculous powers. Padma Sambhava is credited with many miracles, converting sandy tracts into pastures, throwing a silver water-pot into the sky to fetch down holy water, and so on. But the Pönist opposition was always strong. Pu-tön says that, 'The Pönist ministers poisoned the ears of the king in connexion with his miracles. Consequently the king sent Padma Sambhava, accompanied by many attendants and servants, back to India.'[1] Tibetans of the present day believe that the 'Precious Teacher' is now living in a land, inhabited by demons, to the south-west of Tibet. He is teaching religion to these misguided ones.

But Shanti Rakshita remained. And other Indian pandits, aided by Tibetan assistants, translated a number of Buddhist sacred books from Sanskrit into Tibetan. Another Tantrik sage, Dharma Kirti, came from India; Tantrik rites were practised, and the people were seated in magic diagrams. The highest priests gave religious vows to their juniors. Chinese teachers imparted instruction in deep meditation, while Pandits composed works on different subjects. The treasurers kept the properties of the Church, and Buddhist professors preached the religion to the public.

The industry and organizing ability of the Tibetans is made clear. 'In the Dragon year, in the autumn, when the king was residing in the Den-kar palace, the translators made catalogues of the translated Buddhist books then extant in Tibetan territory. They gave for each work the

[1] Fol. 114.

title-page, the number of chapters, the number of verses, at the same time revising these works.'

Shanti Rakshita himself died from the kick of a horse. And this no doubt made it easier for the Chinese teachers, who were in rivalry with the Indians, to raise their heads. The Chinese were Mahayanists, and they 'began to teach thus: "A man will not attain to nirvana by religious observances of body and speech, but by remaining in a state of absolute inaction. They followed the theory of non-existence and gave up accumulating merits through religious devotion and works." The Tibetans mostly liked the theory of non-existence and followed that school; it was but a few who followed the teaching of Shanti Rakshita. They differed both in theory and in practice and therefore both parties quarrelled with one another. The Chinese teaching was known as the *quick progress*; the Indian teaching as the *slow progress*. Thus they taught.'

Eventually an Indian philosopher, Kamala Shila, a disciple of Shanti Rakshita, was brought from India to debate with the Chinese doctor. The stage was set. The king sat in the middle, the Chinese with his followers on the right hand, the Indian with his adherents on the left. Kamala Shila was eventually adjudged the victor, and the Chinese doctor had to offer him the garland of victory and then return to his own land, in accordance with the conditions prescribed before the debate commenced. Some of his followers 'were so greatly ashamed of their defeat in the debate that they died from beating their breasts with stones. Then the king gave order, "Henceforth all Tibetans shall follow the Middle Doctrine[1] of the Great Vehicle teacher, Nagarjuna, and shall act on the ten religious practices and the six transcendent virtues".'[2] It was forbidden to follow the Chinese teacher's theories, but it is interesting to notice that 'his works were collected and concealed as a treasure'.[3] There seems, indeed, some ground for believing that the banishment of the Chinese

[1] *Madhyamika*.
[2] *Paramitas*.
[3] Pu-tön Rim-po-che, fols. 114–16.

was due not so much to their doctrines as to the strained political relations between China and Tibet. The Madhyamika is one of the doctrines which preach the unreality of all things, and it is necessary to mention it, as it has entered into the devotional books, used by the Tibetans. But the mythological trend of Tibetan Mahayanism, the deities, the saints, and the joy of life among the people themselves, kept in check the atheism of this Middle Doctrine.

Kamala Shila stayed on in Tibet and instructed many Tibetans. One of his most illustrious disciples, Jeng, spent years in meditation, studied incantations, practised severe penances, and obtained supernatural powers,[1] and others followed on the same lines. Pu-tön records that the Chinese teacher, many years after his banishment, sent four Chinese butchers who 'killed Kamala Shila by pinching his kidneys with their hands.'[2] In the Tibetan books Kamala Shila is often described as 'The holy Indian'. When speaking of him, they more often call him 'The holy Buddha'. His body was embalmed, and is still preserved in a monastery twenty miles north of Lhasa, where I found it a few years ago in a state of good preservation,[3] an eloquent testimony to the religious devotion that has always characterized these people.

King Ti-song De-tsen died at the age of sixty-eight. He was great in war and great in peace. Successful in his military campaigns, he steered his way between the conflicting religions. Along with Song-tsen Gam-po who preceded him, and Ral-pa-chan who followed later, his reign is regarded by modern Tibetans as their country's Golden Age.

After two more reigns—during the ninth century—Ral-pa-chan, the grandson of Ti-song De-tsen, succeeded to the throne in his seventeenth year.[4] His elder brother,

[1] Tep-ter Ngön-po, vol. iii, fol. 37. [2] Fol. 116.

[3] A description of this mummy is given in my book *The People of Tibet* (Oxford University Press), p. 296.

[4] The eighteenth according to the Tibetan history. I take one year off ages

Dar-ma, was first made king, but being 'on the outside', i.e. a Pönist, was superseded in favour of his Buddhist younger brother.[1] The latter is said to have built a palace of nine storeys with a vaulted roof. Under him Tibet again achieved great military successes. The *Feast of Pleasure* is brief but emphatic.

> At this time China and Tibet fell into disagreement. A fierce and glorious army of great size marched into Chinese territory and gave battle. It conquered many districts in China. It fell headlong on the country, killing soldiers, officers, and braves.
>
> Three stone pillars were set up, one in Lhasa, one in the Chinese capital, and one at Kunga Meru in China, making it the boundary between Tibet and China. On these three were inscribed the terms of peace and friendship.

It was the new religion that made the peace. For, after recording the above military exploits, the *Feast of Pleasure* continues:

> Then the Hwa-shangs (priests) of China and the Translators and Pandits in Tibet became mediators, spoke well-trained words, and made harmony between the king and his maternal uncle (the Emperor of China).[2]

It was indeed a significant meeting, for, ever since that day, Buddhism, a foe to aggression and the taking of life, has stood in the path of Tibetan conquest, has even condemned the training and equipment of soldiers. Tibetans are by nature brave and hardy, but from that time to this, a full thousand years, military glory has found no encouragement in Tibet. 'A great sin; yes, a very great sin,' the people will tell you, at the same time moderately proud —for human nature with them is no less mixed and contrary than with others—of the conquests achieved by the illustrious kings of old.

The history dismisses this great campaign in three lines. Many a novice in his monastery devoting himself peacefully to his studies, is glorified at ten times the length.

as recorded by Tibetans, for it is their custom to count both the first year and the last; i.e. in this case the year of birth and the seventeenth, making eighteen altogether.

[1] *Feast of Pleasure*, fol. 41.

[2] Idem, fol. 43.

Map
showing position
of
TIBET
Statute Miles
0
500
1000
EUROPE
Berlin
Vienna
HUNGARY
Constantinople
Petrograd
Moscow
RUSSIA
SIBERIA
R. Lena
R. Yenisei
R. Ob
Tomsk
R. Irtish
R. Volga
Black Sea
KALMUKS
Caspian Sea
TURKEY
Angora
Cyprus
Mediterranean Sea
SYRIA
Cairo
Jerusalem
Baghdad
PERSIA
Tehran
Red Sea
Medina
Mecca
ARABIA
Aden
Arabian Sea
Aral Sea
RUSSIAN TURKISTAN
Tashkent
Bokhara
Kabul
AFGHANISTAN
BALUCHISTAN
R. Indus
R. Sutlej
L. Balkash
SINKIANG [CHINESE TURKISTAN]
R. Tarim
Yarkand
Khotan
Srinagar
TIBET
Lhasa
NEPAL
Delhi
Benares
INDIA
Calcutta
Chandernagore
Nagpur
Bombay
Madras
Colombo
CEYLON
Bay of Bengal
BURMA
Rangoon
SIAM
Bangkok
FRENCH INDO-CHINA
Saigon
Hanoi
HAINAN
YUNNAN
SZECHUAN
R. Yangtse
CHINA
KANSU
Koko Nor
MONGOLIA
The Gobi
Kobdo
Uliassutai
Site of Karakoram
Urga
R. Kerulen
Irkutsk
L. Baikal
BURIATS
Chita
MANCHURIA
R. Amur
Peking
Hwang Ho
Shanghai
Canton
Hong Kong
FORMOSA
KOREA
Tokyo
JAPANESE EMPIRE
Tropic of Cancer
Arctic Circle
PHILIPPINE ISLANDS
BORNEO
South China Sea
20°
40°
60°
80°
100°
120°
140°
160°

Ral-pa-chan found that both Mahayanist and Hinayanist books had been made in India, Li, Zahor, and other countries. Consequently there was a large influx of foreign words which Tibetans did not understand. And as the spelling lacked uniformity, it was difficult to study the religious books. He therefore revised the spelling and arranged for the compilation of a dictionary in which these foreign words were explained. He is said to have had the earlier translations revised according to the new spelling. He forbade the translation of works, except only those of the Sarvastivadins, a Hinayanist sect, who tried to follow the actual teaching of the Buddha himself, and eschewed subsequent incrustations. He prohibited the translation of works on mysticism. In fact, his object was evidently to purify the Buddhism that came to Tibet, to simplify it, and to render it intelligible to his people. This is of interest, for it is generally held that Tibet is an entirely Mahayanist country. But it is evident from this and other references in the histories that Hinayanist tendencies were from time to time pressed forward by the rulers and other intellectual classes, though it may be doubted whether the masses of the people ever took kindly to them. Religion is developed, and often enriched, when it passes into other countries, gaining new ideas, new adaptations. From hot India to cold Tibet the change is great. The rulers of Tibet at that time could no more block the natural effects of this change than could the ruler of little Sikkim a few years ago.

Ral-pa-chan standardized Tibetan measures, weights, and coins after Indian patterns. To each monk he granted seven households of peasants for his support. Indeed, he went so far as to spread the hair of his head on the ground and allow the Buddhist clergy to walk over it.

Though these kings supported Buddhism, some of their ministers were always of the Pönist persuasion. The histories, being composed several centuries later, are written from the Buddhist standpoint, and often term them the 'Black Ministers', but it is clear that their power was great. The Tibetan documents discovered by Sir Aurel Stein in Chinese Turkistan are reported by the Rev. A. H. Francke, who has examined them, to date from about this period, i.e. the ninth century A.D., or earlier. They were found either at Mīrān near the westernmost end of the present Lob Nor marshes, or at Mazār-tāgh, a low ridge rising in the middle of the Taklamakan desert, on the left bank of the Khotan river. The documents were those of Tibetan garrisons, and refer mainly to the life of the soldiery and some to postal runners. Buddhism seems not yet to have been well established, for

(*a*) The Tibetan names in the writings are mainly non-Buddhist and are not used nowadays.

(*b*) Some of the titles, e.g. various kinds of 'uncle' are reminiscent of the Ke-sar Saga, which is undoubtedly pre-Buddhist.

(*c*) The Pönist form of Swastika, i.e. with the feet pointing in the reverse direction, occurs frequently.

(*d*) The word *lama* is never found. Nor is the formula *Om Ma-ni Pe-me Hum* found. And the style of the documents is quite different from that in the so-called classical language of the religious literature. References are made to religious ceremonies, but it is not known whether they were performed by Pönist or by Buddhist priests. A few documents seem to treat of religious persecution.[1]

In establishing the hierarchy on such a luxurious footing and abasing himself before the new priesthood, Ral-pa-chan went too fast for his people, and the Pönist ministers accordingly took advantage of the public feeling. One of the princes had entered the new priesthood. Some oracles and astrologers—under the influence of bribes, so the *Feast of Pleasure* asserts[2]—prophesied that unless the prince were banished, the kingdom would come to harm. He was banished accordingly to the Chumbi Valley. The queen and the chief Buddhist minister were accused of criminal intimacy, with the result that the minister was assassinated, and the queen committed suicide. And,

[1] *Journal of the Asiatic Society of Bengal*, 1914. [2] Fol. 44.

finally two of these ministers killed the king himself by twisting his face round towards the nape of his neck.

He was still young: some say forty-eight, some only thirty-seven years of age. But he had achieved much. In the books he is known as 'Long Hair' (Ral-pa-chan), but in the talk of the people as 'Enthroned Long Hair, Lord of the Subjects', a name expressed in four short Tibetan syllables.[1] His brother Lang Dar-ma, who opposed the new religion, was again put on the throne.[2]

The foreign Buddhist Pandits (teachers) appear to have come largely from the mountainous lands to the north-west of India and to have studied in the great monasteries and universities in Bengal and Bihar. The Tibetan translators, who went to India to learn the language and study the new religion, were accustomed, so a well-read and careful Tibetan authority tells me, to stop first in Nepal, a cooler land, to learn the Indian languages, and then usually passed on to India, and sometimes even to Burma. Their death roll was very heavy, for the climate of the tropics is deadly to those nurtured in the dry cold of Tibet. Out of a party of eight or ten not more than two or three would usually return to their own country. But death in such a cause was believed to bring a vastly better rebirth in the next life, perhaps a near approach to nirvana itself.

Each Indian Pandit explained the sacred text to a Tibetan translator, who reproduced the meaning with scrupulous accuracy. In China the translators paraphrased the meanings with some freedom, but in Tibet a free paraphrase would have been regarded as a crime. To this day Tibetans regard the printed word, in works on history, medicine or whatever subject you please, as inherently sacred. And the scriptures are all printed, both the Canon and the Commentaries.

The Canon is known as Kan-gyur,[3] i.e. 'The Translated Commandments', and the Commentaries as Ten-gyur,[4]

[1] Nga-dak Tri-ral (མངའ་བདག་ཁྲི་རལ་). [2] Pu-tön Rim-po-che, fol. 117.

[3] བཀའ་འགྱུར་ [4] བསྟན་འགྱུར་

i.e. 'The Translated Explanations'. Pu-tön, one of Tibet's most voluminous writers, is said to have arranged both of these. The former contains one hundred volumes in one version, one hundred and eight in another. It is the Bible of the Tibetan Buddhist, and is to some extent based on both the Indian, and the subsequent Chinese, version of the Tripitaka, the Buddist Canon, but with many Tantrik and other additions. The Ten-gyur numbers no less than two hundred and twenty-five volumes, embracing treatises on grammar, poetry, logic, rhetoric, law, medicine, astrology, divination, chemistry, painting, and biographies of saints. For all these are regarded as the handmaids of religion.

The faithful accuracy of these Tibetan translations—an accuracy that shines forth wherever the Sanskrit originals are available for comparison—endows them with a great value at the present day. For most of these ancient Sanskrit works are no longer in existence. Indian heat and damp render preservation difficult, and repeated Muhammadan invaders have destroyed innumerable sacred writings in India, thinking such destruction to be a religious duty. But Tibet—blessed with a climate both dry and cold, where parchment and writing do not fade, and practically immune from destructiveness—has preserved the translations, so that the lost treatises can be at any time reconstructed from them.

'Some were made to marry.'
Lhasan ladies

V

EXPULSION AND RETURN

RAL-PA-CHAN had greatly favoured the Sarvastivadins, a Hinayanic sect, and in that perhaps lay one of the causes of the assassination of the king and the downfall of the religion. For the mass of the people have always desired deities and ritual, miracles and display, and their own Pönist religion gave them these things. A complicated philosophy that tried to take them away must necessarily have provoked serious opposition, for, like most nomads, they were intensely devoted to their religion. Even now in Sikkim, as we have seen in an earlier chapter, an attempt to return to the teaching of the Buddha—and this was what the Sarvastivadins did—met with uncompromising opposition, and failed. The Tantrik faith also had its vicissitudes in Tibet, but on the whole it stood a better chance. It was nearer to Pönism, and could harmonize.

'Long Hair' having been assassinated, the Buddhist monks were suppressed after the methods of those days in Tibet. Some were made to marry. Others 'were sent to hunt wild beasts with arrows, bows, drums, and tambourines—a magical implement among the Pönists—and those who refused were killed'. The doors of a temple would be walled up and plastered, and on the doors so plastered pictures of monks drinking wine would be painted. The work of translation was of course stopped. But the sacred books do not appear to have been destroyed. Pu-tön tells us that they 'were mostly hidden in the rocks of Lhasa'.[1]

After a brief reign, Lang Dar-ma, in his turn, was murdered by a Buddhist monk, A.D. 900. The latter, so the Tibetan history tells us, was meditating in a cave

[1] Pu-tön Rim-po-che, fol. 117.

with pity for the king, who was accumulating sins by persecuting Buddhism'.

Mounted on a white horse blackened with charcoal, and wearing a roomy woollen cloak black on the outside and white on the inside, he went to Lhasa. With him he took an iron bow and an iron arrow. When he came to Lhasa he saw The Strong One[1] reading the inscription on Long Stone,[2] with his back turned to the Temple and the Chö-ten of Gan-den. He alighted in The Strong One's presence. He bent the bow, resting it on his knee. The king thought he was doing obeisance to him. During the first obeisance he bent the bow; during the second he fitted the arrow-notch to the bow-string; during the third he let fly. The arrow pierced the king's chest.

He stayed to call out, 'I am the demon, Black Ya-she. When anybody wishes to kill a sinful king, let him do it as I have killed this one.' So saying, he fled. The cry was raised, 'The Strong One is killed in Lhasa, pursue the assassin.' But the monk washed the black off his horse in a pond, and turned his cloak inside out. And now he called out, 'I am the god called White Nam-te-u', and continued his flight.

There was confusion as to what route he had taken, and probably he had sympathizers. So he escaped. He went far away into eastern Tibet, taking three of the sacred books with him. Buddhism having eventually obtained the mastery in Tibet, this monk has been canonized, while Dar-ma is reckoned among the fiends.

But the drive against Buddhism continued. Indian pandits were expelled; most of the Tibetan translators fled; executioners killed many of the monks. In fact, as the history says, 'They made it so that the religion was not'.[3]

There was no preaching of sermons, no taking of religious vows, although religious observances were con-

[1] བཙན་པོ་ Title given to the early Tibetan kings. The word implies strictness as well as strength.

[2] One of the monoliths in and near Lhasa. They contain inscriptions of great interest, some of which refer to wars and treaties made by the early kings. See *Tibet Past and Present*, Appendixes I and II.

[3] Pu-tön Rim-po-che, fols. 117, 118.

tinued in a half-hearted manner in the homes of the people. The historian especially reprobates those who practised mysticism in ignorance of the true meaning of Tantrism, for such 'used to indulge in sexual union to attain to nirvana, and practised many other vices'. He finds nothing but condemnation for those who followed the doctrine of the Indian Buddhist school of Shaktism. And, indeed, the doctrines of this repellent school, though they penetrated to Tibet and were followed by some here and there, never seem to have gained the firm hold that was theirs in the soft, voluptuous climate of Bengal.

On the death of Lang Dar-ma the kingdom was divided by his two sons. Subdivisions followed, and in due course the whole country was parcelled out among petty chiefs, each holding what he, or she, could. The ruined forts of these, but more especially of later, days still greet you high up on the mountain sides, showing how they controlled and defended the villages in the valleys below.

The first steps towards the revival of Buddhism were taken in Am-do, a province in the north-east of Tibet on the border of China and far away from Lhasa. A villager there, who had studied the doctrine and was qualified to be ordained as a monk, could not obtain the necessary quota of five monks to perform the ceremony of ordination. At last, however, the number was increased to ten, who returned to central Tibet—then, as always, the nerve-centre of these mountain lands—if haply they might spread the sacred teaching once more. To Lhasa itself they dared not go, for, as the record testifies, 'though Lhasa was formerly the seat of the learned and reverend ones, now it was the place of persecution and punishment'. So they went instead to Sam-ye, which had given a site for the first large Buddhist monastery two hundred years before, and was still faithful. They occupied old monastic buildings, erected fresh ones, and enrolled disciples. Time had passed, and with it the shock of Ral-pa-chan's too strenuous advance. Tolerance had returned, and the work went slowly but steadily forward. The complete suppression of Buddhism lasted, however, for at least seventy years; some of the Tibetan historians have put this dark period at one hundred and eight years, the sacred number of Tibetan Buddhism. And it was from Am-do that the revival came; Am-do, which was later to be the home of Tsong-ka-pa, the great reformer, and has, indeed, so often proved the well-spring of religious devotion, the home of a newer, purer faith. Even to-day the young monks of Am-do are among the keenest, the most intelligent, of all who come for light and leading to the great temples and monasteries of Lhasa.

The work of translating the Indian Buddhist books was resumed. One of the first and most prolific of these translators was a Tibetan named 'The Good Gem' (*Rinchen Zang-po*) who was ordained a monk in the fifty-seventh year after the suppression of Buddhism, and is said to have lived to ninety-eight years of age.

At this time the chief in the Nga-ri province of western Tibet, a descendant of King Lang Dar-ma, renounced his throne to enter monastic life. He believed in the metaphysical school of Buddhism, but doubted the Tantrik school because its followers 'indulged in sexual embrace and committed many other vicious practices. So in order to reform this corrupt Buddhist mysticism,' he sent 'Good Gem' to India as a young man for instruction with a party of twenty-one persons of whom all died from the climate, except himself and one other.

Not only did 'Good Gem' translate books; he also painted images with such assiduity that no other individual, the Blue Treasury affirms, can claim to have done so much in either of these branches. He is also credited with the building of monasteries and temples in western Tibet.[1] Indian pandits came once again, including several from Kashmir; Tibetan students once again sought religious life from India, and cared not though the body perished in the search.

The Indian pandits, too, had their difficulties. Tibetans

[1] Vol. ii, fol. 3.

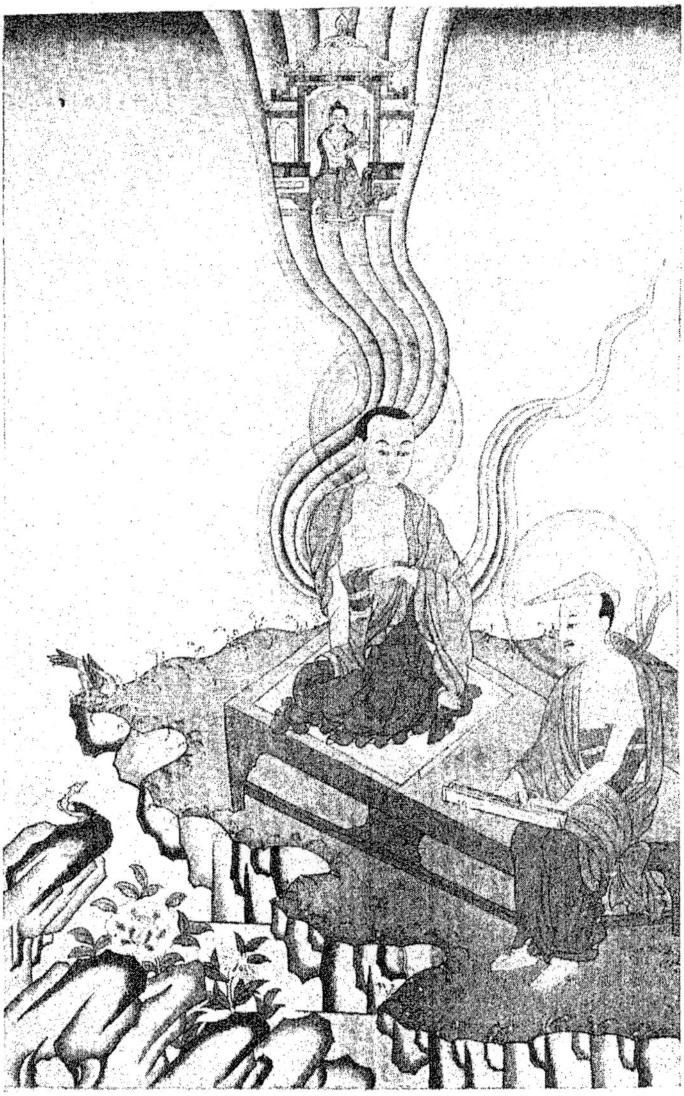

Two Indian pandits, Arya Asanga and Vasubandhu, painted by a Tibetan artist

used to invite these and act as their interpreters. In order to study the necessary Indian languages, they would live in Nepal, and then go to India for a month or two, to bring their pandits to Tibet. One such interpreter died. His pandit, being unable to speak Tibetan, was not recognized as a pandit, and consequently had for a long time to earn his livelihood by working as a shepherd. At length he fell in with some people of learning, and obtained recognition. He then compiled a grammar which he made known as 'The Weapon of the Door of Speech'.

But such difficulties and hardships did but add fuel to the fire. The stream of pandits from India increased in volume. Probably even now, in the welter of twentieth-century upheavals, the quiet thinkers of India would seize a similar opportunity. For always they have been ready to probe into religious and metaphysical dimness, to discuss the relationship of mind and matter.

One of the chief among these was Subhati Sri Shanti—better known to Tibetans as the Great Kashmiri Pandit—who was invited by one of Dar-ma's descendants in western Tibet. Even to-day his name often crops up in conversation, when, as almost invariably happens in Tibet, this veers round to some religious topic. Uninvited also the pandits still came, several of them from Kashmir. At this period it was the rulers in western Tibet, beyond the control of Lhasa, who took the most active part in the re-introduction of Buddhism. One of the princes of this branch of the royal line, so the *Feast of Pleasure* narrates, became himself a translator. Making over his civil administration to another, he led his troops against the Gar-lok, but was subsequently defeated and captured. They insisted on his abandoning his religion or finding his own weight of gold as ransom. This took a long time to collect. When at last it was collected, he said that he was now too old to be of any use even if ransomed. He asked therefore that the gold should be devoted to inviting pandits and spreading the Faith, and, long afterwards, died in captivity.[1] The Gar-lok were apparently Muhammadans; the time was early in the eleventh century.

And with what diligence these reviving Buddhists searched their scriptures! The Great Kashmiri Paṅdit, when visiting Sam-ye, discovered there a lost Indian manuscript, the original of the Tantra of the Secret Essence.[2] The manuscript passed into the hands of another, who gave it to the translator. This last sent it to a man, who was so delighted with it that he practised the prescribed devotions and compiled a manual of devotion and ritual to be used with it. Then another translator took it in hand and made a translation of it, as well as a comparison of its teaching with that of other works on the same subject. Eventually part was lost, and the remainder of the prize came into the possession of the author of the Blue Treasury.[3]

During the eighth and ninth centuries, for a hundred years at least, the Tibetans had been masters of a large area in what is now termed Sinkiang, or Chinese Turkistan. Fighting sometimes alone, and sometimes in alliance with the Arabs then pressing forward in the newly found faith of Islam, they broke the Chinese power at the very time when it had attained its greatest western extension into Bokhara, Tashkent, Afghanistan, and the border districts of India and Persia. They took a yearly tribute of fifty thousand rolls of silk from the Emperor of China. On the latter's death the new Emperor 'considered it unfitting to pay tribute to Tibet', on which the Tibetan commander-in-chief equipped a new expedition, which marched into the heart of China, sacked the Chinese capital, and put the Chinese Emperor to flight.[4] Closely akin as they are to the Mongols, these Tibetan invasions were a foretaste of the conquest achieved by Ching-gis

[1] Fols. 47, 48.   [2] གསང་བ་སྙིང་པོ་

[3] Tep-ter Ngön-po, vol. iii, fol. 1.

[4] These facts appear from Chinese history as well as from the inscription on a stone pillar on the outskirts of Lhasa. For a full translation of this inscription see *Tibet Past and Present*, pp. 273, 274.

Khan and his successors four centuries later, a conquest on a larger scale than any other known to history before or since.

But, as Buddhism increased, preaching peace and forbidding the taking of life, the warlike propensities of the Tibetan tribes diminished. Internecine contests continued, for in the large monasteries themselves there have always been many monks ready for local fights and forays. It is in the blood. But, from now onwards, external aggression died away. And when with its handicap Tibet went to war, it had often to suffer defeat. Thus more and more it fell under the domination of Mongols and other non-Buddhist invaders from the north. After the Mongols became thoroughly converted to Buddhism, their power in like manner declined, and Tibet fell under the sway, sometimes actual, sometimes merely nominal, of China.

During the eleventh century there was a considerable revival of Buddhism in Bengal. Many Buddhist schools flourished there, as well as in Nepal and Kashmir, which had always had Buddhist leanings. Monks of high intellectual attainments were ready to go to Tibet and work there, especially now that Muhammadan invaders were establishing their power in the plains of India and were attacking Hindus and Buddhists alike.

Among all the pandits who flocked to Tibet none exercised so great an influence as Atisha. This remarkable man was a native of Bengal. From the Blue Treasury it appears that he came of good birth, but gave up the luxuries of home, and wandered here and there studying Tantrik and different Mahayanist doctrines. Three of these years he spent on a course of mental training. Later on he lived in Afghanistan on the west, and in Burma on the east, thus gaining a varied experience before his thirtieth year, when be joined the monkhood. When, in later life, he filled the High Priest's office at the Vikramashila monastery, his reputation for learning had spread far afield. It was not until he was sixty years old, in A.D. 1039, that he came to western Tibet. Atisha's teaching was largely based on the Kala Chakra system, one of the most debased forms of Buddhist Tantrism. But it evidently met the needs of Tibet, and in him they had a man who had studied hard and gained a wide outlook. He met 'Good Gem', who was proud of his own learning, upbraided him for being dull-witted and explained his mistakes. In fact the history records his meeting with this Tibetan translator, and other single incidents also, at greater length than the victorious invasion of China or the subjugation of Turkistan. The translator, we are told, far from feeling annoyance, 'was greatly comforted and his mind widened'.

Atisha travelled through Tibet from the west and eventually arrived in Lhasa. The learned teachers of Tibet asked him regarding the qualifications and attainments of those pandits who were in western Tibet. He replied that a certain pandit had so much knowledge and another had so much. When questioned regarding his own attainments, he looked into the sky, saying *Tak tak*, a sound betokening surprise, and adding 'His accomplishments! Oh, his accomplishments!' Thus, says the history, he silenced them.

He then taught the chief who had invited him, and taught others, conferring spiritual powers secretly. The chief further requested that as there were several heretical beliefs a Religious Commentary might be composed to remedy this state of affairs. In this commentary Atisha dealt with the duties in the different stages of a priest's life. He counselled meditation on the Void, i.e. on the unreality of external phenomena. He announced that there were four different kinds of Mantrayanik (Tantrik) initiation, but advised against the second and the third, 'as they would lead one to go astray by wrongly thinking of obtaining salvation by a sort of mystical union'.[1] There was evidently a strong feeling in Tibet against this Indian importation, and Atisha, though largely brought up on the Kala Chakra tenets, was distinguished by a wide

[1] Tep-ter Ngön-po, vol. v, fol. 4.

erudition, and, having come late to the priesthood, seems to have been a man of the world. So, whatever his own views may have been, he bowed to Tibetan opinion. The great teacher did not, indeed, escape scandal, and was consequently careful of his own reputation. At first he refused permission to the young man Drom-tön, who had left home owing to disputes with his step-mother, to be with him, for fear of evil reports. A girl who offered him the precious ornaments which she wore on her head was taken to task by her parents and committed suicide. He left Sam-ye earlier than he had intended owing to a malicious report being spread about him. Drom-tön returned to him later on—a nun advising Atisha that he was coming—and served him ever afterwards with all the devotion that a disciple in eastern lands gives to a spiritual guide whom he reveres highly. Atisha in his turn 'initiated him[1] well, and thereafter allowed him great intimacy in conversation'.[2]

While they were still in the west, Drom-tön had informed Atisha that there were thousands of priests in the monasteries in Ü, the Lhasa province, and Sam-ye. 'Atisha replied that "even in India there are not so many who keep their religious vows; there must be many among them who have subdued the foe (i.e. Arhats)." And he bowed himself down several times in the direction of Ü.'[3] It was now a hundred and fifty years since the suppression of Buddhism. The revival had already surpassed the first coming.

Several attempts were necessary before Drom-tön could persuade his master to visit Lhasa. On the way he arranged for a number of Tibetan priests to receive him. When Atisha saw these with their long-pointed (lit. 'long-nosed') hats, their priestly robes of thick woollen cloth and their many ponies, all stretched out in line, he called out, 'Disciple, many non-human beings are coming'.[3]

[1] *Wang kur* (དབང་སྐུར).

[2] Tep-ter Ngön-po, vol. v, fol. 6.

[3] Idem, fol. 7.

On Atisha's arrival in Lhasa, Chen-re-zi, the patron deity of Tibet, appeared as a white man, and came to meet him.[1] The same deity is reputed to have appeared at Ne-nying Monastery near Gyang-tse, again in the form of a white man. On this last occasion he said, 'In this northern country of Tibet shall be my dominion'. So saying, the white man disappeared.[2] The second occasion may well be much later than the first, and may possibly, though not probably, reflect the visit of some white man, otherwise forgotten.

With the aid of several Tibetan translators Atisha translated Sanskrit works into Tibetan. He was greatly surprised to find such a number of Sanskrit books in Sam-ye, including many that were not extant in India itself. It is usual to ascribe religious losses of this kind in India to Muhammadan destructiveness, but we cannot do so in this case, for the Muhammadan invasions had not yet penetrated into its Buddhist monasteries and homes. Perhaps with the decay of Buddhism the works had fallen out of favour, and none had recopied them before they were devoured by the destructive Indian climate. Atisha indeed expressed the view that Padma Sambhava could have procured them only by non-human agency.[3] His mind turned easily to visions of the supernatural. As for Sam-ye, it is probable that Indian manuscripts or Tibetan translations—and these are remarkably accurate—are still preserved there.

At the place known as 'The Rock of Purity' (*Tra Yer-pa*), sixteen miles from Lhasa, Atisha lived for a time in a cave, and people came to him from Lhasa and elsewhere for instruction. This cave peeps out from high on the mountain side; round it has sprung up a monastery, not, after the more usual Tibetan style, in one massive whole, but dispersed in little buildings and caves. When I stayed there for two September days, the Michaelmas daisies

[1] དེབ་ཐེར་སྔོན་པོ་ Tep-ter Ngön-po, vol. v, fol. 8.

[2] Nyang Chö-jung, fol. 73.

[3] Tep-ter Ngön-po, vol. v, fol. 8.

Two pilgrims from Am-do coming to Lhasa

Small house (left) built over Atisha's cave at 'The Rock of Purity'. The red upper portion shows that it is a sacred building

were still in flower in the valley two thousand feet below, with dandelion, larkspur, and a few primulas flowering continuously since May. Cow-parsley and aconite, thistle and dock and edelweiss grew in great profusion. Round the monastery itself wild rose and wild currant bushes were everywhere, and some stunted junipers completed the picture. At midnight we had a terrific thunderstorm, a real Tibetan one, and I awoke to taste by night, as I had tasted by day, the smell of the rancid butter offerings on the altar, and of the decaying silk pictures on the walls of the dreamy little chapel, which my kind hosts had placed at my disposal.

Atisha indeed had said that he had come to Tibet to help the Buddhist religion there. But, as the storm rent the sky with its vivid flashes, some might have interpreted his spirit as saying that there was no need for me to come there. Hail fell, and conch shells were blown in the monastery to keep it off. Afterwards the hail turned to snow, and by morning the thick white mantle was over all.

During his stay at the Rock of Purity Atisha was very feeble, for he was seventy-three years old, and the Tibetan climate had no doubt tried him. A certain Indian pandit happened to be visiting Nepal at this time. Black Face (*Nak-tso*)—the Tibetan scholar who had brought Atisha from India to western Tibet and still worked with him as a translator—wished to seize the opportunity to visit the pandit, for the latter was an expert on the meaning of a valuable text. But he felt that he could not leave his master in his present state. Atisha, seeing this, permitted Black Face to go to the pandit, at the same time telling him that he, Atisha, was going to die and would be reborn in the Tushita heaven. On this the translator obtained the Lord's permission to make an image of him, and obtained the dying man's blessing on it, and the assurance that he would at his death join Atisha in Tushita. Black Face was criticized greatly for his action at such a time, but the historian supports him.[1]

[1] Tep-ter Ngön-po, vol. v, fol. 9.

An explanation of the Tibetan calendar must be given here. It was instituted according to the era of the 'Wheel of Time' School,[1] and the first cycle commences from A.D. 1027, but other cycles with the same year-names are sometimes used to describe earlier events. Five elements, viz. earth, iron, water, wood, and fire, are joined to twelve animals, dog, pig, mouse, ox, tiger, hare, dragon, serpent, horse, sheep, monkey, and bird. Each element comes twice, first as male and then as female. The elements thus end with the tenth year, the animals with the twelfth. So the first element is joined to the eleventh and twelfth animals. The latter in like manner repeat, and the result is a cycle ending at the sixtieth year.

Wood Male Mouse.
Wood Female Bull.
Fire Male Tiger.
Fire Female Hare.
Earth Male Dragon.

and so on. The particles that denote male and female can be omitted without causing confusion, for the animal changes from year to year throughout the series. This calendar is still in use; we are now in the sixteenth cycle.

Atisha 'ascended to the Tushita heaven on the twentieth day of the middle autumn month of the Wood Male Horse Year'.[2] He had spent thirteen years in Tibet. We are now in the middle of the eleventh century. His tomb is at Nye-tang on Central River (Kyi Chu) about twenty miles below Lhasa. I visited this mausoleum on my way to Lhasa and on my return. The tomb is in the form of a mud-coloured *chö-ten* (tope) some fifteen feet high, and is popularly believed to contain one hundred thousand tiny clay images on which the ashes of the deceased were sprinkled.

In the centre of the mausoleum is an image of Atisha made in his own likeness;[3] it is perhaps the very one that the Master blessed. On the other side is the tomb of a lama of the Sa-kya Monastery. The mausoleum stands

[1] Kala Chakra. [2] Tep-ter Ngön-po, vol. v, fol. 10. [3] *Dra-ku* (འདྲ་སྐུ).

Atisha's tomb

among old willow trees and is severe in its simplicity, as are the two tombs which fill it. It does not appear to receive much attention, though, in the historical books as well as in the conversation of to-day, Atisha is habitually termed 'Lord'[1] or 'Noble Lord', and few are more highly venerated.

He wrote many treatises and helped in the making of many translations. But he did far more than this. He preached public sermons and gave private teaching to his three leading disciples. To Drom-tön, his most intimate disciple and the chief of all, he expounded carefully the doctrines of a new sect, known as Ka-dam-pa, 'The Adviser'. Sects, like religions, need disciples to propagate them. So we read that Drom-tön and the other disciples 'spread the Ka-dam-pa doctrines widely throughout Tibet'.[2] This sect Drom-tön organized and led, becoming its first Hierarch.

The features which set it apart were its elaborate ritual and its powers for propitiating deities. There was not much difficulty in forming a new sect at that time, for Buddhism was at a low ebb in consequence of the anti-Buddhist movement that had only recently lost force. And the full importance of the Ka-dam-pa lies partly in the fact that it was the first sect to be divided off from the main body of Tibetan Buddhism, and partly that it was the parent of the Ge-luk-pa or 'Virtuous Way', which, founded three hundred years later, is now the leading sect.

[1] ཇོ་བོ

[2] Pu-tön Rim-po-che's Chö-jung, fol. 123.

VI

BUDDHISM BECOMES THE NATIONAL RELIGION

In the middle of the eleventh century the revival of Buddhism was in full force. New monasteries were springing up everywhere in response to the demand. And, incidentally, they were the safest places during these centuries when independent chiefs contended for supremacy. For Tibetan monasteries do not trust only to the protection which sanctity confers on religious buildings in a religious land. The walls of monastery and chapel were, and still are, of castle-like thickness, and the whole assemblage of buildings often were, and still are, surrounded by a protecting wall, strengthened with bastions or towers.

On Atisha's death, Drom-tön assumed the leadership among his disciples. He founded the great monastery of Re-ting,[1] sixty miles north of Lhasa, but on a small scale. After his death it was completed by an ascetic who had commenced his monastic career by looking after Atisha's ponies and doing other manual work for him. During his last years Drom-tön devoted himself entirely to teaching. Though well versed in the tantras and in the sutras, i.e. the sermons of the Buddha, he relied mainly on the atheistic teachings of the Middle Doctrine propounded by Nagarjuna, thus following in the steps of King Ti-song De-tsen. Having lived for nine years in his new monastery, he died at the age of sixty. But, in spite of his own beliefs, his last injunctions to his chief disciple, Po-to-wa, were, 'Take the sutras as your teacher; I see no other place of support for you'. Po-to-wa, as a result of concentrated meditation, was credited with the power of knowing events before they occurred. That was not altogether unusual,

[1] ར་སྒྲེང་

but what the historian deems worthy of comment is the fact that, 'He did not attempt to hide his power of foreknowledge, but used to speak openly about it'.[1] Po-to-wa died at the age of sixty-six; he was born in the year of the Fire Dragon and died in that of the Water Dog.

And so the succession runs on in this and other lines, while the historians love to record details in the lives of the different teachers, both Indian and Tibetan; the infant precocity, the school of teaching followed, the spiritual or magical powers gained, the post occupied, be it abbot's throne or hermit's cell, and the passing away from life, leaving perhaps no mortal remains behind.

Twenty-two years after Atisha's death, in the year of the Fire Dragon (A.D. 1076), there was 'a general meeting of all the learned Lamas of Tibet'. Many scholars and translators attended the meeting and a great many translations were carried through.[2]

Tibetan students continued to flock to India and to Nepal, in spite of the hardships encountered. Shaktism unfortunately was still practised by Indian Buddhists. Two of these advised one of the most promising young Tibetan translators to return to Tibet, where 'he would meet an incarnation of the Goddess, known as 'She who Saves'.[3] He was to take her as his consort, and to receive from her the power to meditate upon The Mystery and The Divine Wisdom, and to practise the meditation inculcated in those texts.' This translator for a time, while in Tibet, adopted the garb of an Indian pandit, but, subsequently, reverted to Tibetan dress.

There was zeal everywhere. A young disciple would give to his Master the proceeds of his begging tour, and, by holding religious services for others, gain enough food, used sparingly, to continue his own meditation. And, as knowledge spread in Tibet, Indian Buddhists used to come to Tibetans for instruction.

A remarkable man of this time was Mar-pa, translator

[1] Tep-ter Ngön-po, vol. v, fol. 12. [2] Idem, vol. ii, fol. 4.
[3] Dröl-ma.

and Tantrist, whom the Blue Treasury describes as 'One of the greatest authorities and one of the chief sources of the Buddhist doctrine in Tibet, both in preaching and in the devotional rites and rituals'. He was born in A.D. 1011 in a district in southern Tibet between Lhasa and Bhutan, and was twenty-nine years younger than Atisha.

As a boy, though he learned to read well from his teacher, named 'Eight Serpent Spirits', yet he was so wild and quarrelsome, that he was unwelcome in any house except his teacher's and one other. So his father decided to send him for study elsewhere in the hope that his temper might cool down. With him he sent a good pony and saddle and various other articles as presents for the new teacher. When he was fifteen years of age Mar-pa had learnt sufficient to be able to translate fairly well.

Now he made up his mind to visit India, the fountain head of learning. Returning home, he collected fifteen ounces of gold. He then found a generous friend, who provided him with all necessaries, including caps and boots and an ample supply of gold. In Nepal he met a travelling acquaintance and the two stayed for three years in that country to acclimatize themselves to the heat of India. During this time they learnt Tantras from a Buddhist pandit of the Newar tribe, one of the leading tribes of Nepal.

When the third year was ended, he went on to India and received initiation from Naropa and learnt Tantras from him and others. He then came back to Tibet and set up as a practical Tantrik lama, undertaking the protection of rich and influential persons and their children from evil influences. Each case entrusted to him for spiritual protection brought him a fee of ten ounces of gold. An influential citizen became his disciple and collected still more gold for him.

With the aid of this new wealth he journeyed again to India. He found that Naropa had passed away. But the meditation and prayers, allied with the occult powers, of such as Mar-pa, accepted no such check. In the solitude of an Indian jungle the guru's embodied spirit answered his call. As the result of Naropa's teaching he started a new sect which became known as the Ka-gyü, i.e. 'The Succession of Orders'. It was based chiefly on the Indian philosophy of the 'Great Symbol' (Mahamudra), which Naropa had learned from a fellow Indian, Tilopa, in the tenth century. To this day it has a wide vogue throughout Tibet; in Bhutan it is pre-eminent.

Returning to Tibet through Nepal, Mar-pa, now forty-two years old, married a wife, and also had 'eight other female disciples, who were his spiritual consorts'. All nine were believed to be manifestations of goddesses.

Yet a third time he visited India, met a well-known saint, and listened to more Tantrik texts. 'Now he realized the knowledge of the doctrine of the Great Symbol, and this cut off all thought-forming activity.' In spite of having travelled so much in hot countries he did not die till he was eighty-six years old. His biography depicts him, boy and man, as full of vitality, and it shows his character to have been a curious blend, a puzzle to his neighbours.

I discussed Mar-pa with the late Da-wa Sam-trup, himself of the Ka-gyü sect and a very learned exponent of the religion. Da-wa Sam-trup put it thus:

'Mar-pa was a Bodhisattva, yet he was frequently drunk and showed great avarice. He would take nearly all their possessions from his disciples, and spend them on his journeys to India to collect Buddhist books. And he used to live in comfort, while they endured great hardships.'

'How then was it known that he was a Bodhisattva?'

'By reason of his supernatural knowledge and powers. For instance, he could within two or three months summon a god, which another high lama would take twelve years to call. He would become drunk in order to test the faith of his disciples and thereby advance their spiritual instruction.' Faith in one's guru is a primary rule.

On the same subject the Blue Treasury writes:

Though a highly advanced Yogi, who had mastered 'That Very Self', and dwelt in it like the current of a stream, yet to people at large he seemed a worldly person in his agricultural pursuits, his dealings with his children, and quarrels with his relatives. But to his spiritually developed disciples he appeared another being. He had shown them on four different occasions that he could project his own soul into a dead body and so take that body instead of his own, putting his own mind into it. This was a secret art, known as 'Entering The Dead',[1] which was believed to be within the power of some, especially during later times. Mar-pa was held to be the incarnation of the Indian saint, Dombi Heruka.[2]

It is a remarkable fact that, though the Blue Treasury notices the lives of Atisha and Mar-pa at considerable length, it makes no mention of any meeting between the two. Mar-pa's spiritual gaze was centred on Naropa, not on Atisha; and, judging from the known views of Mar-pa's disciple, Mi-la, one may surmise that Mar-pa disagreed with part of Atisha's teaching. His own fame rested mainly on the large number of translations which he made, but also on the magical powers which he was reputed to have gained through his Tantrik studies.

There are two courses open to a lama, who truly seeks deliverance from the Wheel of Life. He may either teach others how to follow the Way; or he may concentrate on his own mind, practising piety through asceticism, mortifying the flesh that the spirit within may dominate it. The latter is not regarded as a selfish working for one's own salvation. Less visibly than the teaching, but no less certainly, it works for the deliverance of all human beings and animals from the miseries of the Wheel.

Mar-pa had four chief disciples, three of whom took up their work as lamas on the exposition, or teaching side. Well-known among these is Ngok, a translator, who was twenty-four years younger than his master. One only took up the devotional, or ascetic side. This was Mi-la; frequently called 'Cotton Clad Mi-la',[3] because he lived on the

[1] Trong-juk (གྲོང་འཇུག). [2] Tep-ter Ngön-po, vol. viii, fol. 1–3.

[3] *Mi-la Re-pa* (མི་ལ་རས་པ་)

Tibetan mountain sides, clad only in a single cotton garment; but often known simply as 'The Revered Mi-la'.[1] First a wizard, then a saint, and always a poet, his name is a household word; his songs, as well as his biography, are universally read and often quoted. I will refer more fully to him later.

The next leading event is the building of the great monastery at Sa-kya,[2] south-west of Shigatse, half-way to the Tibet-Nepal frontier. The Blue Treasury assigns the sixty-second year (A.D. 1071) of Mar-pa's life as the year of its foundation. Its Hierarchs traced their descent from 'the Inner Minister' of the great king, Ti-song De-tsen.[3] They were not celibate; a son could succeed his father in the post. Sa-kya was of secular, as well as religious, importance. With the assassination of Lang Dar-ma, the line of the old kings had lost their power, and the land had been divided among petty chiefs. But, as Buddhism grew in this land, always so prone to supernatural influences, the political power of its priests grew likewise. And so the new foundation increased its power, ecclesiastical and secular. It was the largest of all the monasteries; capable Hierarchs in turn succeeded to its throne. As to its doctrines the Blue Treasury says that 'the line upheld the school of Tantrik mysticism as well as the philosophical teachings of Mahayanist Buddhism'.[4]

In the thirteenth century they came into touch with the Mongol Emperors. One Hierarch was summoned to Peking to heal an illness of the Mongol ruler of the time. He was successful in this, and his learning—he was known as 'Sa-kya's Great Pandit'—gained wide recognition. A successor, Dro-gön Pak-pa, ministered to the spiritual needs of Prince Khubilai[5] during the impressionable

[1] *Je-tsün Mi-la.* [2] ས་སྐྱ [3] Tep-ter Ngön-po, vol. iv, fol. 4.

[4] Idem, vol. iv, fol. 6.

[5] In the Tibetan history that tells of Buddhism in Mongolia, entitled Hor Chö-jung, by Jik-me Nam-ka, this Emperor's name is spelt Hwo-bi-lai (ཧྭོ་བི་ལའི་)

years of youth, and remained as his spiritual guide when Khubilai gained the overlordship of the vast Mongol Empire, then in the heyday of its power.

Dro-gön was treated with the highest respect, and was asked to introduce the Tibetan form of Buddhism among the Mongols. Probably the Emperor, himself a Mongol, wished his people to have a religion less crude than the early animistic faiths, and decided that, Tibet and Mongolia being nearly related, Tibetan Buddhism would be the best religion for them. So closely do the two peoples resemble each other, that it is even now difficult to tell a Mongol from a Tibetan.

We know, indeed, from the travels of Marco Polo's father and uncle that Khubilai asked the Pope to send him a hundred learned Christian priests to expound Christianity to his Mongols. Two only were sent, and these soon abandoned the long and dangerous journey, frightened by a Mameluke attack on one of the districts that they traversed. This incident serves to show the Mongol Emperor's inquiring mind, but we may doubt whether the Mongols would have followed the distant alien in preference to their own kinsman.

Khubilai asked Dro-gön also to introduce Tibetan characters to clothe the Mongol language, which till then was merely oral. But they were found unsuitable, and eventually a modified and enlarged form of the Uigur alphabet was adopted. This had, in fact, been already used for Mongol by the Sa-kya lamas, and was accordingly introduced by a Tibetan lama during the reign of Khubilai's successor.

The Emperor treated his spiritual instructor with the highest respect, giving him the following title, 'Son of an Indian Deity, Incarnate Buddha, Composer of Writings, Who brings Complete Peace to the Kingdom, Pak-pa Ti-shri, Pandit of the Five Kinds of Learning'.[1]

The religious conversion was, indeed, only partial, and slid backwards again after Khubilai's death, but three

[1] Hor Chö-jung, vol. i, p. 99, of Dr. Huth's edition.

centuries later, again through Tibetan agency, it was pressed to completion.

In A.D. 1270 the Sa-kya Hierarch was given the sovereignty over central Tibet. Each in succession received the title of 'Mighty Nephew',[1] to emphasize his close relationship with the Emperor of China. It was a significant change from the time, four hundred years earlier, when China had been compelled to pay tribute to Tibet, a change due to the softening influence of Buddhism, rendering Tibet unable, in the material things of life, to stand up to their powerful neighbours.

On the decease of one of the Hierarchs, while engaged in building operations on a large scale, his steward assumed the title and completed the work.[2] This brought in a Mongol force, 'who descended on Raven Fort (Cha-rok Dzong) and slew him. Thus was the prophecy fulfilled when the time was due.'[3] Soon afterwards the Hierarch himself was assassinated, apparently by his attendants, and this brought in another Mongol army. *The Feast of Pleasure* says, 'Sa-kya, acting as the nose-string brings the Mongol army into Tibet. And the misery was greater even than among those who have gone into Hell'.[4]

Other large monasteries had meanwhile been built, chief among them being Dri-kung[5] built in A.D. 1177, and 'The Tiger's Prophecy' (Ta-lung[6]), forty-five miles north of Lhasa, the following year. The pandits still continued to come, chief among them being Sakya Shri from Kashmir, who came as an old man, and remained for ten years (1202–12). So great was his fame that the Blue Treasury regards him as one of the future Buddhas,[7] while the local religious history of the 'Valley of Taste', a valley which runs into the Tsang-po at Shi-ga-tse, is equally full

[1] Ön-chen (དཔོན་ཆེན་).

[2] Tep-ter Ngön-po, vol. iv, fol. 6.

[3] *Feast of Pleasure*, fol. 57.

[4] Idem, fol. 57.

[5] འབྲི་གུང་

[6] སྟག་ལུང་

[7] Tep-ter Ngön-po, vol. xv, fol. 1.

of praise.[1] Others came from U-gyen,[2] bringing secret wisdom. Later on there was a large number of highly skilled translators.[3]

It was a time of constant internecine struggles. Even Buddhism could not entirely control the natural ebullitions of Tibetan pugnacity. Dri-kung and Ta-lung were strong and semi-independent. Still less could Buddhism control the armies of Mongolia, whose over-flowing power had not yet come under the restraining influence of Tibetan Buddhism. The secular ascendancy of Sa-kya was unable to survive for longer than seventy-five years.

Many of the Hierarchs were famous for their learning. Sa-kya's general outlook encouraged liberality and breadth of view. Some Tibetans had by this time become so learned that their Indian pandits expressed surprise that they did not work independently. Of one they said, 'Any pandit in India, who possessed but a third part of your knowledge or philosophy, would set about compiling books on sacred subjects.' Of this Tibetan priest it is recorded that he would never reprove anybody unless he knew that the reproof would have a good effect.[4] But Tantrism, magic and mystic, was in full force, and there seems to have been a good deal of Shaktism with it.

The Blue Treasury gives us a glimpse showing how the large libraries in the Tibetan monasteries were gradually evolved during the eleventh and succeeding centuries:

> Tsün-pa Jam-yang sent a large variety of goods to Clear Mind, a priest of the Central Province,[5] and others, and exhorted them to collect all the translated scriptural works[6] for the library of the Nar-tang monastery. Accordingly Clear Mind and two others, with great labour, collected the recent translations, arranged them in order, and added rather more than a thousand new religious treatises. From this collection several others were produced. Each

[1] Nyang Chö-jung, fol. 65.

[2] The modern Swat, east of Afghanistan, the land from which Padma Sambhava came.

[3] Tep-ter Ngön-po, vol. iv, fol. 7.

[4] Idem, iii, fol. 28.

[5] In which Lhasa lies.

[6] By selling these goods.

The monastery of 'The Tiger's Prophecy'

edition underwent correction, and so became more trustworthy. Thus Sha-lu, Rin-pung, Gong-kar, and several other places of learning received revised sets of scriptures, each better than its predecessor, and all based on the Nar-tang copy. This work was entirely due to Translator Ngok[1] and his line of disciples.[2]

It would appear that the original writings and the translations brought from India were examined and revised over and over again with meticulous care. The Blue Treasury sets out the names of nineteen separate translators who at various times translated or revised the 'Tantras of the Wheel of Time'.[3] And so it was with other works in a greater or less degree.[4]

Internal quarrels put an end to the Sa-kya overlordship in 1345, and the power passed into the hands of a man known equally as Si-tu and Pak-mo-tru. He fought with Dri-kung and Sa-kya, and he prevailed over both. The fifth Dalai Lama's history relates:

> Si-tu having defeated Sa-kya, the Chinese Emperor was made aware of this. But Si-tu sent presents and an envoy, who obtained an edict in favour of Si-tu. Thus Si-tu obtained supreme power for a time in Tibet and Great Tibet.[5]

The various chiefs and governors, as the Blue Treasury tells us, surrendered their seals to him. He is said to have enacted a new legal code. Among other changes he abolished capital punishment, prescribing the payment of blood money to the relatives of the deceased. King Si-tu and his successors ruled a large part of Tibet, but to some extent depended on Chinese support.

We are now nearly five centuries later than 'Long Hair', the last of the fighting kings. Much of the country is parcelled out among powerful monasteries, who, while professing the religion of the peace-loving Buddha, fight each other for spiritual and worldly supremacy. For five hundred years have not sufficed to send the fighting spirit

[1] Mar-pa's disciple.
[2] Tep-ter Ngön-po, vol. vi, fol. 6.
[3] Kala Chakra.
[4] Vol. xi, fol. 41.
[5] *Feast of Pleasure*, fol. 80.

to sleep. And invasions of the Mongols, as yet outside the Buddhist fold, added to the turmoil.

The Blue Treasury, writing of this somewhat confused period, sums it up as follows:

> In later years the great Lama Dro-gön Pak-pa succeeded in bringing the whole of Tibet under Sa-kya's sway. Yet internal disputes brought this power to an end after about seventy-five years. Pak-mo-tru then attained sovereign power; but it was not long before that hierarchy also lost its power. Then came the Dri-kung hierarchy: it retained the sovereign rule for the longest period. But, later on, the adherents of Sa-kya raided Dri-kung and set it on fire.
>
> Only the Ta-lung hierarchy, since its inception by the great Ta-lung Tang-pa, has had a long period of undisturbed peace and prosperity, as it did not excite the rivalry or enmity of any other hierarchy or sect. It has had a long line of Hierarchs in succession. Even the invasions of the Mongols left the Ta-lung monastery untouched.[1]

When one has visited the Ta-lung monastery, one can understand this, for it lies tucked away in a fold of the mountains, away from the main lines of communication. And its religious heads were stern disciplinarians.

The revival of Buddhism, beginning weakly some seventy years after Dar-ma's death and steadily growing in strength, had long ago surpassed the efforts of the early kings, and was now the dominant religion of Tibet. Under Atisha, Mar-pa, and others it had taken a strong Tantrik turn. The secret places of Tantrism were more impressive and more congenial to the Tibetan nomad, travelling in wild wastes and facing the unknown forces of Nature on a stupendous scale, than the agnostic disillusionment or the intricate metaphysics of the earlier Buddhist schools.

Let the learned lamas study the latter; that was their business. But he, the plain man, wanted some power that would hold in check the spirits of mountain, of torrent, and of hail; some form of religion that would recognize his Pönist gods and include them in its system. After all they were his old gods. Pure Buddhism did not recognize

[1] Tep-ter Ngön-po, vol. viii, fol. 108.

them, but was it safe to neglect them? One of his acquaintances had done so, and he and his whole family had died. No, it certainly was not safe. Such instances could always be found; they are quoted still, even at the present day.

The Tibetan histories are really histories of Tibetan Buddhism, written by keen Buddhists. We cannot expect impartiality on religious questions in their pages. But even from them we may gather that Pönism was still fighting the victorious invader. We read of a conflict between a Buddhist priest and a powerful Pönist priest in the Pu-rang district of western Tibet. The latter 'used to do as much harm as he could to all Buddhist hermits and ascetic lamas. The Hierarch of the great Dri-kung monastery set himself against the Pönist, and eventually, by one means and another, the latter and all his family were driven from their home. Similarly, disrespectful persons among those who lived near the monastery gradually dwindled in luck and at last died out, so that the number of such disbelievers greatly decreased.'[1] Tibetans believe that good luck is inherent in persons, in greater or lesser amounts, as are bodily strength or brains. But each of these may be increased or lessened by the strong mental power of another concentrated on it. It is the mind that rules.

Similarly, the Blue Treasury records a duel of magic between a Hindu yogi and a Buddhist priest in which the latter, by stupendous feats, proves of course victorious. The history of the religion in the Valley of Taste tells how the son of a Pönist 'through the influence of his good actions in his former life became a staunch believer in Buddhism and learnt the religious subjects thoroughly'.[2]

The Buddhist histories often testify to the influence of Pönism on Buddhism. Naropa, the Indian teacher of Mar-pa, had a wife, and she introduced a set of doctrines which were known as 'The Ripening and Liberating Series'. There was a leading Tibetan priest—a Trup-top,

[1] Tep-ter Ngön-po, vol. viii, fol. 83.

[2] Nyang Chö-jung, fol. 138.

i.e. one that has gained control over a deity—who followed these doctrines, and was proficient also in Sanskrit literature and the 'Wheel of Time' Tantras. This lama 'learnt all the Pönist doctrines from a Master of the Pönist lore, and delivered lectures on them to others. Seven hundred students came to him to study the subject.'[1]

I have met these Trup-tops in Tibet, and can understand that there should be a measure of sympathy between them and the Pönists, for certainly their actions and their equipment are far removed from those of the orthodox Buddhist. When we were in Lhasa, my faithful servant, Rab-den, took a photograph of one for me.

'Your instrument cannot make a picture of me', he said, 'I am a Trup-top.' And then, as an afterthought, 'But if it does, give me one of the pictures'. Seated at his little table, almost naked, he held in his right hand a drum made from a human skull, and in his left a trumpet made from a human thigh-bone. On his table were two skull cups, one for beer, which he offered to his deities, the other for tea, which he drank himself. His bell and sacred thunderbolt rested also on the table. Over his right shoulder passed the hermit's band; at his left side stood the long pole in which dwelt the minds of the deities that he controlled. For the minds are independent and all-important; it does not matter where the bodies are. He did not shave his hair as an ordinary monk does, but wore it long, somewhat after the fashion of Indian Sadhus.

Pönism had, too, a subtle and potent influence in that it coloured the Tibetan translations of the Buddhist Scriptures themselves. The same authority says of a translator, 'His translations were said to be exceptionally faithful ones, not mixed[2] with the Tibetan religion,[3] whereas those of all others were mixed with it.[4] It is of interest to note that even after Buddhism had obtained a firm hold, this Buddhist history refers to Pönism as 'the Tibetan religion'.

[1] Tep-ter Ngön-po, vol. ix, fol. 2.

[2] འདྲེས་པ་

[3] Pö Chö (བོད་ཆོས་).

[4] Tep-ter Ngön-po, vol. vii, fol. 11.

'Seated at his little table, almost naked, he held in his right hand a drum made from a human skull'

Bridge of canes in Sikkim, where Pönism flourishes

We can see what a strong force their old religion has always been to the Tibetan people. They developed Buddhism along the lines that suited them best. Their capacity for building is shown in the massive monasteries that harmonize so admirably with the great mountains round them, their capacity for organization is shown by the completeness of their hierarchy and their monastic discipline. This complex system, however, has perforce to defer to the needs of the ordinary Tibetan, and meet him in respect of spirits, good and bad, and supply, or allow others to supply, the charms and spells that control these heirs of the older Faith. In Burma and other Hinayanist countries one finds the same survivals, to a smaller extent perhaps, but still the same.

The lives of the Buddhist monks, those who stand out above their contemporaries, are individually and fully recorded in the Tibetan religious histories (*Chö-jung*). These are the things that are important to Tibetans. From time to time secular events, a Tibetan invasion of China, Turkistan, or India, or a Mongol invasion of Tibet, flash across their pages, but they come mainly as incidents to illustrate the life and teaching of some saint or disciple; they stand outside the central purpose and are rapidly passed by. The spiritual life is what matters; all else is illusion.

It would be tedious to Western readers were I to detail events in the lives of many of these teachers. But I will pass one or two more in review in order to give life to the above general remarks.

Rim-po-che Kar-ma-pa, i.e. 'The Precious One of the Kar-ma-pa sect', a sect approximating to the Ka-gyü, lived during the time of the Sa-kya Hierarch. Like most of those who distinguished themselves he was credited with great precocity as a child, 'having become proficient in reading and writing when only six years old. When nine years of age, he was believed to have read the scriptures, to be able to repeat them by heart, and to understand their meanings.' This calls for considerable powers of belief, for there are, as already mentioned, one hundred and eight volumes in these scriptures.

When he came to meet a certain high lama, their meeting was attended with auspicious omens, and the lama imparted to him all branches of knowledge. He then meditated for ten years, thereby pleasing his spiritual teacher (*guru*). After this retirement there followed a visit to eastern Tibet, where he exhibited miracles, and over five hundred disciples flocked to him.

His fame spread to the Chinese Emperor of the Mongol dynasty, at whose invitation he visited China. He made the Emperor and his courtiers to embrace the Buddhist faith. He traversed all the dominions of the Mongols and the Chinese. He founded a large monastery in Min-yak Ga. By means of his miracles he converted many to Buddhism.[1]

One of the most pre-eminently learned lamas of Tibet, named 'Self-produced Thunderbolt'[2] had a disciple known as 'The Playful Thunderbolt'.[3] The latter visited China during the reign of the last Mongol Emperor, Tohan Timur. After receiving his invitation, he took two years over his journey to the Chinese capital, where he initiated the Emperor and his sons into the six doctrines of Naropa, the Indian Tantrist. Miracles of Tantrik type are recorded, for it is claimed for this lama that:

Previous to his visit there had been insurrections, and Manchuria had suffered nine years' scarcity of food grains, which sold at five measures of grain for one measure of silver. As a result of the severe famine epidemics were raging, and insurrections had broken out, and the whole Empire was wracked with troubles. But the lama, by quelling and pacifying the local spirits, brought peace to the country. The rebels gradually came and bowed down. By invoking the aid of the Buddha of medicine the epidemics were stopped. By invoking the god of wealth the lama brought such plenty to the land that sixty measures of grain sold for one of silver.

But, as we are told, the lama's reputation kindled jealousy, and so he left China for his own country, refusing all subsequent entreaties to remain.[4] This Emperor,

[1] Tep-ter Ngön-po, vol. viii, fol. 37.
[2] Rang-chung Dor-je.
[3] Röl-pe Dor-je.
[4] Tep-ter Ngön-po, vol. viii, fols. 43, 44.

indeed, was a weak-minded and lazy man, who gave himself up to pleasure, leaving the administration to eunuchs and others. His conduct raised a revolt, and the Mongol rule over China was overthrown.

Of a more ordinary type was 'Magical Void-contemplating Lion'.[1] His house was in a village high up in the mountains. He was born at sunrise; a rainbow settled on the house when he was born. At the age of eight he developed extraordinary powers of love, meekness, and faith; when nine years old he had realized all things to be illusory. One need not therefore be surprised to read that 'at eleven years of age he was pervaded by feelings of melancholy'.

At twelve he dreamt that the sun and moon were shining brightly at the same time. On waking, he saw the Compassionate Lord (*Chen-re-zi*) who said, 'Meditate on the meaning of the Heart's Drop',[2] and disappeared. When twenty-four years old he visited eight learned lamas, one after the other, and acquired knowledge from each, especially in the Heart's Drop doctrine. He passed many years in devotion in remote solitudes. Thus he saved many beings and died at the age of sixty-three. The history has many saints of this kind.

Though they practised austerities, all were not celibate. Of one we are told:

> He had several sons by different mothers. Some of the descendants of these are alive to this day, and they, too, give instruction in the Heart's Drop doctrine. Most of them have attained extraordinary powers and are consequently regarded as Teachers.

To this day one finds lamas of the Red Sect (*Nying-ma*), the original introduction of Padma Sambhava, who have a wife and children, but yet practise most severe austerities.[3]

Another 'forbad shooting and fishing from the province of Kong-po up to the Ye Pass'. Such prohibitions have been greatly extended since his time. At the present day the Dalai Lama has in force a general prohibition against

[1] Trül Zhik Seng-ge. [2] Nying Tik.
[3] An example of one of these is given in *The People of Tibet*, p. 190.

shooting and fishing, which is observed with fair thoroughness in the districts round Lhasa, but is often disregarded in the more remote parts. Meanwhile individual monasteries reinforce this supreme behest with local orders of their own.

During the thirteenth and fourteenth centuries the missionary spirit was still in full swing. People came from the mountainous lands to the north-west of India and from the plains of the Panjab as well as from far-away Utai Shan in China to sit at the feet of Tibetan teachers,[1] for the Tibetan standard of learning was high. Owing to their keenness in study and the accuracy of their translations they would sometimes correct Indian teachers in the interpretation of Indian texts.[2]

But the combative spirit had declined. Mongol invasions are constantly recorded; one Mongol chief burnt eight Buddhist priests alive.[3] Even at the present time Tibetans will frequently point out to you in central Tibet the ruined forts and houses, that bear witness to these invasions.

Some fighting indeed there was. One has only to see the outside of the larger Tibetan monasteries—the same now as they were several centuries ago—to realize their strength in attack or defence with the weapons of those days. If one goes inside and makes acquaintance with the different monks, one finds many who have no learning and pass no examinations, but use their hands instead of their brains and are prepared for any affray. These are the *dop-dop*. They wear their hair long and their skirts short, and paint their faces black. There are *dop-dop* among the lay population also. When a man wishes to hire ruffians to attack somebody or to defend himself, he hires some of the *dop-dop*. Lamas travelling in places infested with robbers take bodyguards of them.

To this day the whole body of monks constitute nominally Tibet's third line of defence against invasion.

[1] Tep-ter Ngön-po, vol. viii, fol. 86.
[2] Idem, vol. v, fol. 15.
[3] Idem, vol. viii, fol. 57.

First come the regular troops, then the lay-militia and then the 'golden army' as the monks under arms are termed. After all, what Tibetans fear in the event of invasion is not so much the loss of their country, though that is bad enough. What they fear most of all is the loss of 'the holy religion'. And the monks may be expected to fight for this. But of course neither the golden army nor the lay militia possess military equipment, nor have they received any military training worth the name. And during the thirteenth and fourteenth centuries, of which we are now reading, they must have been equally lacking in these respects.

It was a time of local uprisings. The Dri-kung monastery stood out against the power of Sa-kya. The Sa-kya Hierarch mustered his minions, subdued Dri-kung, and burnt the monastery down. The Mongols were ever ready to ride out from their homes on an expedition into Tibet, when the fancy seized them, burning monasteries and dzongs. One hierarch of Dri-kung by his spiritual influence prevented 'such misfortunes as the burning of monasteries and massacres of people'.[1]

Some hierarchs disliked exercising the temporal power. Of one at Dri-kung we read that 'he became disgusted with his secular responsibilities, and abandoned them, devoting himself to purely religious studies and meditation for sixteen years, thus gaining divine visions'.[2]

There was no training or cohesion to resist foreign attack. Still there are many indications that the martial energy of the Tibetans, though sapped by Buddhism, has not even now been destroyed. Should Buddhism ever go, the combative spirit will return.

Indeed, Tibet expects later on to fight for her religion. You can sometimes read in Tibetan books about the country called Shambhala. When people talk about it they usually call it 'Shambhala of the North', and describe it as a mystical country which, three or four centuries hence, will be the scene of hostilities, fierce and decisive, between

[1] Tep-ter Ngön-po, vol. viii, fol. 77. [2] Idem, fol. 80.

Buddhists and Muhammadans. One sees paintings representing the battle in Tibetan houses. Bodhisattvas are depicted as joining in the fray; in fact, it is they who decide it. Shambhala lies somewhere to the north-west of Tibet. Dorjieff, the influential Mongol from Russian Mongolia, who used to hold a Chair of Philosophy at Lhasa, claimed that Shambhala is Russia.

In this connexion it is of interest to read in this history, compiled in far-away Tibet, what appears to be an allusion to the warfare between Europe and the Turks. A lama, who died during the first half of the fifteenth century at the early age of thirty-seven, announced that Shambhala was disputing with Mecca and he must go to help Shambhala. There was probably intercourse between Tibet and south-eastern Europe through the Mongols who had conquered Russia and made periodical irruptions into Tibet. There may indeed have been Tibetans in the armies of Tamerlane, the great Mongol conqueror, who routed the Turkish general, Bayezid, in 1402, and temporarily saved Constantinople for Europe.

The connexion between Nepal and Tibet was strong. Apart from the long sojourns of Tibetan students in the country of this southern neighbour, the pandits of the Newar tribe in Nepal came to Tibet and were well received. Nak-tso, the chief translator among those who served Atisha, was aided by a Newar pandit as well as by an Indian.[1] Another Newar pandit, named 'Great Mercy' who was invited to Tibet, received a present of a thousand ounces of gold on his departure for his own country besides thirty-seven offerings during his stay.[2] But Tibet was farther off than was Nepal from the debased Buddhism of India, and the characteristics of its people differ more greatly from those of Indians. Accordingly, to a far greater extent than did Nepal, it evolved its own Buddhist Church in full vigour on national lines.

The late Indian Buddhism in its last refuge in Bengal had a strong admixture of Hinduism. Tibet added further

[1] Tep-ter Ngön-po, vol. v, fol. 10. [2] Idem, vol. vii, fol. 12.

elements from its own Pŏnism, and, thus blended, Tibetan Buddhism came into being as it stands to-day before the ordinary uneducated Tibetan. The administrative ability of the race has organized the priesthood into an effective national Church, which suits the needs of the Tibetans and their Mongol kinsfolk. It has also organized the Buddhas and the numerous gods and demons into an orderly whole, so that the lamas can tell for every department of activity, human or divine, what spirit, mild or fierce, good or bad, in the sky above, in the middle air, or under the earth, is the one in control, the one to be invoked.

And the fighting instincts of the Tibetan were not to be denied. Debarred by this new religion from warfare against material foes, he shifted the battleground to the spirit world. Tibetan Buddhism was not militant in the sense that Christianity was militant, with its armies abroad and its persecutions at home. It has usually been tolerant in these respects, exerting pressure no doubt, but proceeding to extreme measures less often than might have been expected. Its chief fights have been against spiritual foes, the evil spirits that are believed to dwell everywhere, harming man and beast.

VII

COTTON-CLAD MI-LA

None is more highly revered in Tibet than the poet-saint Mi-la, to whom a brief reference has been made in the preceding chapter. The Scriptures, indeed, are recited by the monks; the histories, though forbidden to the monks lest they become too deeply interested, are read by laymen; but the Biography, as well as 'The Hundred Thousand Songs', of 'Mi-la The Revered',[1] is read and quoted by all.

He lived during the latter half of the eleventh century, Mar-pa's most famous disciple, and therefore of the Ka-gyü sect. England was then under the Norman Conquest; India was experiencing the first Muhammadan invasions. In Tibet the Buddhist revival was in full blast, while the people had strengthened their own primitive methods with the advanced civilization of China. And the biography and songs—written in simple language—give us not only the glimpse of a great man, but also a study, valuable for historical purposes, of Tibetan life and Tibetan religion during the eleventh century. And, as literature, they give us the real literature of Tibet, far more living and redolent of the soil, than the Scriptures and the Commentaries, these so-called classical works, which are but close-fitting translations from Sanskrit originals. The last are held in high respect for the religious teaching embodied in them. But 'Cotton-clad M-ila's'[2] life and songs are read and quoted by learned and simple, by rich and poor, a prized national possession. The late Da-wa Sam-trup, to whom reference will be made in the chapter headed *Sources*, read a large part of the Biography very thoroughly with me, and expounded its inner meanings.

Mi-la was born in the Fire-Dragon year (1038 A.D.) at a place called Kya-nga Tsa in the district of Gung-tang, near the frontier of Nepal. His father was away trading at the time, and was so delighted to hear the news of the son's

[1] Je-tsün Mi-la. [2] Mi-la Re-pa.

birth that he gave him the name of Tö-pa-ga, 'Delightful to Hear', Mi-la being the family name. The father was a prosperous member of the community, but died when Mi-la was only seven years old, and his sister three years younger. He entrusted his widow and young children together with the property to the charge of a cousin and the cousin's sister. These, however, proved unfaithful to the trust, and succeeded eventually in turning out the rightful heirs and keeping the property for themselves.

The boy had a strong physique and a beautiful voice, so that the neighbours were agreed that his name 'Delightful to Hear' had proved to be peculiarly well-fitting. But the family was desperately poor. One day the boy came home singing and somewhat tipsy. His mother, who at the time was roasting barley, felt furious that he should have the heart to sing when she and they were so unhappy. Dropping her tongs and her roasting-whisk, she came out with a stick and a handful of ashes. Throwing the ashes in his face, she belaboured him on his head with the stick, upbraided him—and then fainted. He was stricken with remorse and promised to do whatever she asked. 'Learn the Black Art,' she replied, 'and kill our enemies by magic.'[1] Mi-la departed and joined himself to a band of companions. They travelled together and eventually found that a man named 'Wrathful Conquering Teacher' was the most powerful of all the Tantrik sorcerers. This Black Magician was at first unwilling to impart his precious secrets. He amused young Mi-la and his fellow-students with high-sounding pursuits, that satisfied the others, who all returned home. But Mi-la remained and entreated the Magician to impart to him a really efficacious charm.[2]

The latter reminded young Mi-la that many appeals had been made to him by people anxious to learn his peerless art. These had sent gold and turquoises from Nga-ri (western Tibet), silks and tea from Kam and Am-do

[1] *Milarepa*, by Evans-Wentz, p. 62.
[2] Tep-ter Ngön-po, vol. viii, fol. 12.

(eastern Tibet), grain, butter, and woollen fabrics from the central province, cattle and ponies from the south-east. But Mi-la not only had a pitiful tale to tell, but offered himself—as a complete disciple should do—body and life, to the Magician. The latter at length agreed that the instruction should be given, but he had a partner living at a distance, and their mutual agreement was that those wishing to learn how to kill by magic should be sent to the partner, while those who wished to bring down hail-storms and destroy the crops of their enemies should be sent to the Black Magician himself. Mi-la learnt both. His magic brought down a house where his uncle's eldest son was celebrating his wedding feast, thus killing thirty-five persons, though the uncle and aunt—for so he terms these cousins—being outside at the time, escaped. Some of those who sided with Mi-la's family were on their way to the house and witnessed the occurrence, as did a maid-servant who had come out of the house to fetch water. Outside the house was an enclosed yard. In this appeared a seething mass of scorpions, spiders, snakes, frogs and lizards, among which one gigantic scorpion was clawing and tugging at the main pillar of the house. The ponies, which, as is usual in Tibet, were tethered below the house, became excited. Some burst loose, the colts rushed on the mares, the mares kicked, and eventually the main pillar of the house was knocked down. Mi-la followed this up with a hail-storm which destroyed the barley crop of the district.

Thus he trod the path of darkness. But repentance followed. Seeking for a Teacher who should lead him along the path of light, he heard the name of Mar-pa and felt the strong call of faith. Yet he must first endure a most rigorous and protracted penance to pay for the evil deeds which he had accumulated during his career as a death-dealing sorcerer. Mar-pa made him build a house, and, when built, pull it down again. Not only that; he had to carry back the stones to the site from which he had removed them. This was repeated several times, one house being nine stories high.

A Tibetan sorcerer

At length the disciple ventured a humble remonstrance. What was the *Guru's* reply? 'The first time I did not give the matter enough thought, the second time I seem to have been tipsy and so gave you a mistaken order.' The drunkenness was merely feigned.

When reading of Mar-pa's methods, I was irresistibly reminded of a Living Buddha, the Grand Lama of Urga, who died a few years ago. Europeans would find him drunk and question members of his flock how they could believe in such as he showed himself to be. But the reply was, 'He is not drunk, but this he does to test our faith. True believers can see him for what he is.' So it was with Mar-pa. In the heart of Asia faith is not confined within the bounds set by western Europe.

Mar-pa would fall into a temper, beat his disciple, knock him down, and set him other hard tasks to test the young sinner's faith and devotion. Mi-la's back was one large festering sore, and sometimes he ran away, but he never failed to return. He was made even to injure and kill human beings and animals by sorcery. A great sin, no doubt, but to disobey one's *guru* would be a sin far greater. Always he hoped to receive from Mar-pa the Initiation and the Teachings, and always the latter held them back.

Mar-pa's kind-hearted wife, who was also a skilful cook, helped him in his troubles. Hearing from her about Mi-la's back, Mar-pa showed him how pads are put on the sore backs of donkeys and ponies, and advised him to do the same for himself.

'What is the use of a pad? The whole of my back is one large sore.'

'Well, it will help to keep the earth from penetrating the sore and making it worse,' said Mar-pa. 'This is nothing to the trials that my *guru* endured. Go on with your work of carrying the earth and stones.'

The Reverend Mother, as he terms Mar-pa's wife, even helped him to run away, and gave him the necessary presents to enable him to engage another lama.

Not only the drunkenness, but the anger and cruelty

which Mar-pa displayed were but pretences, the outcome of a double purpose. Firstly, they served to purge young Mi-la of the terrible sins of sorcery and taking the lives of man and beast and bird. Secondly, they tested the faith of the disciple in his *guru*. Unless this faith is complete, there can be no spiritual advance in the disciple. We have travelled far now from the teaching of Gotama, who made but little appeal to faith. Rather we are with the form of Buddhism that has been mingled with their old Faith, and thus the more fully adapted to the needs of the great Tatar branch of humanity.

On and on went the penances, almost unbearable and seemingly unreasonable. But at long last Mi-la's faith and perseverance were rewarded; he received from his *guru* the Initiation and the Teachings. Both *guru* and disciple drank the consecrated wine out of the *guru*'s cup, made from a human skull, an emblem that reminds how transitory is human life. Mar-pa told those assembled for the Initiation his reasons for afflicting Mi-la, and added that the latter still retained a small portion of his evil *karma* owing to his consort's ill-timed pity and narrow understanding. Happy times followed. Instruction, isolation in 'Copper Cave', meditation, and development of the understanding, and thus several years passed by. Mi-la was thirty-eight years old when he first came to Mar-pa.

But eventually, now forty-four years of age, Mi-la yearned for his home. On arrival there he found the dried bones of his mother inside his house, which had been long dilapidated, with its ruined turrets, 'like the ears of an old donkey'. He made a pillow of his mother's bones and remained for a week in religious meditation, during which he realized that he could save both his father and mother from the miseries of worldly existence. His sister was away begging her daily food. More than ever convinced of the illusory nature of all wordly things, he was strengthened in his resolve to devote himself to the ascetic life. The mortification of the body is a religious longing that lies deep-rooted in the philosophy of Asia. The Buddha himself, though renouncing it as useless for deliverance, could not uproot it, no, not even in those who professed to follow his teaching. Mar-pa, seeing his pupil's capacity for it, had ordered him to follow this side of the religious life rather than the other side which spends itself in teaching.

His resolve Mi-la carried out with terrible severity. His aunt and her brother, living in their respective yak-hair tents, set their dogs on him, pelted him with stones, and belaboured him with a tent-pole. For himself he did not mind this: it helped to cleanse the stain of his evil deeds. But he grieved for them accumulating stores of sins for themselves.

As for food, he imposed on himself the self-denial which the Buddha had abandoned. Meditating in his cave, high on the mountain side, he would not descend to the village below, even to beg for food. It was a waste of precious time. Let him devote every possible minute to the deep meditation which he had learned. The attainment of Buddhahood was a very difficult feat. He would do not only this: he would achieve it in a single lifetime, and thus qualify himself to work for the lasting benefit of all 'mind-possessors', i.e. man, beast, bird, fish, every one. Outside his cave the nettles grew; on these he lived for nine long years. Telling his life story to Re-chung, his disciple and biographer, he says: 'As I had no clothes on my outside, and no nutritious food in my inside, my body became like a skeleton, and of the colour of a nettle. Green, drooping hairs grew on it.'

Though the cold was arctic, his sole clothing was a single cotton garment; this wore out, till replaced by Pe-ta, his sister, or by Dze-se, the woman to whom as a boy his parents had betrothed him. 'How constant you are, Dze-se,' he said at one of her visits, 'never to have married'.

'I would marry nobody else,' was Dze-se's reply. 'And, knowing your powers in the Black Art, none dared to ask me; they feared the deities that stand behind you.'

Mi-la's story continues. 'My clothes were all worn out.

I thought that for use as clothes and bedding I would stitch together the few remnants of the ragged skin coat, the empty sack of flour, and the cotton cloth. But I abandoned the idea, thinking that, if I died that night, the stitching would be useless. Yes, it would be better to continue my meditation.'

Throughout his religious career runs the idea that as life is uncertain, he must use every available minute of his time in that form of religious meditation which is known to Indians as *samadhi*. 'For there will Buddhahood be obtained.' He sings one of his numerous songs, dedicated as usual to his *guru*, now passed away.

Hail' son[1] of the Lord Naro[2] and Way of Deliverance!
Send the waves of grace over[3] this beggar that he may cling to the solitude.

Keep me free from the distractions of Evil Ones and the World
Grant me advance in *samadhi*.

Grant that I may not yearn for the pond of the lower peace.[4]
Let the flower of super-consciousness[5] be formed in me.

Let not the hurly-burly of formed thoughts arise in me.
Promote the foliage of the unformed state.

Make me single-minded in the House of Devotion.
Cause the fruit of Knowledge to ripen.

But his fasting had weakened him, so that 'I could not subdue the air of my body and thus did not gain the ecstatic warmth. My body was very cold.' It is believed that three nerves meet below the navel. By meditation on these warmth is generated, but long meditation after a prescribed pattern is necessary.

So he prayed earnestly to his *guru*. One night during conscious sleep[6] some women appeared to him in a vision

[1] Spiritual son. [2] Mar-pa's *guru*, an Indian.

[3] བྱིན་གྱིས་རློབས་ Lit. 'Make blessings to flow like waves over'.

[4] The first stage of *samadhi*, in which all thoughts are absent.

[5] The second stage of *samadhi*, in which the devotee realizes his state.

[6] *Ö-sel*, in which the sleeper knows that he is sleeping.

and showed him physical and breathing exercises by which he could obtain it. He fights on lest he be pressed down by the 'five poisons of ignorance': to wit, wrath, pride, jealousy, covetousness, and sloth.

Among the common features of Tibet, then as now, were the stalkers,[1] who ranged the mountain sides with their slim, long-nosed dogs, in search of the wild sheep, wild goats, and gazelle. In these cold expanses there is nothing that grows more than six inches high, and the Tibetan, unaided, cannot approach near enough for his primitive weapons to take effect. So the dogs find the quarry and corner it, maybe on the top of an overhanging rock, until their owners can come up.

This tracking and killing is not only opposed to Buddhism; it is also difficult and uncertain. Hunters often come half-starved to the saint's cave, and, believing that he has a hidden store of food, maltreat him. A thief comes by night for the same purpose. Mi-la bursts into laughter and calls out, 'See whether you can find by night, where I cannot find by day'. The thief also laughs and goes out.

The hunters usually fear at first to enter, believing him, all emaciated as he is, to be an evil spirit. He reassures them, and on one occasion they give him food, and ask him to pray that the animals which they have killed may be reborn in a higher state, and so gain, not lose, by the killing. Mi-la has no qualms about taking this meat food. He finds that it benefits him spiritually as well as bodily. But he uses it sparingly, that it may last a long time. Eventually it becomes full of maggots. And now he leaves it, not because he objects to food gone bad, for to that he is accustomed, but because 'I should be snatching away food which has been already allotted to the maggots'.

Pe-ta and Dze-se try to induce him to lead an easier life, but without avail. 'Your devotion will not run away, if you have some good food and clothes,' says Pe-ta. They bring him food and a blanket, for which he is duly grateful

[1] In Tibetan *kyi-ra-pa*, which might be translated 'dog-goat-man'.

He had been checked in his spiritual progress by inability to concentrate owing to lack of food. One cannot do much on nettles alone. The gift of wine and good food, though at the time it entailed 'physical pain and mental commotion', helped in the end. But it had to be accompanied by physical and mental exercises. And so he gained what he sought. 'My mind obtained a state of tranquillity, clearness, and freedom from obstruction.'

Thus, following the Way, he obtained in the end full control over his mind. To the Tibetan the mind is the Universal Cause of all things. It can influence external phenomena; it can, for instance, control the weather, for, in fact, these external phenomena are but illusory; the mind alone is real. Mi-la had realized the supreme wisdom of 'The That'. The Blue Treasury, which deals with his career at some length, says, 'While to others he appeared to be suffering the last extremities of want, he actually enjoyed the highest spiritual joy and fitness of body'.[1] He was by nature endowed with a strong constitution. Religion held every ounce of him; he had no worldly anxieties. His disposition was cheerful; he frequently burst into song. And thus he lived to his eighty-third year,[2] far beyond the normal of this somewhat short-lived race.

For protection against the great cold he had developed the power of internal warmth by which devotees, as is claimed, can dwell naked in the snow. And he is believed to have gained other occult powers; that of flying like a bird, of transforming his body into a flame of fire, into a sheet of water, into a running stream. He could multiply his body into hundreds of bodies and each would go to the Realm of a Buddha, listen to religious discourses, return and preach the religion to others.

His occult powers being known, he felt that worldly people would flock to him to use his power in warding off calamities from them and in advancing their worldly ends.

[1] Tep-ter Ngön-po, vol. viii, fol. 15.

[2] Eighty-fourth according to Tibetan reckoning.

In him, too, would be generated 'the demon of the son of the god', to wit, pride. Worldly fame would cause a break in his meditation and darken the spiritual outlook.

Accordingly, leaving his cave, 'White Cave of the Horse's Tooth', he set out for 'Between the Rivers at Lap-chi'. Lap-chi is a hihh mountain in the neighbourhood of Mount Everest. The Blue Treasury tells us that he had already lived for nine years on nettles, and that his six best-known caves during that period were situated in the Kyi-rong district, on the Tibet-Nepal frontier, about one hundred and fifty miles north-west of Everest.[1]

His earthen pot breaks on the way. He has no other, but he welcomes the loss, for it shows the impermanence of all things.

The earthen pot now is, and now is not.

. . . .

My sole possession.

By breaking, it has become a Lama,

For it has preached an admirable discourse on the impermanence of things.

Mi-la's religious outlook was based on *karma*. Good deeds, words, or thoughts cause good results, evil deeds, words, or thoughts produce evil in countless future lives. All is based on that.

He believed in the doctrine of Voidness. In one passage, speaking of worldliness on one side and the spiritual life which leads to nirvana on the other, he says: 'I understand for certain that the essence of both is the clear light of voidness'. That is, approximately, a state of mind in which the pure consciousness is untouched by any ideas—for such would lead it aside from the true path—and flows on uncontaminated. Mi-la constantly prays to be delivered from 'the obstructing thoughts', which hinder from 'the Final Goal'. An outlook still held by many millions of Asiatics, constituting one of the firmest barriers between their continent and the bustling races of the West.

[1] Tep-ter Ngön-po, vol. viii, fol. 15.

While Buddhism recognizes eighteen stages of Voidness, Tibetan Buddhism concentrates on four.

(1) Realization of the impermanence of forms.[1]

(2) This realization attended by a state of ecstatic bliss.[2]

(3) The second stage attended by vividness. He becomes super-conscious.[3]

(4) Here the devotee realizes the nature of this state of super-consciousness.[4]

He will tread the Way of total self-denial.

I will have no attachment to the Wheel of Worldly Existence;
If one does, the Cord of Deliverance is severed.

. . . .

The affection of one's relatives is the castle of the Evil One;
Accumulation of property is but heaping up provisions for an enemy.

To drink wine or tea for pleasure is to drink a brew of aconite;
It severs the Cord of Deliverance.

. . . . . .

. . . . . .

. . . . . .

I subdue devils through pity;
I scatter evils to the wind;
And set my own face upwards.

We have seen that he avoided popularity. He would kill the 'Evil Spirit of Egoism'.[5] Tibetans believe that everybody has an evil familiar spirit which tells him that self is permanent, a personification of that form of ignorance which regards self as permanent.

And at the end of life Mi-la wishes for a death in solitude.

My growing old unknown to my friend;
  My sister unaware of my last illness.
If I can die in this solitude;
  This devotee will be fully content.

[1] སྣང་སྟོང་ [2] བདེ་སྟོང་ [3] གསལ་སྟོང་ [4] རིག་སྟོང་

[5] རང་འཛིན་ཀྱི་འགོང་པོ་ Lit. 'The Demon who grasps the "I".'

A hunting dog

'In a rocky cave in an uninhabited country'

My death unknown to any being;
  My rotting corpse unseen by the birds.
If I can die, &c.

No footprints at the entrance;
  No bloodmarks in the cave.[1]
If I can die, &c.

None to ask where I have gone;
  No place to point to, saying 'There'.
If I can die, &c.

May the prayer regarding the death of this beggar
Be fulfilled for the benefit of all beings
In a rocky cave in an uninhabited country!
Then will my mind be fully content.

He is against all conventionalism and prudishness. Both his sister and Dze-se find him very troublesome, 'clinging to uninhabited rocks like a wild beast pursued by dogs'. And his sister upbraids him for going about naked. She gives him a blanket that he may sew it into a garment and cover his organs for decency's sake. He cuts it up and makes coverings also for his head, feet, and fingers.

On returning and finding how he has cut up the hard-won blanket, she is indignant. 'You are not to be classed as a human being; you have no sense of shame;' she flings at him; 'you have spoilt the blanket which I prepared for you with so much trouble.'

Mi-la replies, 'As the limbs are also organs of this same body, I thought that I was expected to cover them too.' Men and women, in fact, have their natural forms; he finds nothing shameful in that.

'But, if you find shame in my form, you should find shame in your own. It is better to remove an object of shame than to keep it. With all speed therefore remove your own.'

Pe-ta lowers sullenly at him, and holds her peace. He continues, as is usual, in prose and then in verse, during

[1] Such as there would be, if killed by a wild animal or murderer. Let the solitude be complete.

the course of which he points out what is really shameful in a list comparable with that given by the Founder of Christianity:

> The daughter of shame is bought with a price;
> The son of shame is taken on the lap.
>
> Covetousness, ill-will, scepticism;
> Evil deeds, deceptions, thefts, robberies;
> Cheating relatives who confide in you;
> These are disgusting and shameful. Yet few abstain.

Pe-ta remains sullen. 'In any case, brother,' she says, 'you won't do what I advise. But I cannot give you up.' So she gives him the food for which she has begged, and they stay and use it together. At length, we are told, 'I convinced her of the truth of religion, and made her a little less dilatory in practising it'.[1] The wicked uncle died; the aunt repented of her crimes and came to the cave to beg for forgiveness. He sings to her, recounting her cruelties, and preaches sermons on the Law of Karma. She is 'turned to religion', gives herself up to penance and meditation, and becomes a devotee to this extent that she is able to gain deliverance for herself, though not for others. Mi-la himself, of course, is held to have assisted towards deliverance all those who believe. Pe-ta and Dze-se also gain deliverance in the end.

Mi-la, like Mar-pa, was Tantrik, occult. We know, not from his own biography, but from the impartial pages of the Blue Treasury, that he condemned the Ka-dam-pa teachings of Atisha. Speaking to one who came to him for instruction and was destined afterwards to be his chief disciple, the Lord Gam-po-pa, he asked him whether he had received any Tantrik initiations.

'Yes,' said the young expectant, 'I have experienced the unbroken calm of *samadhi* for a period of thirteen days.'

[1] Lit. 'I drew her to a knowledge of the religion, and the direction of her mind became a little shorter.'

Mi-la burst into a loud laugh, saying, 'The gods of the Physical Universe and of the Formless Universe[1] pass aeons of time in that unbroken calm. That will not help you to gain nirvana. You do not win oil by pressing sand.

'The Ka-dam-pa have teachings, but practical teachings they have not. The Tibetans, being possessed by evil spirits, would not allow the Noble Lord (Atisha) to preach the Mystic Doctrine:[2] Had they done so, Tibet would have been filled with saints by this time.'

He praises the Mystic Doctrine, which enables one to use even worldly goods, e.g. good food and clothing, on the Path. It is a short cut to nirvana.

His instruction to his disciples is, briefly, as follows:

'Believe in the Law of Karma.[3] If you do so, the thought of the miseries of lower states of rebirth will fill you with dread and make you zealous to obtain Buddhahood. Ponder on the lives of the saints, the causes and effects of actions, the evils of worldly existence. Remember that it is difficult to be reborn as a human being in such a position as affords facilities for following religion. Remember that the time of death is uncertain. Believing, pondering, remembering these things, apply yourselves assiduously to the study and the practice of the Mystic Doctrine.

'As for me, I made up my mind to renounce food, clothing, and speech. Setting bravery in my mind and humility in my body, I bore up against every hardship, and meditated alone on mountain sides where men are not. Thus knowledge, the fruit of experience, was born in me. Enter, all of you, into my footsteps, and gain the True Knowledge in a practical way.'

The teaching of Mi-la, and indeed of many Tibetan Buddhists, has points in common with that of the early Christian Gnostics. The ascetic life, the high moral code, the belief in a 'secret teaching' of the Founder, the doctrine of transmigration were all common to both.

1 The Formless Universe is a higher stage than the Physical.

2 Sanskrit *Mantrayana*.

3 Lit. 'the Fruit of the Primary Cause'.

The Biography relates that his passing away evoked marvellous signs. The sky showed the colours of the prism on a background geometrically arranged. In the centre were lotuses, and on the leaves of these appeared mystic formulas. Coloured clouds took the shape of royal umbrellas and banners. Other clouds settled on the mountain peaks in the form of *chö-tens*, each with its head pointing toward 'Between the Rivers', the place where Mi-la died. Showers of blossom fell; gods came down and talked with men.

The Blue Treasury, as befits a history, is more impartial and less detailed. It has to deal with all the saints and all the sects. But it agrees that he attained nirvana.[1]

We can picture this poet-saint with his healthy, powerful frame, his tuneful voice, his occasional flashes of humour, and his delicate love of nature, which last is evidenced rather in his other book, 'The Hundred Thousand Songs'. We can feel his indomitable will, his incessant concentration, whether in the pursuit of the Black Magic of old times, or in the teachings of the new religion. Some of those in the restless West will call him crazy. But some even of these will admit that it is just those forms, of what you may term methodical madness if you will, that have moved masses of humanity not only in Asia but throughout the world. In Tibet he is loved as few are loved.

[1] Tep-ter Ngön-po, vol. viii, fol. 16.

VIII
THE YELLOW HATS

TOWARDS the close of the fourteenth century, while England was making use of her growing strength to attack the territory of her French neighbour, ardent spirits in Tibet were engaged in fighting the spiritual evils that had come in the train of their twilight Buddhism. The leader in the reformation was one named Tsong-ka-pa[1] (1358–1419), 'The Man from Onion Land', a district in the province of Am-do, which borders on the Kansu province in north-western China.

As was usual among those destined for the clergy, his training was laborious; indeed, his studies were continued till his thirty-sixth year and were extraordinarily varied. He then put out some of his knowledge in commentaries and books of wise sayings. To great skill in argument were added rare gifts of elocution, so that he could be heard throughout a large audience. The feature of his delivery that aroused especial admiration was that it 'was uniform, being without variation in the pitch of his voice'. This curious form of restraint is still the aim of preachers, actors, and other speakers in Tibet to-day. It is also recorded that, 'being free from any kind of disease, either of mind or body, he preached both by day and night with untiring zeal'. The French traveller of the eighteen-forties, Abbé Huc, mentions a tradition at Kum-bum in north-eastern Tibet, that Tsong-ka-pa in his early youth was taught by a priest from the West with a large nose and gleaming eyes, features that suggest the European cast of countenance, I myself heard no talk of this in Lhasa or elsewhere, and the Tibetan histories do not mention it. But Tsong-ka-pa may well have conversed with Nestorian Christians from western China or Mongolia. The Nestorians were still strongly established in those countries,

[1] ཙོང་ཁ་པ་

and zealous to extend Christianity, while Tibetans have always been zealous in inquiring about other religions. Certain it is that anybody who sees a service in a Tibetan temple at the present day is struck with the similarity of part of its ritual to that in a Roman Catholic Church.

But among the older Japanese sects there is also some similarity, and these can hardly have copied from Christianity. The case, in fact, is not established.

A strong body, a rich brain, and the will to work immeasurably, all these combined to put him in the forefront of the missionary movement. The Buddhism of Tibet, as we have seen, was mixed not only with Pönism but with Tantrik extravagances, and the debasing sensuality inherited from Bengal. Few among the Tibetan clergy abstained from women or wine. Preaching observance of the laws of discipline, Tsong-ka-pa revived the religion in a purer form. His writings were accurate, concise, clear, and well-arranged, so that even the general reader could understand them. Other teachers could not compete with his forcible arguments. So his reforms went through.

When fifty years old, he founded the monastery of Gan-den, 'The Joyous', the name being derived from *Ga* (joy). His followers became known as *Ga-luk*, 'The Ganden Way', but as this seemed to suggest the way of pleasure, a slight change was made, and it became *Ga-luk*, 'The Virtuous Way'. Discarding the red hats of the original priesthood, they adopted yellow. People generally, uncertain perhaps whether virtue walked this way or that, found it easy to refer to them as the 'Yellow Hats'.

In the same year he introduced into Lhasa the festival of 'The Great Prayer', which was destined to become the most important of all the gatherings in the Holy City, a strong weapon in the armoury of the priesthood. The Tibetan New Year commences with the new moon in February, and the Great Prayer begins a few days later. It continues for about three weeks, and during this time services are held thrice daily in the Temple, and are attended by ten to twenty thousand monks. Twenty to thirty thousand of the laity and forty to fifty thousand monks crowd into the Holy City.

Among various other religious events is the service held by the Dalai Lama himself on the fifteenth day, when he reads from the Scriptures and preaches a sermon. Though the temperature is far below freezing point, he does this at dawn in an open square near the Temple.

'The Man from Onion Land' came now to be known as Je Rim-po-che, 'The Chief of Great Price'. His priests were celibate and more austere than those of the older sects. He did not abolish the Tantras; the most powerful reformer, had he even wished, could not have carried a magic-loving people so far. But he discriminated between Tantra and Tantra. A popular and convenient tradition ascribed one, named 'The Secret Collection',[1] to the Buddha himself. It had been handed down, after the manner of the East, by Indian and Tibetan teachers. This he popularized throughout Tibet.[2] It is esoteric, of the Mahayanist school, and explains the natures of all the Buddhas, who are here treated as a collective body. It is consequently regarded as the highest of all the Tantras.[3]

The Emperor and Government of China, recognizing the Precious Chief's power over his religious-minded countrymen, wished to secure his friendship. But the Imperial invitation to visit the Chinese Court was declined. This man of the people, with his knowledge of human relationships, was not to be side-tracked from his life's mission by worldly honours and rewards. Though his home was vulnerable in its nearness to the Chinese frontier, he had the courage to refuse. He replied that 'If he, the Master, went, great hardships would result in what was a matter of small necessity'.[4] He knew well the

[1] གསང་བ་འདུས་པ་ [2] Tep-ter Ngŏn-po, vol. vii, fol. 7. [3] Idem, fol. 3.

[4] Page 122 of the Tibetan text of the 'History of the Religion in Hor', Jik-me Nam-ka's (འཇིགས་མེད་ ནམ་མཁའ་) *Hor Chö-jung* (Georg Huth's *Geschichte des Buddhismus in der Mongolei*, Truebner, Strasbourg, 1892). I have not followed Huth's translation entirely.

burdens that the visit of a saintly personage to the Son of Heaven would lay on the Chinese villages passed through. His retinue must be large, to mark the importance of the occasion; each member must be provided free of charge with food according to his rank, and with men or other beasts of burden to carry his belongings. So he sent a deputy to China, and continued his work in Tibet.

The teaching of the new 'Virtuous Way', followed the main lines marked out by Atisha in his Ka-dam-pa school. This, my Ge-luk-pa acquaintances assure me, lightened the master's task. But priests of the older sects, whose power was permanently reduced by the reformer, are naturally antagonistic. They tell one of a sinister alliance by which the new school was forced through, and this aid was, as usual, supernatural. The priests of the Ka-gyü sect, which dominates Bhutan and the lower reaches of the Chumbi Valley, make this quite clear. Their version runs as follows:

'Walking one day near the Temple in Lhasa, the saint heard his name being whispered from under the ground. Laying his ear to the spot, he detected the whispering of the "Nine Brother Sprites", who told him that Padma Sambhava had imprisoned them there immediately under the central eye, the invisible Eye of Wisdom, in that holy of holies, the central figure of the Buddha. They promised to help him always, if he would obtain their release. He gave them leave to go, but they confessed that whenever they tried to emerge above ground, the Eye of Wisdom forced them down again. Accordingly, Tsong-ka-pa placed a circlet over the Buddha's brow. The eye thus veiled, the sprites escaped, and redeemed their promise by bringing the Mongol armies to Tibet. These overran the country time and again, and eventually handed it over to Tsong-ka-pa's successor of that period, the fifth Dalai-Lama. But in the process they brought much suffering on our land.'

The old Governor of western Bhutan, whose mind hovered between religion and politics, stressed the destruction of Old Sect monasteries, which crumbled before the

The Ruler and Council of Bhutan, with the author
The Ruler is the third from the right, the Governor of Western Bhutan second from the left

Mongol onslaughts, while those of the new teaching were reverently protected. True, Buddhism is a religion of peace, but Mongol and Tibetan have the nomad's instinct for an occasional outburst, and therefore these things happen.

By whatever means he did it, there is no doubt that Tsong-ka-pa achieved a great and lasting success. Among the Yellow Hats he is known as the second Buddha. Talking with Tibetans from the Central Province, on any subject you please, his sayings are apt to come into the forefront of the conversation. In Lhasa and the districts around I found his image everywhere. And one thing noticeable about it was that its expression was varied, and it seemed to have been done from life; so different from the uniform calm that almost everywhere throughout Asia enwraps the features of the Buddha and his saints. One in the large monastery of Re-ting, north of Lhasa, is especially marked. From its broad smile it is known as 'Laughing Tsong'.

Tsong-ka-pa died in 1419 at the age of sixty-one. His tomb is in his own Gan-den Monastery, and the fact that he lived there and is entombed there gives Gan-den, 'The Joyous', an added sanctity which even its great brothers Se-ra and Dre-pung cannot claim. Whether any white man, except Kennedy and myself, has seen the tomb, I do not know; but it is certainly famous throughout Tibet. You enter a large red building with a gilt pagoda-like roof, and you find the tomb in a small chapel of its own. It is enclosed in a circular Mongol tent, whose walls are of felt, overlaid with silks and supported by pillars of red-lacquered walnut wood. The tent encloses nearly the whole of the chapel.

In the foreground, as we enter, is a large raised platform partly of plain wood, partly silver-gilt, including figures of elephants, of sacred gems, and seven or eight goddesses, whose duty it is to make offerings to the Saint. The profusion of barley grains on this platform showed the wish of all to give.

Further back in the centre of the tent is a golden image of Tsong-ka-pa, three feet high, seated Buddha-wise. In the dimly-lighted background, taking leave, as it were, of the garishness of the world, is the tomb itself. It is of gold, shaped somewhat like a *chö-ten*, and about twelve feet high. My Tibetan companion offered the white silk scarf of ceremony[1] on our behalf, and prayed with great earnestness. There was already a scarf on the tomb in a prominent position, and a writing with it, long and yellow after the fashion of Tibetan letters. It was a prayer to the Chief of Great Price on behalf of one who had lately died.

The tent inside the chapel gives the latter a very unusual appearance. 'It was presented', as I am informed by the 'Peak Secretary' (i.e. a Secretary of the Dalai Lama), 'by a Mongol chief of the Dzungarian tribe, who entered Lhasa with his troops some two hundred years ago. This chief destroyed temples and images of the unreformed Red Hats, but helped the Yellow Hats, for Tsong-ka-pa was always a good friend to the Mongols, and even now Gan-den always has a large number of Mongol monks on its roll. Though he invaded Tibet, the Ge-luk-pas certainly did not look on this Mongol chief as an enemy. The Chinese drove him out, because they never like to see the Tibetans friendly with other people, lest they may lose their own power in Tibet.'

Round the sides of the chapel, arranged outside the tent on platforms seven feet above the ground, are the tombs of many of the successive high priests of the monastery. Each of these is appointed as an old man, for seven years, and is known as 'Gan-den's Enthroned'.[2] He is the highest of all the priesthood, at any rate in central Tibet, except for a very few of the Living Buddhas. The tombs are of silver to distinguish their lesser importance in comparison with Tsong-ka-pa and the Dalai Lamas.

Every morning a service in honour of the great reformer is held in Gan-den to this day; and a still longer

[1] In *The People of Tibet*, pp. 248–50, I have described and explained these scarves.

[2] *Gan-den Ti-pa* or *Ti Rim-po-che*.

Gan-den Monastery

Tsong-ka-pa's tomb is in the red building (left centre); close to this on the right, with four pillars, is the monks' Assembly Hall

service, lasting from early morning till after sunset, worships his Guardian Spirit, 'The Maker of Fear'.

Tsong-ka-pa passed from the world on the twenty-fifth day of the tenth Tibetan month. The anniversary in 1920 fell on the 5th December, while I was in Lhasa. The great Potala palace was illuminated, and the religious service which was held in commemoration was perforce attended by all the high State officers.

This anniversary has a further, indeed an intimate, significance for all who serve the Government. It is the official beginning of winter. Our ministers of state, civil servants, and clergy would resent being compelled to wear an overcoat on a warm day, or forbidden its use when an icy wind was scouring the land. But in Tibet the rule is inflexible. On the anniversary of Tsong-ka-pa's death winter begins; on the eighth day of the third Tibetan month it ends. This fixes winter between a date in the first half of December and another in the last half of April. Between these two dates all officials—half belonging to the laity and half to the clergy—must wear fur hats and cloaks strictly in accordance with the patterns prescribed for each grade. Outside these dates, however cold the day, they must appear only in their summer silks, gorgeous, indeed, in their yellow and blue, but affording cold comfort where the land is raised twleve thousand feet above the ocean.

Tsong-ka-pa's mantle fell on the son of a herdsman, whose ancestors had lived, as Tsong-ka-pa lived, in eastern Tibet, a home of much keenness and ability in Tibetan religious life. They had, however, moved across the country to the western highlands, and here Protecting Thunderbolt and his wife, Sky Happiness, had a family of five, four boys and one girl. The third son, Lotus Thunderbolt, was born in 1391 in the cattle enclosure. That very night robbers came and attacked the little home. Lotus's mother hid the boy between some stones and fled. Returning on the morrow, she was surprised to find the baby still alive with a crow watching over him and keeping all birds and animals away.

When only five years old, he tended the goats of a wealthy neighbour, and used his time in carving sacred inscriptions on the rocks. Two years later his father died, and he entered the Nar-tang Monastery, a few miles from Shi-ga-tse, as a servant. He was nicknamed Young Brass from the yellow robe that he wore. A high lama, called Excellent Knowledge, travelling from monastery to monastery—for all Tibetans are fond of travel—saw that the boy was full of promise, and had him entered as a novice. He showed the usual precocity, compiling discourses and books, one of them, indeed, 'for the remission of his father's sins'. All his writings were, as he claimed, 'free from the three faults of More, Less, and Mistake'.

At the age of twenty he took the full vows of monkhood, having been taught by different priests, forty or fifty in all, the branch of knowledge in which each excelled. He became officially known as Ge-dün Trup-pa, which may be translated as 'The Perfecter of the Priesthood', or 'The Perfecter of Those who Yearn for Virtue', but in the biography, as in the current speech, he is 'The Excellent One'[1] or 'The Revered One'.[2]

It was now that he fulfilled his dearest wish, to meet the venerable Tsong-ka-pa. The Master received him favourably, added his teachings to the rest, and, somewhat like the prophet of Israel, presented him with one of his own skirts as an omen for the young priest's future success. We need not, therefore, wonder that, seven years later, the poor herdsman's son was able to found the monastery of Dre-pung, 'The Rice Heap', four miles west of Lhasa. Its yellow-hatted monks now number more than ten thousand, overcrowding the most powerful monastery in Tibet, the largest in the world.

Ge-dün Trup-pa's biography, 'The Rosary of Jewels'[3] —for which, with so many other Tibetan xylographs, I am indebted to the kindness of the Dalai Lama—is my

[1] རིན་པོ་ཆེ་ [2] རྗེ་བཙུན་

[3] 'The Rosary of Jewels, which sets forth that tale of surpassing wonder, the life of the Omniscient Lord, Glorious and Good, the Perfecter of the Priesthood.'

chief source of information in the history of this remarkable man.

At about the same time (A.D. 1419) another home of religion was founded by one of Tsong-ka-pa's leading disciples two miles north of the capital. The monastery was then, the Peak Secretary tells me, a small one, and surrounded by bushes of wild rose, and so became known as Se-ra, 'Wild Rose Fence'. Now, it is second only to Dre-pung. These two, with Gan-den, are popularly known as 'The Three Seats'. Mustering between them twenty thousand irreconcilables in the vicinity of Lhasa, they have from time to time dominated Lhasa, and controlled the destinies of Tibet.

Knowledge Lion, the most constant of the Revered One's teachers, fell ill. Following the age-old custom, the Scriptures were read and offerings made in the temple to restore his health. For his own health, Ge-dün struck out on a different line. His broad forehead and his high nose proclaimed his intellect and force of character. From his babyhood, indeed, he had been healthy and high-spirited. But his life was strenuous in studying, preaching, travelling, founding monasteries. When, therefore, at times he overtaxed his strength and illness supervened, he took to meditation, in order, as the book expresses it, 'to protect himself from evil'. And not for a day or two, but for ten or eleven months at a time. The simple and scanty fare of a hermit's retreat and the pure air of the solitude combined to bring peace to spirit and to body.

The mind was turned inwards. There were visions of deities, and, though he diligently enforced the new rule of celibacy, there were visions of women, and sometimes of white women. Whether human or divine, women were his frequent helpers.

When Knowledge Lion died, his revered pupil wished to set up a memorial, 'as a substitute', in his own monastery at Nar-tang. It was evidently something on a big scale, for his followers demurred to the heavy toil and cost. He then tried one monastery after another; but each one definitely refused. Ge-dün Trup-pa, however, had from boyhood been accustomed to make shift to meet his needs, and grew up full of resource.

> He made an examination of the land. He increased the ceremonial observances used in making offerings to the local spirits.[1] Then he made deep foundations for the whole temple, centre, and sides, and built Ta-shi Lhün-po as an independent monastery,[2] splendid with its extensive lands, more regal than all.[3]

Thus, even after its purification, Tibetan Buddhism had to make its peace with the Pönist gods of the soil. No doubt they were feared, for they, too, were 'very, very old'.

Ge-dün Trup-pa had succeeded beyond all expectations. This great monastery is now the seat of him whom Europeans and Indians know as the Ta-shi Lama, but Tibetans usually as the Pan-chen Rim-po-che, 'The Great Pandit of Great Price'. He ranks almost equal with the Dalai Lama, the Supreme Head of the Church.

Several years (1447–1453) were needed for the building and furnishing.[4] The Revered One lived in a white tent in the courtyard of the temple. The size of the sanctuary was the space of six pillars, that of the monks' assembly hall forty-eight pillars. Now came the question of the name. Some were for calling it 'Religion's Increase', others 'Glory Gained'. The Revered Lama pondered, as he sat in his little white tent, and on the morrow all were made aware that the voice of a goddess—one who had already appeared to a professor meditating on the hill-side—had given him the name as 'Mount of Blessing'.[5]

The central image was one of the Buddha himself. It was twenty-five spans[6] in height. In the heart were de-

[1] གཞི་བདག་

[2] གླིང་ This denotes a monastery of large size, and independent of other monasteries.

[3] Ge-dün Trup-pa's Biography, fol. 28.

[4] Nyang Chö-jung, fol. 199.

[5] In Tibetan, *Ta-shi Lhün-po* (བཀྲ་ཤིས་ལྷུན་པོ་).

[6] One Tibetan span is the measure from the tip of the thumb to the tip of the second finger at full stretch.

The 'Mount of Blessing' ('Ta-shi Lhün-po) Monastery
Shi-ga-tse fort on the extreme right

posited relics of holy men, including the skull of Knowledge Lion himself. The lower part received sacred books, and, as a special offering, the great Tsong-ka-pa's skirt. Some hundreds of years later when, on behalf of the Viceroy of India, I gave the present 'Precious Great Pandit' (Panchen Rim-po-che)—as the Grand Lama of Ta-shi Lhün-po is styled by Tibetans,[1]—an ancient stone image of the Buddha brought from India, he laid it soon afterwards in a gigantic image of the Coming Buddha, which he was fashioning. Thus is a holy image saved from theft and breakage.

Ge-dün Trup-pa set up also an image of himself. Nepalese were employed to make it, 'as they were skilful and cheaper'. But disputes arose between the Tibetans and themselves, and they retired in dudgeon. After many vicissitudes he found a new designer, who had stood apart from all the wrangling. 'It is best', said Ge-dün, 'to use the tongs, when the pan is hot.' The artisans did not fail. 'Working with their hands by day, and with their minds by night, the work was done soon and done well.' In the fifth month of the Sheep Year (1453) it was consecrated, and as he sat by night at the feet of the image and worshipped, he saw the great Buddha of the future, King Love himself, appear as a monk and absorb into the image again and again. So, too, it was when he consecrated images that he had engraved or books that he had written. They were visibly inspired, for they glittered while the divine wisdom absorbed[2] into them.

In the illness of his old age he was reluctantly induced to intermit his religious striving and to seek new health, as many Tibetans do, at one of the hot springs which gush from the mountain sides here and there throughout Tibet.

[1] I sometimes style him Pan-chen Lama for the sake of brevity. His own people in Tsang apply to him the same titles—'Precious Protector', 'Precious Sovereign', &c.—as Tibetans in general apply to the Dalai Lama. Europeans usually call him 'Tashi Lama', but it would be better to abandon this latter title, which is applied by Tibetans to lamas of inferior position, who attend weddings.

[2] ཐིམ་པའི་ཕྱུང་བ་

He did not, however, gain the usual benefit, for his open-air sulphur bath was in the upper Valley of Taste,[1] bleak and wind-swept beyond the average. Attacks of vomiting are not unusual in this treatment, but on him they fell so strongly as to drive him away. He resumed his missionary tours, carried from place to place in a sedan chair, a vehicle which in Tibet is reserved for the highest of all. A rainbow struck the fore-part of the chair, and when he came to his old monastery, Nar-tang, it stood there as a pillar.

He tried his old cure for illness, deep meditation. But tears were seen to flow from the eyes of a golden image in the monastery and he heard the weeping of the goddess who had spoken to him before. The time to pass on had come. He gave his last instructions:

'Remember the teaching of the Buddha and the happiness of the people, and especially remember the doctrines of Ta-shi Lhün-po. Live here and preach and meditate in accordance with the vows of religion. That alone will fulfil my desire.'

For a moment none dared to answer. On the promise being given, he said, 'Then I shall pass away without regret,' and rubbed his head.

'Shall we offer prayers?'

'No; it is no longer necessary.'

Deities appeared to him as he spent the night in meditation, during which he passed into Buddhahood. 'His body, his illusory body, shrank a little owing to fatigue, and then suddenly shone with such brilliance that one could hardly look at it. The light turned into red and gold, white and gold, and then into pure gold.'

Two high officers were on their way from China with offerings to the holy man, but arrived too late.

On Ge-dün Trup-pa's death in 1475 there was considerable discussion as to his successor at Ta-shi Lhün-po. He himself had in his mind either of two men as 'worthy of taking charge of the monastery'. His flock preferred

[1] *Nyang Tö.*

Priests of the Ka-gyü sect

A Nepalese Brahman

another, named Great Saint, who seems to have taken the lead among his disciples. This man, as we are told in the biography, had been associated with the Revered One in many previous lives, 'sometimes as pupil and teacher, sometimes as child and parent, and sometimes as a friend who is like one's right hand'. Indeed, he had been in charge of the monastery for about three years during the Lama's absence in the Lhasa Province. But in this present life he had been born into a somewhat low social position—always in Tibet a barrier against preferment, though nowadays no great barrier in a priest's career. He therefore gave a half-refusal. At length the whole following of the deceased Lama, both the teachers and the pupils, united to choose another successor.

Ge-dün Trup-pa was one who from boyhood upwards took his own line regardless of what others said about him. His great driving power enabled him to begin and to finish, though no doubt on a smaller scale than they now occupy, the powerful institutions at Dre-pung and Ta-shi Lhün-po. It would be hard to find in Tibet to-day two monasteries with a stronger spiritual and political influence than the Rice Heap and the Mount of Blessing.

His influence went even further than these, for soon after his death the system of incarnation from man to man was developed. The incarnation of God in man was known from the first; we find traces of it in some of the earliest Tibetan records, the inscriptions engraved on the stone monuments at Lhasa. There, of a bygone king we can read, 'After having been a god in the heavens he reappeared as a king of human beings in the lofty land with the mountains of snow.'[1]

Again, the idea of reincarnation from man to man, derived from Hinduism, passed on into Buddhism. It is customary to speak of reincarnation: we might term it soul-transference or mind-transference; but the Buddha, in fact, refused to define what it is that passes from one life to the next. This idea, indeed, had come down through the

[1] Inscription on the eastern face of the stone pillar by the Temple in Lhasa.

ages, but in fifteenth-century Tibet it was developed and directed along particular lines of hierarchs, in order to maintain the authority of the highest priesthood.

Sa-kya had passed on the power of the high priests, spiritual and temporal, from father to son, but to the celibate priests of the Reformation this was no longer possible. So the difficulty was met by the return of Ge-dün Trup-pa himself in the body of a boy born soon after his death. He had attained the rank of a Buddha, and was therefore entitled to pass into the particular heaven to which his stage of Buddhahood entitled him. But when this Buddha returned in human form to guide and succour humanity, and the whole animate creation, birds, beasts, reptiles, insects, fishes, each and all, there was the germ of a great change. No longer was there a contest between several learned lamas, each desiring the headship, a Pope elected by the votes of his colleagues. The religious authority of each successor was clear from the first and was indisputable.

It has generally been assumed by earlier writers that this new system came into force immediately upon Ge-dün Trup-pa's death. But from the latter's biography in my possession it would appear that this did not happen for a good many years. After reciting various miracles that accompanied the Revered One's funeral, this biography—printed clearly, as is usual with those which the Dalai Lama himself gave me—says nothing about his spirit passing then or afterwards into a baby successor, but describes the measures taken in the ordinary way to choose the next occupant of the Chair. The Revered One, in fact, had said that he and Great Saint would be reborn in China, as teacher and pupil respectively, and would work there. He does not appear to have envisaged a return to Dre-pung or Ta-shi Lhün-po.

The great teachers then ordained the Lama, named Excellent Wisdom,[1] as owner of the religious kingdom, in recognition of his

[1] མཁྱེན་རབ་

religious service. In memory of the Revered Lama a very large image of the Buddha and two large images of the Revered One himself were made of copper gilt. Paintings were made for the hall; and flags, umbrellas, and banners were hoisted.

Excellent Wisdom preached the doctrine for ten years for the benefit of the followers, and then went to live in solitary places for meditation. After this, although he was not qualified to take the seat of the Revered Lama, yet through their connexion in former lives, and still more through the cherishing compassion of the Lama himself, in the fortieth year after the founding of Ta-shi Lhün-po, being the twelfth year after the Revered Lama had shown the method of passing from sorrow (i.e. had attained nirvana), on the third day of the Horse-Rider month (September–October) of the Fire-Horse year, he ascended and sat on the Revered Lama's Throne of Religion. He prayed for blessing from the Lama, the Tutelary Deities, and the Protectors of the Doctrine, that he might live long and do good work.

It is clear, therefore, that the present system, by which each Grand Lama is reborn in order to take up his life's work again, did not come into force at Ge-dün Trup-pa's death, nor for several years afterwards. But eventually such a successor was recognized in the person of Ge-dün Gya-tso, 'Ocean of Yearning for Righteousness'.

The biography of Sö-nam Gya-tso, the third of the series, dealing with events some seventy years later, about the year 1542, treats this system as firmly established, with Ge-dün Trup-pa as its origin. The light of reincarnation was now focussed on the succession of spiritual sovereignty. Applied in this way for choosing the High Priests of Drepung, the Dalai Lamas of the future, it was found to confer undisputed authority, and was therefore extended everywhere, so that to-day there are several hundred Incarnations scattered throughout Tibet, each with his own appointed monastery. Organization comes easily to the Tibetan, and his talent is employed unstintingly in religion, for it is religion that dominates his life.

IX

BUDDHISM CAPTURES MONGOLIA

WHEN in 1543, the 'Ocean of Merit' (*Sö-nam Gya-tso*) succeeded the 'Ocean of Priesthood's Perfection', succession to the post by reincarnation was firmly established. The change was greater than the two names would indicate, for none of these high Incarnations laboured so effectively for the extension of Buddhism as did Sö-nam Gya-tso. His Biography is aptly named 'The Ocean Chariot of Real Attainment'. In it we are told:

> Ge-dün Gya-tso, the omniscient, was aged, and wished to serve as a young monk. It was prophesied that his rebirth would take place from three to five years after his death. He, therefore, entered the womb of Pal Dzom-bu-ti, the mother. His father's name was De-wa Trak-pa-Nam-gyal. His body showed all the signs of greatness; he was found to possess all the good qualities; and he identified his possessions in his former life. People from all sides flocked to visit him. They were satisfied with his acts and with his speech. He was, accordingly, recognized as the incarnation of Drom-tön, the source of religion.

A Living Buddha, thus returning to earth, proves his identity by recognizing his rosary, bell, and other religious implements, as well as servants, ponies, &c., that were with him in his previous existence.[1] He is expected to do it, indeed, as a boy of two or three years old, and the belief is universal that he does so.

Sö-nam showed the usual superhuman proficiency in education, and displayed such miracles as convinced all that Drom-tön, Atisha's chief disciple, was once again with them in the flesh. He wrote books and preached; he fashioned images with his own hands and painted pictures of deities: but was ever careful to renew his inspiration and strength by frequent periods of secluded meditation. Like the Founder of Christianity and his own predecessors, he

[1] *Tibet Past and Present*, p. 51.

frequently 'went out into the mountain to pray'. Here and there he founded new monasteries, for he was full of the missionary spirit, intent on spreading the law as taught by the great Tsong-ka-pa.

At this time Altan Khagan, the chief of several tribes of the Tumed Mongols, was the dominant power in eastern Mongolia. His frequent raids into China, where the Ming Dynasty was now decadent, had spread terror over the north-western provinces, and the Biography of the 'Ocean of Merit' treats him as a king among lesser princes. During one of his raids a lama from north-eastern Tibet was carried off. Through him the chief was attracted to the form of Buddhism practised by the Tibetan Yellow Hats. Altan's great-nephew added his influence and urged the Khagan to send for Sö-nam Gya-tso.

Altan was no doubt conscious of his own military power, and could hardly fail to recognize the growing strength of the Tibetan priests, a people akin to his own. None knew better than he how strong throughout Asia is the power of the priesthood. If Mongol soldier and Tibetan monk could work together, perhaps the glories of the great Khubilai—who also had made use of Tibetan lamas—might be repeated in him. So an envoy was sent to invite Sö-nam to the court of the Mongol chief. Declining the first invitation, Sö-nam accepted the second, and travelled to Mongolia.

Buddhism after the Tibetan pattern, as we have already seen, had been introduced into that country during the time of the Sa-kya hierarchs, and especially by Dro-gön Pak-pa. The Sa-kya Pandit's tutor had not failed to inform his master of the prevailing prophecy that he would be invited to propagate the religion among a border nation, who wore hats like falcons and shoes like the snouts of pigs. Accordingly, we can read in the narrative of William de Rubruquis, the Flemish friar, who visited Karakoram, the Mongol capital, in A.D. 1253, a description of the temples and monks there, and in it we see a picture not greatly differing from present-day Tibet. The heads of the priests were shaven; they lived one hundred or two hundred together 'in one cloister or covent'. In the temples 'they sit upon foormes like singing men in a quier, namely the one half of them over against the other. . . . There they read softly unto themselves not uttering any voice at all. And these do always utter these words: '*Ou mam Hactani*".' Go to any monastery or chapel in Tibet to-day and you will see the same thing throughout. Indeed, for Om Ma-ni Pe-me Hum—the earliest known reference to which is in this account of Rubruquis—you need visit no home of religion. From any man, woman, or child, anywhere and at any time, you will hear it unceasingly.

It is of interest to note that there were celibate priests before Tsong-ka-pa's time, for de Rubruquis makes mention of them. The whole credit for celibacy is not due to the Reformation.

When, however, the sceptre fell from the hands of the Mongols, they tended to relapse into their former Shamanism, which resembled the Pönism of Tibet. Sö-nam Gya-tso, therefore, when he responded to the renewed summons of Altan Khagan, knew well the nature of the opposition that stood in his path. The loyal Biography hastens to tell us that he countered this, as we should expect, by miracles. The climate of Mongolia in winter is arctic, but the 'Ocean of Merit' turned it into a balmy summer's day. A river is impassable. He throws 'an angry glance at it, and instantly men and animals are able to cross it in peace'. And, what is no less wonderful and important, from inside a large rock he takes a conch-shell that winds the reverse way.[1] A discovery of a right-handed conch is usually noted in the Tibetan histories as an event of outstanding importance. To this day they are treasured with reverence in the Tibetan temples.

As he rides with his followers across a broad Mongolian plain, two hundred horsemen ride into his presence. Their leader, who indicates that he is a Pönist by the hat he wears, dismounts, bows to the ground, and shows veneration, but only for a day. The princes, sent by the

[1] Sö-nam Gya-tso's Biography, fol. 91.

A mountain stream, in the Kam-pu valley, near Chum-bi

king to welcome him, make gifts of silks, jewels, and food supplies 'completely free of meat'. But they do not pretend to believe in him.

However, the Chiefs, though in accordance with the exhortation of the Great King, they came before the Lama, yet were but barbarous border folk, who had no faith either in the Lama or in the Buddhist religion. Understanding their minds, he knew that he must subdue them. Accordingly he pointed a threatening forefinger at the head waters of a stream and showed the miracle of turning it back and making it flow upwards[1] for a little.

We are assured that the people thus obtained steadfast faith.[2]

In Tibet and Mongolia, when one man meets another from a distance there is an exchange of presents, among which is a white silk scarf.[3] The presents indicate the friendship; the white scarf shows how pure is this friendship. If converts come into the presence of a Grand Lama, the presents are vastly increased, and still more lavishly when Lama and Great King meet. Ponies and cattle, Mongolia's staple products, are offered by the thousand. The king himself 'wore a white robe in order to convert into a white country the dark lands of the barbarous border tribes'.[4] All the Eastern love of display enlivened that Mongolian steppe. Four or five deputations preceded the actual meeting, and the last of these was careful to start on the day of the full moon, the most auspicious day that each month can show to the Buddhist of Tibet. With their banners glistening in the strong sunlight, and their musical melodies borne on the desert air, the five hundred horsemen advanced in strict order of rank, for many among them were 'men of learning, of authority, of good birth. The procession was like the deathless elephant, Sa-la-rap-ten, ranging at leisure through the bathing pool of power'.

1 The Tibetan word here is *gyen*, which denotes a steep slope upwards. If you are told that a hill is *gyen*, you know that you are in for a stiff climb.

2 Biography, fol. 93.

3 For a description of these scarves, see *The People of Tibet*, pp. 248–50.

4 Biography, fol. 94.

The Chinese did not intend to be left out of these pregnant events. Their embassy to the holy man not only gave presents, but, in accordance with Chinese custom, proceeded to an athletic display. Then, in the presence of a vast concourse of Mongols, Chinese, and the herdsmen of the highlands, the 'Ocean of Merit' made his pronouncement. No longer shall they live in darkness, but in accordance with the ten virtuous laws. No longer when a Mongol dies shall his wife, servant, pony, and cattle be burnt alive. 'Whoever kills a man as in the past, his life shall be separated from his body. If you kill pony or cattle, your property will be confiscated. If you assault a priest, your house will be destroyed.' Animal sacrifices to their god were to be discontinued. Indeed, the image of the god himself was to be burnt in fire. But they were not to be left without a Protector, for a new and greater substitute would be found for him, the six-armed Buddha, and he should be worshipped only with milk, butter, and curds, unstained with human or animal blood. Periodical fastings were prescribed, and raiding in China and Tibet was forbidden. The nomads of Mongolia were certainly no more able to abandon these profitable adventures at the earliest dictation of the religious teacher than were the nomads of Tibet when they first tasted Buddhism. But bit by bit the prohibition took hold; China and Tibet obtained gradual relief, and the Chinese Government were not slow to realize the advantage of an alliance with the Head of a Church that could command the situation so effectively. Leading Tibetans, looking to the north and east, still tell one that Tibet is the Root of China. Accordingly, if Tibet does not remain happy, China will not be prosperous.

To the Mongol himself the result was not altogether advantageous. His raiding tendencies, the nomad's natural instinct, were stopped down, and his limited education gave him nothing in their stead, except the newly-acquired religion. To that he has applied himself devotedly. Yet, even now, it is the companion of but three

Mongols. A priest seated, with two laymen, come to Lhasa to sell ponies

or four centuries, and one cannot help feeling that if the river of agnosticism, which has come flooding into so many Asiatic countries, slops over into his land also, the fighting instincts will revive. Perhaps, however, education, and the consciousness that her neighbours are now more powerful, will direct Mongolia down the peaceful avenues of commerce.

A Tibetan seldom fails to present a situation, at any rate a religious situation, with shrewdness. Certainly Sö-nam Gya-tso did not fail before Altan Khagan. He called into play the doctrine of rebirth and a Pontiff's power to demonstrate the links in a chain of lives. It was, he showed, not the first time that their two destinies had been united. His royal convert was inclined to believe that in a former life he was the great Khubilai himself. The Lama confirmed this, and asserted his own identity with Dro-gön Pak-pa, that Emperor's spiritual guide. Now, as aforetime, he must teach to the returned Khubilai the great truths of Buddhism. For the Mongol the link with Buddhism went back even farther, for when the Buddha lived on earth, Altan was the King of Kosala. So close, indeed, was his connexion with the Holy Faith, and so unfailingly had Karma, irresistible Karma, thrown king and priest together. Thus was Altan Khagan, the most powerful of the Mongol chiefs, the terror of China, converted to Buddhism. In due course lesser chiefs and subject populations followed his lead.

On his side the Warrior King gave to the 'Ocean of Merit' the title of Talai (by Europeans called Dalai) Lama. It was extended posthumously to the first two, and has been held by each successor in the line. Tibetans, however, in ordinary conversation prefer to use their own titles, 'Inmost Protector', 'All-knowing Presence', and so forth.[1]

The All-knowing Lord then visited China at the Emperor's invitation, and passed on to south-eastern Tibet. He built a monastery at the important centre of Li-tang

[1] See *Tibet Past and Present*, p. 55.

near the Sino-Tibetan frontier. Though independent of China, he was at one with the Chinese in desiring a friendly relationship between the two countries, and accordingly appointed a local governor to see to this, or, as he phrases it, 'to enlarge the golden bridge between China and Tibet'.[1]

Meanwhile the Great King felt forlorn with the Master so far away. But Sö-nam Gya-tso had too much on his hands; the eastern regions needed his thrusting personality, and perhaps central Tibet also. As a temporary substitute he delegated one Yön-ten Gya-tso. The Chinese Emperor sent presents and the inevitable edict to the new arrival.[2]

Eastern Tibet has always been a stronghold of the older Faith; accordingly, the new monastery at Li-tang was taken as a challenge. When, therefore, Sö-nam Gya-tso pitched his tent close to a Pönist home of religion, its magicians flung a hailstorm at him. But the Biography assures us that the storm was returned to the assailants with an added violence.[3]

Far away to the north the Warrior King lay dying. He was in his seventy-sixth year, and his life had been a hard one. But his followers, sore stricken with grief, fell to reviling the vanished priest and the new religion that, in spite of all the vaunted miracles, could not save so valuable a life. Yön-ten rose to the occasion, restored the king to health, and preached a sermon on the impermanence of all things. He also assured the people that their chief would pass to something even higher, being exalted to Buddhahood, the highest state of all. On his recovery Altan Khagan rebuked his princes and his peoples, inquiring whether, 'before the religion was introduced into the country, you have seen any one who has not died but has remained in life'. Even the Lord Buddha had passed that way. Altan received one year's fresh lease of life,[4]

[1] Biography, fol. 99. [2] Idem, fol. 99.
[3] Idem, fol. 100.
[4] The Hor Chö-chung, by Jik-me Nam-ka, p. 142, Huth's edition.

dying in 1582, and was succeeded by his son, Seng-ge Du-gu-rung.

Five years later, at the new chief's earnest request, Sö-nam Gya-tso returned to Mongolia. Passing a district where there was a grave dispute between the Chinese and a border tribe of graziers, the Lama adjudicated on this, and peace was restored to the people. The value of his goodwill was evident, and another invitation came from China.

The Chinese Emperor sent innumerable presents and prepared a reception-hall of silver, measuring two pillars. A chair also was sent, borne on the necks of eight carriers, and inscribed with letters of gold.[1] The invitation was accepted, but signs of heavy illness showed themselves. He wrote his last instructions in verse, surrounded by the sorrowing Mongol princes, who urged him to take rebirth as a Mongol.[2] He expressed pleasure that he had preached the religion and sorrow that he was parting with his disciples and congregations, and prayed that he might have similar opportunities in his next life.

In memory of his body his image was painted on cloth, in memory of his speech a Kan-gyur was printed in letters of gold, and in memory of his mind the people erected a silver tomb to the height of thirteen cubits.[3]

Thus were Body, Speech, and Mind, composing one of the may Buddhist Triads, honoured in accordance with Tibetan custom.

The desire for rebirth as a Mongol was fulfilled. In fact, during the following year, 1589, the new incarnation was recognized in the son of Seng-ge Du-gu-rung himself. Mongol co-operation was thus assured. He, too, was named Yön-ten Gya-tso; and he remained in Mongolia till thirteen years of age, when of necessity he had to install himself at Lhasa, sending a high lama to represent him in the land of his birth.

Mongolia stands apart from the other Buddhist nations in that she did not receive the religion from India, from

[1] Biography, fol. 105.
[2] Hor Chö-chung, p. 144.
[3] Biography, fol. 105.

which, indeed, Buddhism had long disappeared. It was from Tibet that the inspiration came, and by Tibetan agency the work was carried through. And carried through it was, for hitherto no people in the world have shown more steadfastness in their Faith than those of Tibet and Mongolia.

X

THE PRIEST ENTHRONED

AMONG a people so devoted to their religion as are the people of Tibet there are bound to be keen religious differences. From what one reads in other Tibetan histories, and from what one sees and hears in Tibet to-day, it can easily be inferred that the advance of the Yellow Hats in spiritual and material power was neither so constant nor so universal as their own histories would wish us to believe. The strong conservatism of the Tibetan impels him, even while clinging to his spiritual guide, to yearn secretly for those old gods whom his guide has discarded. Thus it happened that during the first half of the seventeenth century, between 1610 and 1642, the Yellow Hats suffered a set-back. The ruler of Tsang[1] belonged to the old Kar-ma-pa sect. His fortified head-quarters on the little hill above Shi-ga-tse were strongly built; his authority throughout this western province of central Tibet was supreme.

To this day the memory of his outstanding personality is preserved among all sects, new and old. During my long years in Tibet I paid a week's visit to Shi-ga-tse and the Pan-chen Lama, the Grand Lama of Ta-shi Lhün-po. While returning up a broad valley, my Tibetan companion, himself a distinguished priest of the Yellow sect, pointed out a cave in the mountain-side as the birthplace of this self-made chieftain. Certainly it was a lowly origin, but Tibet has never been entirely a land of feudal privilege. It has continually thrown up from below, mainly through the priesthood, but sometimes also through the 'black heads', as the laymen are termed.

'How did he rise?' I asked.

'Well, his mother was a she-devil, and that accounts for much.'

[1] Known to Tibetans as *De-si Tsang-pa* or *Tsang De-pa*.

His father was but a groom in the service of a local chief. The boy proved quick at letters and figures, and was therefore put into the office of the controller of the household. His talents were now employed in buying and selling articles for his master. He continued to do well, and in the fullness of time came to hold charge of the silver and gold, the store-rooms of barley and peas, the leather bags of mustard oil, the wool, the silk, and the bricks of tea, in fact, all the miscellaneous property which a Tibetan fort requires and maintains. This gave him the control over a large staff of employees.

One day he had to visit Shi-ga-tse, then, as now, a prosperous commercial town, in order to buy two hundred good needles, which were not very easy to procure in the wilds of Tibet. His master gave him a letter to the authorities there, requesting their help in the purchase. In this visit the ambitious young man perceived the chance of a lifetime. The Tibetan word for 'needle' is *kap*, and by adding an *r* after the *k*—which, in Tibetan, requires only a straight line under the *k*—*kap* is changed into *krap*,[1] the latter meaning 'a suit of chain armour'. The addition being neatly effected, the young man acquired two hundred suits of armour. He was in close touch with the villagers, for it was from them that he collected the money, grain, oil, wool, and other taxes. His employees recognized his forcefulness, and obeyed his orders; his armoured suits were therefore quickly filled.

Thus equipped, he marched against his master, who—the story goes—was so struck with his cleverness that he surrendered forthwith, remarking that a man of such resource was far fitter to rule the territory than he was. Master and servant exchanged places. Wisdom, knowledge, cleverness have always been esteemed by Tibetans as the highest of virtues.

During this period Tibet was mainly under the rule of local chiefs, each governing by force whatever tract of country he was able to control. The she-devil's son, by

[1] Pronounced *trap*.

Tsang woman (right) with a friend from a robber tribe

various stratagems subdued the neighbouring chiefs, and in due course became the ruler of the whole of central Tibet. His capital he maintained at Shi-ga-tse, where he lived in the present fort, on which, say the people of Tsang, the famous Potala at Lhasa was subsequently modelled.

We have an interesting sidelight on this remarkable man from an unusual source. For now at last the white man has pushed his way into the heart of this hermit land, Fathers Stephen Cacella and John Cabral, two Portuguese Jesuits, visiting Bhutan in 1628. Marco Polo, who recorded the wonderful power of the Tibetans as magicians, had apparently been in the neighbourhood of the Szechwan-Tibet frontier in 1277, but had not penetrated far, if at all, into Tibet, though he may well have seen Tibetans at the court of Khubilai.

Meeting with hostility in Bhutan, Cacella passed on to Shi-ga-tse, where he was subsequently joined by his companion. They received a friendly welcome from the king, who, as such lay rulers usually are, was by nature tolerant. Moreover, having risen from the ranks, he had plenty of enemies, in addition to those of the yellow priesthood, and perhaps hoped for help in some form from the white strangers. He lent them a house, gave them supplies of food, and appointed one of his servants to keep him acquainted with their needs.

Far away, in the west of Tibet at Tsa-pa-rang, another member of the Society of Jesus had pushed up his little Mission, and received support from the local chief, who permitted the preaching of this new 'holy law', expecting perhaps to find in it a new sect of Buddhism. A church and a house were allowed to be built and a garden to be made, houses being demolished for these purposes. This Father Andrade, writing in 1626, gives some interesting details of the Tibetan priesthood. He found both Red Hats and Yellow Hats settled in the same district. 'The monks were', he writes,[1] 'divided into ten or twelve kinds, differing from each other by their rites and ceremonies.

[1] Letter of 16th August 1626; *Lettere annue del Tibet*, pp. 6–9.

They do not marry; some live in communities, others each in his own house. They wear one sleeveless garment, leaving their arms bare, and over it another that comes down to their feet. Their wearing apparel is generally red; their head-dress is either red or yellow. At their religious celebrations they use trumpets, which are usually made of metal, but sometimes of the bones of human arms or legs. To remind themselves of death they wear necklaces made of human bones, and for the same reason they use skulls as drinking vessels.' We could apply the above catalogue equally to the priesthood of the present day.

During the following year the King of Tsang sent an invitation, but it does not appear that the distant call was ever accepted. The monks of Tsa-pa-rang were always in bitter opposition to the missionaries, who came preaching that the Tibetan religion was false. They inflamed the people; there were uprisings, and eventually the Mission buildings were destroyed. Partly on account of his support of the Jesuits, the Chief of Tsa-pa-rang was himself attacked and captured, and carried off into exile at Leh. Thus, storm succeeding storm, the Mission was abandoned a few years later. Visiting Tsa-pa-rang in 1912, nearly three hundred years afterwards, Captain G. M. Young found no tradition of a Christian Mission, and only one trace, but that unmistakable. 'A row of white-washed *chö-tens* stands near the Dzong-pön's house. One of them, some forty feet high, towers above the rest; and on its summit there lies horizontally a weather-beaten cross of wood.'[1] Why was it so placed? Perhaps, as Captain Young surmises, somebody wished to lay up treasure for himself in both the Buddhist and the Christian heaven.

The king is described as a young man of twenty-two, of a fair complexion, in good health, very religious, and generous towards the poor.

He and his attendants live in the fort on the top of a hill with a guard of soldiers. The insides of the houses are gilded and painted,

[1] *Early Jesuit Travellers in Central Asia*, by C. Wessels, S.J. (Martinus Nijhoff, The Hague), p. 88.

and the wing containing the king's apartments is really worth seeing, more especially some rooms full of trinkets, which he has of every sort, for being a rich man, he has the best of everything from everywhere. Hangings are much used in all his rooms, the plainer ones being of Chinese damask, but the others are equal to the very best in Portugal. The king's retainers dress very neatly.[1]

Even in those early years of the seventeenth century the transmission of news in Tibet was remarkably efficient. Father Andrade's Mission at Tsa-pa-rang was over a month's journey from Shi-ga-tse. The Tsa-pa-rang Monastery was under the great monastery of Ta-shi Lhün-po, which lies only half a mile from the Tsang capital, and the monks were able to give to the Portuguese Fathers daily tidings of their distant compatriots. It is the same in Tibet to-day. Tireless messengers are mounted on relays of ponies, provided by intervening villages as part of their rent, and carry letters from one government officer to another, and between the great houses of religion, whose ample estates, furnishing ponies and riders, are never far away.

Though the king began in friendliness, the monks were hostile from the first. It was given out that the two strangers had come to pull down their temples and destroy their religion. The king wavered, and became 'more reserved towards us'. He did not approve of their intercourse with Ta-shi Lhün-po, the chief home of his enemies, the Yellow Hats. 'These lamas are not very favourably regarded by the king, because he says they are a bad sort.' And probably he found, as the lesser chief had found, that intercourse with the foreign priests lowered him in the eyes of his people.

The missionaries did not remain long, departing through Nepal. There were other visits three years later. Cacella, broken down in health, though only forty-five years old, died at Shi-ga-tse seven days after his arrival. The king, still friendly, sent for Cabral, who went again

[1] Account by Cabral, quoted in *Early Jesuit Travellers in Central Asia*, p. 154.

in 1631, but appears to have made only a short stay. However, from this time until 1733, Roman Catholic missionaries were frequently in Tibet. From them we gain information concerning Tibetan Buddhism, as seen through the eyes of European Christian priests. Tinged, no doubt, by a natural bias, both racial and religious, but still of great value.

In Lhasa and in the Tibetan histories emanating from the Ge-luk-pa sect the King of Tsang was, and is, anathema. The young Dalai Lama, born in 1615, could gain no wide recognition, for this Kar-ma-pa chief ruled the country, and in fact, as the present Reincarnation informed me, sent men to kill the young Dalai. In this they failed, but they succeeded in killing his mother by throwing her from the upper storey of her house. The Yellow Hats, in fact, were pressed down; the power of the old sect was in the ascendant.

But the Lama, too, had his ambition, and had not forgotten the Mongol connexion. When he was more than twenty years old, he appealed to Gusri Ten-dzin Chö-gyal, the chief of the Oelöt Mongols. In Mongolia the Yellow sect was supreme; indeed, Gusri and the young Lama had studied under the same spiritual teacher. Gusri, in alliance with other Mongol chiefs, was too strong for the King of Tsang, whom he eventually defeated in 1642. A history, in sympathy with the Ge-luk-pas,[1] writes:

> At that time the king (Gusri) rose up with a great army against Ü and Tsang. He conquered all the armies of the De-si Tsang-pa, seized him and his ministers, and imprisoned them in their own homeland at Ne-u in the province of Ü. He collected[2] the whole territory of Ü and Tsang under his power. He became king of the three divisions of Tibet. The white Umbrella of Law encompassed his whole domain up to the summit. He completely cut off all uncivilized persons who contended with the Ge-luk.

So writes one of the Yellow Hat chroniclers. But the

[1] Hor Chö-chung (Huth's edition), p. 158 of the Tibetan text, p. 252 of the German translation.

[2] བསྡུས་ is the Tibetan word.

leading Bhutanese history, whose Ka-gyü sympathies are opposed to the Tsang ruler and still more strongly to the Dalai Lama, points out that the former's Treasurer, named Nang-so A-u, helped to promote this invasion, whose progress is thus portrayed.

The Ü and Tsang provinces of Tibet were turned into a land of hungry ghosts, like the domains of the Lord of Death. From that time the spiritual sway over the entire Tibetan nation passed over to the Dre-pung Incarnation,[1] while the temporal power was divided between Nang-so A-u and the Mongol ruler Ten-dzin Chö-gyal.[2]

The invasion was rendered possible by the internal factions and intrigue, which then, as ever, divided the loosely-knit Tibetan communities. Bhutan also was attacked by a Mongol-Tibetan combination, but without success. The hardy Bhutanese have never been inclined to serve others, even their kinsfolk beyond the Himalaya. They follow their own sect of Buddhism, and have retained their freedom against both Chinese and Tibetan.

In the chief campaign Bhutan was attacked simultaneously from five points along its northern frontier, and the fighting lasted for nine months. Some of the invaders penetrated down to Dewangiri on the southern border, but the huge Bhutanese forts were proof against all attacks. The Chronicle says: 'It seemed as though they had come merely to die and leave their bodies in Bhutan. . . . They never besieged or stormed any of the Bhutanese forts, but simply filled the wilderness of Bhutan and Tibet with useless forts and redoubts.' It attributes the ultimate discomfiture of the force to 'the injustice of their cause and their consequent dread of the occult power of the Grand Lama of Bhutan'. The latter, we are told, had undergone a special training in that form of occultism which serves to repel foreign invasions. The great Dalai Lama is referred to contemptuously as 'The fifth Dre-pung hierarch'.

Eventually the Sa-kya hierarch acted as intermediary,

[1] i.e. the fifth Dalai Lama.

[2] Lho-i Chö-jung, fols. 38, 39.

and Bhutan escaped further invasion for a period of thirty-seven years. It was a religious, rather than a racial war, an attempt by the Yellow Hats, flushed with victory over the Kar-ma-pa sect in Tibet, to crush the Ka-gyü in Bhutan. There was no tolerance at that time; battles were fought and monasteries were pillaged.

The high priest of the Tsang ruler sought sanctuary with the Bhutanese king, who delighted in holding religious discussions with him. The exile became a professor in the State monastery, wrote commentaries on the history and meaning of the Bhutanese sect, and trained young priests.[1]

Gusri's conquest appears to have been fairly complete throughout Tibet, embracing the central, eastern, and north-eastern territories. He made Tibet over to the fifth Dalai Lama, and from that time to the present each succeeding Dalai Lama has been not only the spiritual head of Tibet but the ruler in things temporal also, though this latter power has usually lain in abeyance. Where, however, as in the case of the present Dalai Lama, the temporal power also is firmly gripped, there results an autocracy such as perhaps no other country in the modern world can show.

The conquest gave a strong and continuing impetus to Buddhism, especially that of the Yellow Hats, in Mongolia. Mongol priests entered the different monasteries in Tibet to study the sacred literature; and on their return to their homes founded schools there. Still do they come pouring into Lhasa—as I so often witnessed during my stay there—to drink of the holy teaching at its source. None are more keen than they, using to the full the time and the money they spend on the long, arduous pilgrimage.

The doctrines of the new religion were examined with the minuteness in which Mongol and Tibetan intellectuals have always delighted. The study of dialectics was introduced, and with such effect that the Mongol is now fully equal to the Tibetan in this coveted field of the

[1] Lho-i Chö-jung, fol. 39.

Pa-ro Fort, Western Bhutan

There is not a nail in the whole of this huge building; the wood is dovetailed

higher priesthood. In the Hall of Audience in the Potala, while attending the Dalai Lama's great yearly Reception, Colonel Kennedy and I witnessed a contest between two of the leading dialecticians in Lhasa, one of the main items to be staged before the exclusive audience that attends this function. Both contestants were Mongols.

The Tsang king now disappears almost completely from view, but his memory, though unwelcome to the good people of Lhasa, is revived year by year in the Holy City. After attending the Dalai Lama's Reception, we two white men went up on the roof of a house in Potala Shö, the village nestling at the foot of the Palace. There we witnessed a strange ceremony. Three Tsang-pas, i.e. men of Tsang, one after the other, slid down a rope attached from one of the lower buildings in the Potala to the obelisk inside the precincts, a distance of some two hundred and fifty feet with a descent of one hundred.

Standing in his loneliness on the near corner of the flat roof, the Tsang-pa offers up his prayer in a loud voice that the whole hushed multitude can hear, as they watch him eagerly from every possible view-point in the village. He follows up the prayer with an offering of barley flour, which he scatters upwards and outwards into the strong wind that is blowing. Then, strapped to the rope by a leather thong, he commits himself to the descent.

The first two come down easily enough, but the third turns upside down after describing only a quarter of the distance, and hangs head downwards for what seems an age, before he succeeds in his hard efforts to right himself. This misadventure caused the Dalai Lama, who was watching from above, grave anxiety lest the man fall; for it meant not only death to the poor man, but an evil omen for all in the year then beginning.

Formerly the rope was attached to the top of the Red Palace on the summit of the Potala right down to the ground outside the village below, a drop of three hundred feet or more. But this was discontinued, after one of the performers had been killed, his abdomen ripped open.

This annual event, provided and paid for by the Lhasan Government, refers to Gusri's defeat of the King of Tsang, and is intended to prevent the Tsang province from gaining power again. For the descent, belonging as it does to the category of things that are inauspicious, works against the return of the kingdom of Tsang. This explanation, given by our Tibetan friends, was subsequently confirmed by the Dalai Lama himself in one of my conversations with him. However, to prevent bad fortune from falling on Tibet as a whole from an inauspicious performance, one always climbs up the rope a short distance after the three descents are completed.

Having witnessed this hazardous performance on a frozen day in February, we thread our way through the dense crowd, and ride homewards in one of those tempestuous dust storms that occur all too frequently throughout the Tibetan winter. It is fortunate that it did not chance to burst fifteen minutes earlier when the man was still on the rope.

Some two years before his defeat, the Tsang chief had written to the Chinese Emperor, seeking to enter into friendly relations. The young Dalai Lama had also done so, and to him simultaneous advances appear to have been made from the Chinese side, where the new Manchu power was now growing.

At this stage of Tibetan history we may summarize the political background as follows:

In Tibet the Yellow Hats were struggling into a position superior to that of the other sects. The Tibetan population, especially in the provinces of Ü and Tsang, recognized their moral appeal and their growing power, but were not disposed to abandon the older sects in which their forefathers had been brought up.

The Mongols, thirsting for one of the forms of Buddhism that Tibet could give them, had fallen mainly under the spell of the Yellow Hat school, and therefore used their military powers in its support. Their leaders, too, hoped that the religious influence of the lamas would

Shi-ga-tse Fort

'He commits himself to the descent'

aid them in re-establishing Mongol dominion over China.

The Chinese, indifferent to Buddhism for its own sake, were, nevertheless, resolved on political grounds to gain power with the Tibetan lamas, in order to control the Mongols through them.

With the enthronement of the fifth Dalai Lama as sovereign over the whole country, the power of the Yellow Hats was greatly increased. The priest was on the throne, and he was more than a mere priest, for he had attained Buddhahood, the right to return to earth no more, being recognized as the Incarnation of Chen-re-zi, the patron deity of Tibet. One may speak of all these Incarnations, the lesser as well as the greater, as Living Buddhas, for this is how the ordinary Tibetan regards them. He in fact uses *Sang-gye*, i.e. 'The Fully Cleansed', his term for a Buddha, in two senses. Firstly, of those supreme ones, Gotama Buddha (*Chom-den De*) himself, and of his predecessors and successors who follow each other at intervals of some thousands of years. Secondly, of those who, by a succession of good lives, have awakened from the slumber of ignorance, the root-cause of evil, and become fully cleansed.

I asked my friend Ku-sho Pa-lhe-se, a well-educated member of the Lhasan nobility, his opinion as to the propriety of using the term Living Buddha, which is sometimes disputed by Europeans. His reply was, 'I do not know what explanation the lamas would give, but we laymen look on all Incarnations[1] as Buddhas.[2] The Buddhas are innumerable. The Incarnations are those who have attained Buddhahood, but have left their heavenly homes[3] and returned to earth in order to help all animate beings. One may therefore call them Buddhas, but we Tibetans usually refer to them as Incarnations of Chen-re-zi, Ö-pa-me, Je-tsün Dröl-ma, &c. It is another way of expressing the same idea.'

Having thus attained the sovereignty, the young Dalai

[1] *Trül-ku.* (སྤྲུལ་སྐུ་) [2] *Sang-gye.* (སངས་རྒྱས་) [3] *Zhing-kam.* (ཞིང་ཁམས་)

left the Dre-pung Monastery, where, like his predecessors, he had lived and studied, and moved to the Red Hill,[1] the home of the early Tibetan kings. Here his chief minister commenced to erect again the fortified palace, which had first been set up by King Song-tsen Gam-po, and destroyed by a Chinese invasion after the great king's death. The new palace was on a much more generous scale. Grueber, who made the earliest European picture of it,[2] had seen but a part of it in 1661, as it was not finished till twenty-eight years later, being over forty years in building. Since those days there have from time to time been small additions, for in honour of a victorious war it is customary to add to the Potala[3], as was done, for example, after conquering the province of Nya-rong in the eighteen sixties. It was named Potala after a hill on the southernmost tip of India, a hill sacred to the cult of Avalokita, the God of Mercy. By Tibetans he is named Chen-re-zi, and by them each Dalai Lama is recognized as his embodiment on earth.

Tibetans, when using the word Potala, always prefix *Tse*, i.e. 'Peak', to it, for it stands on the summit and side of a hill, three or four hundred feet high, which rises directly out of the level plain. It was clearly built as a place of defence, and in relation to some other places and events it is still known as the Fort. A horse race held on the plain behind it is 'The Gallop behind the Fort'; the beautiful little chapel which nestles with its lakelet and old gnarled willow trees immediately below the towering walls is known as 'The House of the *Lu* behind the Fort',[4] to distinguish it from chapels to these powerful serpent deities in other parts of Lhasa.

The Potala is of a size to dwarf the palaces of Western monarchs, but there is in it nothing of ostentation. In the beauty of simplicity its massive stone walls slope upwards and inwards, nine hundred feet in length and seventy feet

[1] *Mar-po Ri.*

[2] *China Illustrata*, by Athanasius Kircher, S.J., Amstelodami, 1667.

[3] The second syllable should not be accentuated.

[4] *Dzong-gyap Lu-kang.*

The Potala, with a procession of monks passing below it, and on its face two huge pictures, each about eighty feet high and seventy feet broad

higher than the golden cross surmounting St. Paul's Cathedral. They seem to grow out of their rock foundations and to stand in sympathy with the wide plain and the bare mountains around them. The main building is whitewashed every year; the central topmost block, in which are the chapels, is dark crimson; and a small adjoining block is yellow. Dotted about on the great flat roof are gilt pagoda awnings. Few who have seen it, lit up maybe by the afternoon sun in the clear Tibetan air, and backed by the soft purple of the eastern hills, will deny that here is one of the most impressive buildings in the world. Eleven months spent at Lhasa could but enhance day by day my admiration for this marvel.[1]

The interior also is full of interest. In the part behind the red walls, known as 'The Red Palace', are numerous chapels with old images, many of which came from India in the early days of Tibetan Buddhism. Here we find a room sacred to the great conqueror-king, Song-tsen Gampo, with an image of him and of Tōn-mi Sam-bo-ta, who is said to have introduced the Tibetan alphabet from India in the seventh century of the Christian era. Both wear red turbans or hats shaped very much like the black hats worn nowadays by Parsees. There are many indications that Tibet obtained its Buddhism largely from Kashmir, Afghanistan, and neighbouring territories. The Indian ministers to the Chinese Court in the seventh century, as represented in the Tibetan play 'Chinese Princess, Nepalese Princess', might almost be modern Afghans.

The fifth Dalai Lama, too, has his own room. His image represents him with a strong, but somewhat angry face, conveying the impression that, even when secluded, he was unwilling to relinquish the worldly power. In one of the chapels his boot is still preserved, encased in a thick gold covering, at the foot of the most precious image in the whole Potala. Long ago, tradition says, a sandal-wood

[1] For an excellent description of the exterior of the Potala the reader is referred to *Lhasa*, by Perceval Landon (Hurst & Blackett), vol. ii, pp. 184–91.

tree in India was split, and this image of the Lord of the World (*Lokesvara*), with three others, appeared fully-formed inside it.

Along the western side of the Potala lie the mausolea of the Dalai Lamas, commencing with the fifth, and excepting the sixth, since he did not pass away in Lhasa. They are shaped somewhat like *chö-tens*, that of the fifth being sixty feet in height. All are overlaid with gold, and the framework is reputed to be of solid silver. In them are set diamonds, turquoises, corals, sapphires, and other precious stones. Cloisonné jars, large and beautiful, though now much worn with age, are often placed on each side of a tomb, usually a couple on each side.

In addition to the numerous chapels and apartments room is found for the 'College of Victorious Heaven', housing one hundred and seventy-five monks, who constitute the personal monastery of the divine ruler.

One of the Dalai Lama's most intimate subordinates,[1] lately deceased, who combined the duties of Lord Chamberlain, Cabinet Minister, and Chief Physician, told me that this fifth Dalai conducted the secular affairs of his State for no longer than three years. He then retired into religious seclusion, leaving the worldly government to a Regent, who consulted him but little. And this was the form of government which presented itself to the Jesuit fathers Grueber and D'Orville, who stayed about one and a half months in Lhasa in 1661, the first white men to reach the Tibetan capital. Secluded in sanctity within that home of religion, extending his claim to be regarded as an Incarnation of the patron deity of Tibet, the Lama wielded a more potent influence than as a priest of Dre-pung seated on a worldly throne. The upraised mass of the Potala which towers above the city of Lhasa, resting a mile away on the flat plain, exemplifies the dominance of the priesthood over the people of Tibet. It was not until the time of the present thirteenth Dalai Lama that this Incarnation of Chen-re-zi,

[1] *Chi-kyap Ken-po* (སྤྱི་ཁྱབ་མཁན་པོ་).

fortified by over two hundred and fifty years of possession, has held firmly to the twofold power.

Though he came to live in the palace, his apartments at the Dre-pung Monastery, the same as those occupied by all his predecessors, were, and still are, preserved as a sacred bequest. They are kept by a 'house steward',[1] who is appointed for seven years. In March 1921, during my mission to Lhasa, one such period of seven years expired. The Dalai Lama's secretary, who attended on my party, had to be present during the transfer, in order to see that all the property was intact.

The Regent, who was himself a lama and was named 'The Ocean of Buddhahood' (*Sang-gye Gya-tso*), enlarged the festival of the Great Prayer, ordained by Tsong-ka-pa to be observed at the commencement of each Tibetan year. At the end of it come five days of racing and other sports, based on Mongol customs, and presided over by two Tibetan nobles, who, like most of the nobility, are in the service of their Government. These Masters of Ceremonies are dressed in priceless robes, which give the general effect of Mongol princes of three hundred years ago, in honour of him who gave the sovereignty to the fifth Grand Lama.

In 1652 the Dalai Lama visited the Emperor of China in Peking. He was treated as an independent sovereign, for his spiritual authority, backed by the Mongol armies and the single-hearted devotion of the Mongol peoples, ensured respect from the rulers of China who were constantly afraid of Mongol attacks. The Manchus had recently wrested the throne from the Mings, a Chinese dynasty, and were ruling with all the vigour of youth. Tibetans are by nature more in sympathy with Manchus, whom they regard as of their own religion, than with Chinese, whom they regard as without any real religion at all. Thus Emperor and Lama could help each other; and on the whole they worked in harmony during the years that followed.

[1] *Kang-nyer*.

Among other presents the Emperor conferred on the Lama a gold tablet inscribed with the title which he had given him.[1] When I attended the Dalai Lama's annual Reception in the great hall of the Potala, I noticed over his throne an inscription in large gilt Chinese letters with a Tibetan translation below. The Secretary of His Holiness identified it as this very tablet, and gave the substance of its meaning as 'The Excellent One, who Draws up, is Merciful, and sheds his Light in all Directions'.

The vigorous regency of the 'Ocean of Buddhahood', resting on the Dalai Lama's sanctity, was a time of great movement in Tibet. Power, temporal as well as spiritual, was steadily concentrated in the Lhasan Government. The petty chiefs and monasteries, that ruled their little territories, could not withstand the pressure of the Yellow Church backed by the Mongol power. Parts even of Mongolia acknowledged the Lama's sovereignty.[2] As we have seen above, the new Government failed to extend its power over Bhutan, and probably also over several of the outlying parts of Tibet. But throughout a large area it became supreme. As you travel down valley and plain in central Tibet you cannot fail to be impressed by the number of ruined forts placed here and there in commanding positions. You ask when they were abandoned, and usually the answer will be, 'During the time of the Great Fifth'.

In 1680, on the twenty-fifth day of the second Tibetan month, the Dalai Lama 'departed to the heavenly fields'. Sang-gye Gya-tso concealed his death for several years, telling the people that he was in religious retirement in the Potala, and must not be disturbed. Lamas occasionally go into retirement for years at a time, and, no doubt, the Regent wished to have the prestige of this Dalai Lama behind his administrative acts. Tibetans have told me that he was particularly anxious to finish the Potala before announcing the passing away of the God-king. Stones

[1] Sheng-wu chi, v. 4b (Rockhill's *Dalai Lamas of Lhasa*, E. J. Brill, Leyden, p. 18).

[2] Rockhill, *Dalai Lamas of Lhasa*, p. 21.

'Ruined forts in commanding positions'

The 'Tree of Sorrow'

had to be carried and other heavy work done, all without payment. The faithful would do this for their supreme Divinity, but hardly for a mere Regent. The Emperor of China in due course protested that he had been kept in ignorance of the death for sixteen years, but a Tibetan friend with whom I discussed the matter put the period of concealment at nine years. There was certainly a protracted delay in recognizing the new Incarnation, a boy who had been born in southern Tibet ten months after his predecessor's death. After his recognition, and after, no doubt, due preparation, he took the vows of priesthood before the Pan-chen Lama at Nor-bu Kang in the neighbourhood of Lhasa, receiving at the same time his priestly name, Tsang-yang Gya-tso, the 'Ocean of Melodious Purity'. He was then thirteen years old. When, two years later, he was installed on the throne, the Emperor of China was represented at the ceremony.

The period of the fifth Dalai Lama marks a turning-point in Tibetan history. Now at last the priest is enthroned, a Living Buddha, holding the twofold power. For Dalai Lamas are entitled to rule on the material as well as on the spiritual side. Though they have generally found the former to be irksome and too full of worldly contaminations, yet some have ruled thus for a time, and the present Dalai Lama has done so throughout manhood's years. The High Priests of Sa-kya had indeed reigned as kings, but they had not the same full flavour of divinity. Their domination was smaller, and their dynasty held sway for only some seventy years.

To the Tibetans he stands out as a compelling figure, the 'Great Fifth'.[1] Disregarding the verdict of history that his death was concealed, they will tell you that when he passed from the world, all the flowers drooped. There are a few weeping willows in Lhasa and the neighbourhood. You will hear from some of the simpler folk that it is only since this calamity that the branches drooped, whence they call it the 'Tree of Sorrow'. Even those who use the

[1] *Nga-pa Chem-po.*

ordinary name, 'Chinese willow', aver that since those days all trees and flowers have drooped a little.

Of all the mausolea in the Potala that of the Fifth is the most striking. Every day a religious service is held before it by the chief priest[1] in charge. At sunrise it commences, at noon it ends; then all entrances to the vicinity are closed, and none is admitted.

Several books are attributed to the Fifth. His biography, which is in six volumes, totals three thousand nine hundred pages.

After 'The Great Prayer', established on its present lines by the fifth Dalai Lama, 'The Offerings of the Assembly', established by Sang-gye Gya-tso, the Regent, ranks next in importance. It fills the last ten days of the second Tibetan month—early April or thereabouts—including the death anniversary of the Fifth, and commemorating his memory. Offerings are laid before him and prayers sent up to him by priests and fairies, by Oracles and the 'Eight Great Kings'. The dances of heaven are performed before him. Thus will this great Vicegerent of the Lord Buddha be pleased, and his blessings will fall on his own land of Tibet.

[1] *Um-dze* (དབུ་མཛད་).

XI

CHRISTIAN MISSIONARIES IN LHASA

THE rules which govern the up-bringing of a young Dalai Lama are of unbending severity. His young compatriots may drink wine and spirits; he does not. But the restrictions go much further than this, for after the first three or four years of his life, he meets no women—not even his own mother. With all Living Buddhas persistent care is taken to impress on them a firm belief in their divine origin and mission. The present Dalai Lama was taken from his mother when barely three years old, and brought up entirely by priests. Whether or not this moulding of the youthful mind is the cause, it is seldom that Dalai Lamas have been accused of straying from the path of virtue. In fact, out of the thirteen there is only one clear case, and to that case we have now come.

The sixth Dalai Lama missed this early up-bringing, for, owing to the concealment of the death of the fifth, he does not appear to have been recognized till he was ten years old. Certain it is that, as he grew to manhood, his mind was found to have developed on unusual and difficult lines. He delighted in beautifying the great palace that had been so recently completed. He arranged for the construction and decoration of the 'Serpent House', the building dedicated to the *Lu* under the northern escarpment of the Potala. He delighted also in the drinking of wine and in nightly assignations with girls from the town. These he would meet in the Serpent House, in the long upper room with its view across the dark water into the gnarled trees beyond. The dances of the girls he would view in a palace which he built close to the Temple in the heart of Lhasa.

He composed verses, mostly love songs, which are now read and quoted with pleasure. The following translation, though crude, adheres closely to the sense of the original.

It nearly represents the metre also, which prescribes three trochees (–⏑–⏑–⏑) for each line; but, Tibetan being so highly condensed a language, I have of necessity added a fourth.

Yellow mouthed, but black within it,
Cloud, the source of frost and hailstorm.
He, that 's neither grey nor yellow,[1]
Is the foe of Buddha's teaching.

Melting snow with ice beneath it
Is no ground to loose a pony.
To a sweetheart newly fancied
Never tell your inmost secrets.

. . . . .

Now the cuckoo from the lowlands
Comes, and comes earth's yearly moisture.[2]
I have met with my beloved;
Peace has come to mind and body.

Dog, that 's tiger-dog or leopard,
Give him food, comes near all-friendly;
In my house the long-haired tigress,
When she 's near, stands up in power.

Drawing diagrams, I measured
Movements of the stars in heaven;
Though her tender flesh is near me,
Yet her mind I cannot measure.

. . . . .

Lhasa gathers large assemblies,
Chung-gye holds the fairer maidens;
'Tis in Chung-gye that my loved one,
'Little Intimate', is living.

. . . . .

[1] i.e. neither true layman nor true priest. The latter are so described from the yellow hats of the dominant sect; the former often wear grey-white clothes.

[2] In central Tibet it is usual to have dry weather from September to May, when the 'yearly moisture' may begin, giving showers till the following September.

'The Serpent House under the northern escarpment of the Potala'

Righteous king of hell, whose mirror
Shows all deeds, both good and evil;
Justice is not found on this side,
Grant it there, when I pass over.

. . . . . .

Now in this short life lamenting,
So much have I said, but shall we
In our next lives come together,
In the years of early childhood?

. . . . . .

Lo! the snake gods and the demons
Lurk behind me, stern and mighty;
Sweet the apple grows before me;
Fear leads nowhere;[1] I must pluck it.

Thus 'Melodious Purity' lived and sung. We need not wonder that men questioned whether he could be the true Dalai Lama. The Emperor of China and the Mongol chiefs in Tibet held that he was not. He himself at Ta-shi Lhün-po renounced the vows of celibacy and monkhood. Sang-gye Gya-tso, now aged, stood by the young Dalai, and plotted against Latsang Khan, the Commander of the Mongol forces, but the latter had the power of his soldiery behind him. He attacked the Regent, who fled to a fort near Lhasa, but surrendered on being persuaded that the Dalai Lama had so ordered. He was immediately put to death. This was in 1705.

Sang-gye Gya-tso had governed the country for a very long time with rare ability. Capuchin missionaries who visited Lhasa forty years after his death paid tribute to his wisdom.[2] In addition to his administrative acts, many—perhaps too many—books are attributed to him; a work on medicine, another on astrology, while a third embodies political discourses. If you visit the Police Court in Lhasa, you will find his image there, sitting back against the wall, with the white silk scarves of ceremony placed reverently

[1] Lit. 'Fearing and not fearing is not'.
[2] *Alphabetum Tibetanum*, by A. A. Georgi, p. 329.

over his shoulders. In front is a holy lamp, fed by butter, in a frame of green gauze. Above the lamp is a prayer wheel of silk and paper, turned—of course in the right direction, i.e. the way of the sun—by the draught from the flame of the lamp. These stand on a small square table, which here serves the purpose of an altar. In front of the lamp seven small bell-metal bowls of holy water are alined. Thus does the great Regent receive divine honour in the heart of the administration which he did so much to shape.

There is another Court of Justice at the foot of the Potala. This, too, was established by Sang-gye Gya-tso. Here his throne is preserved; it is not used, but is kept as an object of veneration.

'Melodious Purity' did not long survive his Regent. Latsang Khan appealed to the leading lamas to depose him. A council was held. Most of the lamas present at it expressed the view that the Dalai Lama's mode of life was due to the fact that there was no 'spirit of enlightenment'[1] in him, but none dared to suggest his deposition or to declare that he was not the true Dalai Lama.[2]

Foiled in this endeavour Latsang resolved to use force. In 1706 he sent the young man on a journey to Peking, to visit the Emperor, and did not omit to send one of his trusted ministers and a strong Mongol escort with him. The feeling of the Tibetan priesthood at this outrage was shown by the monks of Dre-pung, who broke out and rescued the Dalai from the soldiers. But the Tibetans having no army, the Mongol troops stormed the monastery and recaptured Tsang-yang, who died shortly afterwards. Some accounts affirm that he was murdered at Nag-chu-ka, and with them the Capuchin friars, who visited Lhasa soon afterwards, are in agreement. The Chinese chroniclers maintain that he died of dropsy somewhere between Nag-chu-ka and Koko Nor. This latter view was confirmed by the Dalai Lama's secretary, who accompanied me in Lhasa. He told me that the death

[1] *Chang-chup.* [2] Georgi, op. cit., p. 251.

'You will find his image sitting back against the wall'

took place at Par-lam Tso-ka, a place in the Chang Tang near the frontier of Mongolia. No doubt it was hastened by the treatment that he received.

One might suppose that the Tibetans would wish to be rid of a Dalai Lama who interpreted his Buddhahood as did Tsang-yang. But this would be to underrate the deep religious loyalty and faith of the Tibetan mind. His subjects could not question his acts. The ministers of a Dalai Lama are freely blamed if things turn out badly, but the God-King is above human criticism. Even with the Grand Lama of Urga, who was the spiritual head of Mongolia and third in the Lamaist hierarchy, it was the same.[1] The Tibetans do not willingly allow anybody to interfere with their Grand Lamas. The Chinese Government twice endeavoured to depose the present Dalai Lama; firstly, after the British military capture of Lhasa in 1904; secondly, after the Chinese capture in 1910. On each occasion the Tibetans treated the proclamation with contempt and continued to refer matters for the orders of His Holiness.

Whatever may have been the opinions of his contemporaries, it appears that the present-day Tibetan is at no loss to explain the young Incarnation's unusual development. A Tibetan friend put it in this way:

'The sixth Dalai Lama had the power of assuming several forms. His own body used to be in the Potala Palace, while a secondary body used to roam about, drink wine, and keep women.'

Quoting the verse about 'Little Intimate' in Chung-gye, he continued:

'The girl mentioned was a goddess who would have borne a son to the Dalai Lama. This son would have grown up to be a famous king, ruling over three thousand countries. The people of Tibet would have enjoyed great power and prosperity during his reign, but for this very reason they would have lost their religion.

'Tibet with three thousand nations as its vassals would

[1] See Chapter VII.

have become the most powerful country in the world. The conquest of these nations would have entailed many wars, the taking of very many lives. Herein would have been great sinfulness and slackening of religion. And, becoming powerful and prosperous, the Tibetans would thereby also have slackened in their religion, as is the custom among powerful and prosperous people. Therefore the king was not born.'

Some no doubt believe that the Chinese realized the danger, and removed him before it could materialize, but many hold the more spiritual reason given by my friend. Gotama Buddha himself was free to choose whether he would become a World Conqueror or the Buddha. There is no question which is the higher.

Latsang endeavoured to set up as the next Dalai Lama a young man of some twenty-five years of age, treating him as the Incarnation of the fifth, and ignoring the sixth. The Emperor of China supported him, but the Tibetans would have none of it. In one of his verses the late Tsang-yang had written that he would fly with the wings of a white crane to Li-tang, and return from there. This was held to be a prophecy that the Reincarnation would take place in this village in south-eastern Tibet.

In due course there was found in those parts an infant who had announced that he was the Dalai Lama and wished to return to his home in Lhasa.[1] The Emperor and Latsang were alarmed, and in 1717 had the boy confined in the Kum-bum Monastery near Sining in Kansu. Another Mongol chief came to the help of the Li-tang Incarnation, captured Lhasa, and defeated Latsang, killing him and his ministers in December 1718.[2] He then proceeded to sack monasteries of the older sects, and raised again the predominance of the Yellow Hats. There was no tolerance in those days on the part of the new sect and its

[1] Orazio della Penna, *Breve notizia del Regno del Tibet* (1730), Klaproth's edition, p. 41.

[2] C. Wessels, S.J., *Early Jesuit Travellers in Central Asia*, p. 224 (The Hague, Martinus Nijhoff, 1924).

Mongol supporters; nowadays there is no more than quiet pressure. Old and new as a rule live together harmoniously, and often in the same monastery.

The Emperor Kanghsi sent a force to restore order, but it was defeated by the Mongols and their Tibetan friends, and massacred almost to a man. He then realized the opposition with which he was confronted, recognized the Li-tang boy as the Incarnation, and sent him to Lhasa with a strong army. The Jesuit Father Desideri, who was in Tak-po at the time and therefore an eye-witness of these events, writes:

'Had I not seen it with my own eyes I would not have believed it, but no sooner had the Chinese penetrated into Tibet than the country literally ran over with silver. To supply his wants every soldier had received advance pay for five years in bits of uncoined silver of various sizes. The Tibetans were at a loss how to dispose of this abundance, and sent most of it to Nepal to exchange by weight for the currency of the country, out of which transaction the Nepalese made a handsome profit.'

Very different has been the practice of Chinese troops in Tibet during recent years, when, receiving no pay from their own officers, they have had to live, by force or fraud, on the country that they were nominally protecting. In this campaign the large influx of money no doubt helped to render the Chinese army popular. And in any event, now that their true Divinity was being brought to them, the Tibetans opposed no longer. Indeed, many joined the Chinese against the Mongols. Even Desideri received orders under pain of death to join the Chinese army within twenty-four hours, to provide himself with a horse and arms, and to bring two followers, also armed. But on the intercession of the local governor the order was countermanded.

Thus the Chinese, with some Tibetan allies, had only the Mongol occupants of Lhasa to deal with, and these they overcame. In 1720 the Tibetans received their Lama, 'Ocean of Good Fortune', and the Chinese at length gained real power at Lhasa. They annexed a large slice of eastern Tibet, garrisoned Lhasa as well as the route from Tachienlu, and appointed their own nominees as ministers at the Tibetan capital.

Shortly after the death of the sixth Dalai Lama, Christian priests came again from Europe to Lhasa. In 1707 Capuchin fathers arrived there, coming apparently from the mission station at Kathmandu in Nepal.[1] They were received without marked disfavour by the rulers and people, who were fully occupied in their own political upheavals. The missionaries on their side worked quietly. From the authorities and colleagues of their own Mission came but scanty support, each missionary receiving only ten to twenty pounds a year, in spite of the appeals for assistance that they circulated to their brethren at other stations. One of them, Da Fano, soon returned, and in 1711 the others left both Tibet and Nepal, and came to Chandernagore in Bengal. During ten years fifteen fathers had gone out to Bengal, Nepal, and Tibet, but had made only two converts to the Christian faith. We may with some safety assume that neither of these two were Tibetans.

Fresh efforts were, however, made, and in October 1716 Capuchins came again to Lhasa. Owing to the invasion of Tibet by the Oelöt Mongols in 1718 the missionaries opened a second station in the province of Tak-po, about one week's journey south-east of Lhasa. The Capuchins appear to have been treated well both by Latsang Khan and his successor. In 1724, three years after the seventh Dalai Lama was installed in the Potala, they received permission in a lengthy official document[2] to build a 'little Convent and a Church' . . . 'because they came to Tibet and remain here simply for the good of their fellow-creatures and to help them; not, like so many others, for their own gain and benefit.'

Hostility of course soon developed among the Tibetan

[1] *Alphabetum Tibetanum*, by A. A. Georgi (1762), p. 331.

[2] *The Exploration of Tibet*, by Graham Sandberg (Thacker Spink, Calcutta), p. 42.

monks and the populace, always ready to follow the lead of their priestly advisers. During the following year the river burst its embankment and flooded Lhasa, a sign that the gods who dwelt in the ground were angry at this desecration of the Holy City. A mob assembled at their door and was restrained only by being shown the edicts of the Dalai Lama and of the Regent stamped on yellow satin and supported by the Emperor's seal. But the mobs returned, and if they ventured into the streets the missionaries were molested. At length the Regent issued a proclamation affirming that he had consulted the Oracle at Sam-ye, on the Tsang-po, south-east of Lhasa, and its god had declared that the flood was due to the sins of the people themselves. This was a view which the people were quite ready to accept, and the molestation accordingly ceased for a time. The fathers started translating into Tibetan, Cardinal Belluga having a fount of Tibetan type cast at his private expense on models sent to him by one of the devoted band. They extended their influence also, as so many Missions in the East have since done, by medical work among the people.

The Christian priests appear to have had their own internal dissensions. It is alleged that the strong Jesuit influence at Rome was worked against them, and when they came again to Lhasa in 1716 they found a Jesuit priest, Father Desideri, residing in Se-ra Monastery. As for themselves in the city of Lhasa, then as now the favourite fighting ground of turbulent priests, their troubles grew and grew again.

In 1727 a fresh Tibetan rebellion broke out at Lhasa, instigated, it is alleged, by the seventh Dalai Lama and his father, and the Prime Minister was murdered. The Governor of Tsang, 'Power-Man Po-lha',[1] marched on Lhasa, put down the rebellion, and maintained his position there with Chinese help. The rebel ministers were put to death by the 'slicing process', and the Dalai Lama was

[1] མི་དབང་པོ་ལྷ

carried off and confined in eastern Tibet in the Ka-ta Monastery, close to a Chinese garrison. His father was summoned before the Emperor of China, chained to his two new wives. He was forbidden henceforth to reside permanently in Lhasa, but was permitted to make visits not exceeding a month at a time. A Chinese garrison of two thousand men was divided between Lhasa and Shiga-tse. After seven years' absence, however, in order to appease the Tibetans, the Dalai Lama was brought back to the Potala.

With all this there was no abatement in the hostility of the Tibetans and but a poor measure of support from home, so that in 1733 the Capuchin Mission at Lhasa came to an end. Such record as we have of this period seems to show that they worked in a humble, kindly way, alleviating bodily suffering also among a people who could do little to cure themselves. These probably are the reasons that enabled them to survive civil war and remain as long as they did.

Meanwhile two more Jesuit priests, Fathers Freyre and Desideri, were posted to Ladakh, and thence travelled on to Lhasa, arriving on the 18th March 1716. Freyre stayed only a few days, returning to India through Nepal. For a time Desideri was alone in the capital, for the Capuchins did not return till seven months later. A few days after his arrival he was summoned by the Commander-in-Chief, who, as sometimes happens in Tibet even in these days, spent his early years as a monk, but evolved later into a successful military commander. 'Longlife Purpose-fulfilled'—for such was his name—after listening to the Jesuit politely, put a few pertinent questions. 'Whence had I come? What was my station in life and profession? With what intention and on what business had I visited that country and kingdom? And, finally, how long did I desire to remain?'

Desideri replied fully on each point. As to his business, 'I had not come to Tibet on any mission save to teach our holy faith, and to guide in its ways all who desired to embrace it', adding that, 'as long as I was not impeded either by the authority of the king or by the orders of my superiors, I desired nothing else than to be allowed to continue the undertaking I had begun until death'.

'By the will of God my answers made a good impression on the General, who with warm expressions of cordiality and satisfaction, cheered me by saying that not only would I not meet with any opposition to my aims, but that even the king and court would willingly listen to such a great, just, and relevant matter as that which I had described.'

A few weeks later Desideri had an audience with the Regent (whom he styles 'king', for that is the literal meaning of the Tibetan word), and was accorded permission to preach.

He worked hard. 'From that day to the last which I passed in that kingdom I studied from morning till night.' By the end of the year he had finished a summary in Tibetan of the Christian religion, and presented it to the Regent in January 1717. A friendship grew up between the Regent and himself.

The latter advised him to retire into a monastery, and consult the most famous exponents of the Faith. He gave him permission to see and use all the books that he desired, and issued instructions to the lamas to explain difficult points. Accordingly, the zealous father entered Ra-mo-che Monastery, in the city, and lived there from March to July, examining the Kan-gyur. In August he moved to the monastic university of Se-ra for further study, his object being to write in Tibetan a refutation of Tibetan Buddhism coupled with a defence of Christianity. At Se-ra comfortable quarters were placed at his disposal. Not only could he say Mass in his private oratory, but he was permitted to use the libraries and to converse with the most learned among the professors.

But on 30th November the Oelöt Mongols of Ili captured Lhasa, looted it for three days, and put to death among others the Regent who had befriended him. The mission house of the Capuchins did not escape the loot, and one of them received personal injury. 'During these tragic happenings', writes Desideri, 'I remained hidden in the university and monastery of Se-ra.' Then, for greater safety, he fled to the refuge which the Capuchins had opened in Tak-po, where he remained till April 1721, with the exception of a few months at Lhasa. He completed his book in three parts. The first argued against the doctrine of transmigration or rebirth; the second against that of the Void,[1] which occupies so large a space in Tibetan theology; while the last explained the manner of learning the Christian doctrine, and was in dialogue form. This work 'was well received by the Lama and doctors, who read and examined it, and used to come in great crowds to re-read it and study it together'.[2]

Desideri's personal relations with the Capuchins appear to have been amicable, but there was rivalry between their respective orders for the possession of the Tibet mission field, and victory rested with the Capuchins. From Rome came the command that the Jesuit should leave Tibet. Accordingly, in April 1721, Desideri set out for Nepal, five years after he had entered Lhasa. One of the Capuchin friars accompanied him as far as Nepal.

Desideri's account of Tibet in general and of Lhasa in particular shows us that the last two hundred years have effected hardly any change. Having been fortunate enough to remain in Lhasa longer than any white man since the time of these Italian missionaries, it is easy for me to recognize the Lhasa of to-day in his well-knit description. One change there is; the city wall of those times is no longer, and was indeed demolished, in 1720, before Desideri's departure.[3] In his book he writes:

> Formerly the city of Lhasa was not enclosed within walls, but this was done in the time of King Cinghes-khang,[4] doors and battle-

[1] In Sanskrit *Sûnyâta*; in Tibetan *Tong-pa Nyi* (སྟོང་པ་ཉིད།).

[2] See Carlo Puini, *Il Tibet secondo la Relazione del Viaggio del P. Ippolito Desideri*, vol. x, Roma, 1904, pp. 61–5.

[3] Rockhill, *Dalai Lamas of Lhasa*, p. 42.

[4] The Regent, Latsang Khan.

Monks outside the Assembly Hall of a college in the Se-ra Monastery

ments being placed in various parts. It is very extensively populated, not only by the people of this country, but also by a very large number of strangers from diverse and remote lands: by Tartars, Chinese, Muscovites, Armenians, Kashmiris, Hindustanis, and Nepalese, who establish themselves here to trade, and grow exceedingly rich.

As a Buddhist sanctuary and as a trade centre Lhasa has always attracted a cosmopolitan population; but at the present day strangers, except Mongols, Nepalese, and Kashmiris, find no easy admittance.

As one looks back across the years, one cannot fail to recognize that, wide in his learning and keen in his study of all things Tibetan, Ippolito Desideri was among the most brilliant Europeans who have ever travelled in that country.[1]

In 1740, after an absence of seven years, another party of Capuchin priests, headed by Orazio della Penna, returned to their old hospice in Lhasa. They were sufficiently well received by the Regent. When, in the following year, they visited the Chinese Resident, the latter paraded his superiority of status by keeping them waiting for some time 'at the outer gate of the palace (which is the best in Lhasa), being detained by the lengthy inquiries of their interpreters concerning our state and condition. When we had been admitted, we were again kept in an outer apartment, and finally introduced to audience'. On departure scarves were placed round their necks, a sure mark of inferiority, but the fathers appear to have regarded it rather as a mark of distinction.

They became friendly with the Regent and with the Dalai Lama's father, a well-built man of gigantic stature, who had been expelled from the Dre-pung Monastery in his youth. He had proceeded to marry three Mongol wives, then a Tibetan, next to her two more Mongols, and finally two daughters of the Tibetan Prime Minister, the Dalai Lama being the son of one of the first three Mongol

[1] For these and further details of his work and writings see (*a*) Carlo Puini, op. cit.; (*b*) C. Wessels, *Early Jesuit Travellers in Central Asia*.

women. This is the energetic interventionist who helped to promote the uprising of 1727.

But the priests were no more ready than before to welcome competitors in their line. The Regent's patronage of the Christian missionaries appeared to them intolerable. It was only four months after their arrival in Lhasa that they experienced the first outburst.

> 'The ferment went on gradually increasing, until one fine day several hundreds of Buddhist priests, gathered from the different convents of Lhasa and the neighbourhood, invaded the royal palace and upbraided the King for his partiality. The latter, being terrified and dreading to meet the fate of his three predecessors, declared forthwith that the Fathers had fallen from his favour; he enjoined them to preach no more in Tibet except to traders that came from beyond its confines; and at the same time he caused the converts to be searched for and had them exposed in the Chinese wooden collar, while the few of these who refused to recite the watchword of the faith he caused to be bloodily flogged. Whereupon the missionaries, though formerly well received, became the laughing-stock of the people, and could no longer appear in public without being exposed to ridicule and insults.'[1]

In the hope of mollifying the priests the missionaries reduced their number. But things went from bad to worse. Eventually, after they had struggled on for four years, the Regent—who had already ordered that no other missionaries were to be allowed inside Tibet—permitted them to preach 'only on condition that they should declare the Tibetan religion to abound in goodness and perfection'. That ended the uphill fight. On the twentieth day of April 1745 the Capuchin fathers left Lhasa for ever. Some twenty-three years later the Mission was expelled from Nepal by the newly risen power of the Gurkhas, who were intensely suspicious of all European influences.

It was just a hundred years after their departure from Tibet that, in 1846, two French Lazarist missionaries, Huc and Gabet, entered Lhasa from the north. They, too, were well received by the Regent of the time, but the Chinese

[1] Sandberg, *The Exploration of Tibet*, p. 98.

Resident would have none of it, and after two and a half months they were driven forth. Apart from this brief exception, no Christian missionary, since 1745, has worked in the Rome of Northern Buddhism, nor probably in any of the vast areas of Tibet that are under Tibetan control.

There is a marked sameness in the history of all these devoted bands of Christian priests. First a welcome, or half-welcome, by the secular rulers, later to be followed by opposition from the Tibetan priesthood, growing in violence as the time passes. The priests are by far the stronger power; the secular government must either abandon the Christians or go under. So it was at Tsa-pa-rang, so it was, time and again, at Lhasa. Capuchins, Jesuits, and Lazarists, all fared alike.

Yet it was not only mob violence with which the Christian missionaries had to contend. There were two other obstacles. Firstly, the wide range and complicated structure of Tibetan Buddhism, and the long, sustained study which its cleverer priests devoted to it. Had the Christian fathers sufficient knowledge of all this to enable them to combat it? Desideri, indeed, fought the doctrine of the Void, but that is only one of many. The studies of a Tibetan monk may be very wide. Those of the Abbot of Sum (1702–74)—a man, no doubt, of unusual learning—embraced metaphysics, logic, rhetoric, poetry, liturgy and ritual, and the differences between the various Buddhist schools. He also learnt medicine, as well as music and the art of sacred painting. He further added some proficiency in astrology. With these stores of knowledge he wrote books as follows:

(*a*) Three books on medicine.

(*b*) A work on the structure, proportion, and form of images.

(*c*) On rhetoric and drama.

(*d*) On the history of the religion in India, Tibet, and Mongolia, a well-known work. One of its specialities is a valuable chronological table.

(*e*) A work on Buddhist charms to enable its students to work miracles.

(*f*) Geography of the world. Lit. 'A General Account of the World'.

(*g*) A work on Yoga.[1]

(*h*) On fortune-telling and divination.

(*j*) Another work on meditation.

Even though such works appear faulty and weak to Western minds, they confer great prestige among their own countrymen, and it is to these that the Christian teachers have to carry conviction. The writers, too, of books like these have necessarily gained the power of exposition and argument.

A second obstacle lies in the piety and stern asceticism of many Tibetan priests. Not only is celibacy widely practised, but many take no food after midday. Some retire to caves in the snow, and remain for several days with but scanty clothing or food. Others immure themselves alone in gloomy cells for three years at a time. During the years that I spent in Sikkim one lama there used to retire to a high snow-mountain each autumn for meditation, cut off from the outside world until the summer sun melted enough of the snow to enable the devoted worshippers from the village below to bring a fresh supply of food. If his food supply failed, he must necessarily die, for on his snow-mountain none other was procurable.

Tibetans believe strongly in both learning and asceticism, the two parallel roads of their religion. All this has to be met and fought by one who would convert them to Christianity. Mere keenness in preaching is not enough, love is not enough; there must also be knowledge of Tibetan Buddhism, and an over-riding wisdom.

Neither of Jesuit, nor of Capuchin, nor of Lazarist does any house or chapel now remain. None has been able even to identify any of the sites on which they worked. One small trace, however, I found in Lhasa. During my visits to the great Temple in the heart of the city, I used in-

[1] Abstract meditation practised as a system.

A blind minstrel and other Nepalese

Snow mountains in Sikkim

variably to go into the Holy of Holies, the chapel in which the image of the Buddha—brought to Lhasa in the seventh century—is enshrined. A little passage leads to it. Suspended from the ceiling at the entrance to this passage was a large bell, and on the bell were incised the words *Te Deum Laudamus.*

XII

MODERN TIMES

THROUGHOUT the past centuries the people of Tibet have always kept in remembrance the times of their great kings —'The Religious Kings,' as they are termed—who not only conquered other countries, but introduced 'the holy religion'[1] into their own. They have never been content to remain under alien rule. That love of independence, strong in the nomad and strong in the mountain-born, is among them still further intensified through fear of what the alien may do to the religion, which to them means even more than their fatherland itself.

A year or two after the departure of the Capuchins in 1745, Power Man Po-lha died and was succeeded by his son, who arranged an uprising against the Chinese in Lhasa. It failed, and for a time the Chinese garrison was strengthened, and the influence of China increased. In 1758 the seventh Dalai Lama 'retired to the heavenly fields'. His spiritual reign had been of unusual length, and he ranks high in Tibetan estimation, though during his time the Chinese grip on Tibet was increased. Still the Chinese Government has usually been wise enough to realize that outlying dependencies must be left largely to their own rulers, provided that a nominal supervision is maintained, and—in the case of Tibet—its spiritual power secured for the furthering of Chinese aims. It seems clear that, in spite of the decrees that the Chinese Emperor issued and the seals of office that he bestowed, the actual control of China in Tibetan affairs was spasmodic, and limited to the neighbourhoods of their garrisons. If they could but range on their side the spiritual influence of the Lama, and 'save face' by an appearance of sovereignty, the Chinese cared very little for the rest.

1 དམ་པའི་ཆོས་

During the reign of the eighth Dalai Lama it is the Pan-chen Rim-po-che who looms largest in Tibetan history. An Incarnation of wide learning, he exercised great influence, and, therefore, in accordance with the usual practice was invited to the Chinese Court. He refused at first, through fear of small-pox, of all illnesses the most dreaded by Tibetans. But eventually, 1779–80, he was persuaded to quit the cool heights of his native country for the lowlands of the 'Black Expanse', the name by which Tibetans know China owing to its great size and the dark garments of its people. When in Peking, he pressed for the restoration of their powers to the high Lamas of Tibet, and especially to the Central Government at Lhasa. But before his representations could bear fruit, he died of the very small-pox that he feared.

One of his brothers, who held office as his Treasurer and was himself a high lama in the Yellow Church, brought his remains back to Ta-shi Lhün-po and was appointed governor of the Tsang province. He took possession of all the great wealth that the deceased Pan-chen had acquired, and refused to disgorge any of it, either to relatives on the one side or to monasteries on the other.

At this time the Gurkhas had recently by their martial prowess established their sovereignty over Nepal, and were overflowing with energy. They were inclined to raid Tibet in the hope of rich loot from the great monasteries and the houses of the nobility. And they found an unexpected ally in the younger brother of the late Pan-chen. This man, who was settled in Nepal, belonged to the Red Hat sect, and was incensed at being denied all share in the Pan-chen's property. Animated both by personal bitterness and by a desire to strike a blow for his own sect of the religion, this Red-hatted Hutuktu[1] encouraged the Gurkhas to loot the Yellow temples. Pretexts being easily found, the Gurkhas occupied, in 1788, some Tibetan border districts, and three years later pushed further in

[1] A very high rank among lamas.

and sacked Ta-ṣhi Lhün-po, the rich monastery of the Pan-chen Rim-po-che himself. A Chinese force, with some Tibetan assistance, marching through Tibet during the height of winter, drove out the Gurkhas, invaded Nepal, and dictated terms of peace within a short distance of the Gurkha capital. After this event the Chinese for a time strengthened their control over Tibet.

The Chinese official history of this war, speaking of the tribes which were brought into relationship with their representatives in Tibet, mentions a tribe of foreign barbarians in India who made their capital at Calcutta. The British, however, refused the Gurkhas' appeal for help, and the mediator whom Lord Cornwallis dispatched arrived too late to influence the settlement.

Both the Chinese Government and that of the Dalai Lama have from time to time interfered with the rebirths of men who have attained Buddhahood, refusing to those whom they hold guilty of crimes the right to come again on earth. A recent instance of such intervention in the affairs of the next world was that of the Seng-chen Lama, who, in 1882, helped the late Sarat Chandra Das—a noted Bengali explorer in Tibet and a scholar in things Tibetan—to reside for over a year in Ta-shi Lhün-po and to visit Lhasa. For this and other things he was put to death and forbidden to reincarnate. Prithivi Narayan, Gurkha and Hindu, who in 1769 conquered Nepal, similarly attempted to prevent the rebirth of a powerful foe, whom he had defeated in the fight for power, fearing lest the rebirth should upset his dynasty. But among both Gurkhas and Tibetans many were found who doubted the efficacy of these prohibitions.

After their defeat of the Gurkhas, the Chinese used their increased power in Tibet to regulate the appearance of these high Incarnations. They were especially perturbed at so many of those in Mongolia appearing in princely families, thereby increasing the power of chiefs who, from the Chinese viewpoint, were more than powerful enough already. They were able to point to irregu-

Tibetan guns showing the prongs of antelope horn which are planted on the ground when firing

larities, alleging that a forthcoming birth, which the Lhasan Oracle had earmarked for the new Grand Lama of Urga, had eventuated in a girl.

In 1793 a golden urn was sent from China. The names of children who had been reported as likely to be the re-embodiment, were to be written on slips of paper, and placed in the urn. A religious service was to be held, and at its close in the presence of the Amban a name was to be drawn from the bowl, and held up for all to see. Nevertheless, at the choice of the next Dalai Lama, the ninth, the rule was disregarded. This is he whom Manning, the eccentric English traveller, saw in Lhasa, the Lama at that time being about seven years old. Manning writes, 'His face was, I thought, poetically and affectingly beautiful He was of a gay and cheerful disposition; his beautiful mouth perpetually unbending into a graceful smile, which illuminated his whole countenance.'

Ten short years rounded his span of life (1805–15), and the next died in 1837 at the age of twenty, the Regent being suspected of hastening his death. During the life of his successor, the eleventh, the Regent's rule became so oppressive that the Pan-chen Lama of the period and the members of the Lhasan Government forwarded a representation to the Emperor. Accordingly there came a new Amban who seized the Regent and deported him to Manchuria. And in his case, too, the Emperor judged it wise to prohibit his reappearance on earth. But in spite of these precautions this Grand Lama died in 1853 at the age of seventeen, and his successor, the twelfth, in 1874, when only eighteen years old.

It may be of interest to quote a Tibetan view regarding the qualifications desirable in a Regent. Discussing these with Colonel Kennedy, the late Prime Minister expressed himself as follows:

'In the government of a country the first necessity is to have a ruler who is both strong and just. It does not matter his being severe, provided that he is just. That is why the Dalai Lama's rule is so good for Tibet. If His Holiness died, I should have to govern the country. But ten such as I am would not make up for the loss of the Dalai Lama, because he has the twofold power' (i.e. the ecclesiastical and the secular administration).

He then related an incident that occurred during the regency of 'Wise Power',[1] while the twelfth Dalai Lama was a minor, the Premier's father being at that time a magistrate in Lhasa. This Regent was a strong man, well able to maintain his authority. An abbot of the Gan-den monastery through intrigue gained the post of Lord Chamberlain in the Dalai Lama's household, a post that ranks equal with that of the Councillors of State. He then commenced to undermine the Regent's authority. Pressing the Councillors relentlessly to support him, he went so far as to murder one who refused, having him tied in a leather bag and thrown into the river. Another, to save himself from a similar fate, had resigned before the trouble came to a head.

But now he found things too hot for him and fled to Gan-den. A force of soldiers attacking, he continued his flight eastwards. The pursuing soldiers drew near. So he suggested to his chief adherent, a Dza-sa[2], that he should transfix the Dza-sa with a spear, while the latter shot him with a gun. The shot took effect, but the spear failed to drive home, wounding the Dza-sa in the side. The wounded man was soon captured, brought to Lhasa, and put to death.

As for the Lord Chamberlain, the soldiers brought his body to Lhasa, fixed on a pony, the head and body supported with sticks as though he was actually riding. After reaching the capital, his head and hands were cut off and exposed to view; the populace spat on them and reviled his memory. His body was flung out into a field. The young Dalai Lama, then a lad of fifteen, was so greatly affected by his Chamberlain's grim fate, that he would not allow

[1] *Kyen-rap Wang-chuk.*

[2] A high rank, often hereditary, given both to ecclesiastical and secular officials for services rendered, or to support a high position.

anybody near him, and used to wander about alone like one demented.

Whatever be the causes which ended the lives of his four predecessors so prematurely, the thirteenth, at any rate, escaped their fate, for it is he who still rules Tibet.

As these four Dalai Lamas in succession died young, though most of their predecessors had lived to a good age, one can only infer that the lives of some, at least, were shortened by the Regent. For the latter would naturally be unwilling to release his grip when the young Incarnation of Chen-re-zi, reaching the age of eighteen, became entitled to grasp the temporal as well as the spiritual government.

A Tibetan explanation throws considerable light on the early passing of these four. There is a lake called 'The Heavenly Lake of the Victorious Wheel of Religion'[1] in the province of Tak-po, a hundred miles south-east from Lhasa. Every Dalai Lama visits it once in a life-time, for it shows him the future events of his life and the manner of his passing away.

Near the lake is a 'Protector's Room'[2]—i.e. a room sacred to protecting deities of a particularly fierce type—and in it is an image of Mar-sor-ma, the terrible goddess who presides over the lake. So dread is she that none but the Dalai Lama himself can venture inside the building. He enters it alone, and speaks to the goddess there. The ninth to the twelfth Dalais paid their visits between the ages of nine and seventeen. Young as they were, they had not sufficient knowledge to persuade her to turn away the wrath, which comes so easily to her, and, accordingly, they died soon after the meeting. The present Lama was twenty-five years old when he visited the lake and the fierce goddess, and had gained sufficient knowledge to enable him to persuade her to help him.

The Chinese in Tibet had become so thoroughly accustomed to Dalai Lamas dying after travelling to this lake,

[1] *Chö-kor Gyal-kyi Nam-tso.*

[2] *Gön-kang* (མགོན་ཁང་).

that some looked on the visit as a means of getting rid of the Precious Protector, the only person in Tibet who could hold their Amban in check. The Chinese colonel who commanded his troops in the Chumbi Valley a good many years ago, was a jovial, out-spoken soldier, who disdained the crooked by-ways of politics. He told a friend of mine that his compatriots were greatly disappointed when the present Dalai Lama did not die after his visit to the lake.

Some believe that the Regent's party, or the Chinese, used to bribe the Dalai Lama's cook and thus work their will by poison, relying on the story of the angry goddess. The present Lama has always been careful to have his food tasted; being older than his predecessors when he visited the lake, he was able to protect himself. From time to time the Lama's physician gives him a certain pill, known as 'the ball of great price'. 'This', say the Tibetans, 'renews his vitality and makes his body shine'. If the Amban or Regent did actually poison the young Dalai Lamas, it may be that this pill afforded the opportunity.

The manner of discovering which is the true rebirth of a Dalai Lama, a Pan-chen, or indeed any of these high Incarnations, has, so far as I am aware, no parallel elsewhere in the world. High lamas, of the reformed sect at any rate, are celibate. There is no son to succeed as in the hierarchy of Sa-kya during the thirteenth century.

Before a Dalai Lama 'retires to the heavenly fields', he may indicate where he will be reborn. For instance, the poetic sixth wrapped it up in one of his verses. In any case, within three or four years after his death the oracle at Ne-chung and Sam-ye give particulars as to his house and family, the land and trees and the country round, his parents and himself. The most learned of the lamas, including the three great State monasteries, Se-ra, Dre-pung, and Gan-den, set themselves in motion to discover, subject to the guidance already laid down, what boys have been born under unusual circumstances, and show on their bodies the marks that distinguish the embodiment of the four-handed Chen-re-zi from lesser mortals. Among such signs are:

(i) Marks as of a tiger-skin on his legs.
(ii) Long eyes and eyebrows that curve upwards on the outside.
(iii) Large ears.
(iv) Two pieces of flesh near the shoulder-blades, indicating the two additional arms of Chen-re-zi.
(v) An imprint, resembling a conch-shell, on one of the palms of his hands.

The names of three or four boys may be written on strips of paper, and placed in the golden urn. A religious service is held, after which one of the slips is picked out with a pair of chopsticks. When the Chinese were in power, this was done by the Amban. The boy so chosen is always able to identify various articles, religious and secular, belonging to his predecessor, or, rather, to himself in his previous life. The present Dalai Lama told me that the custom was to place two religious implements, i.e. bell, dor-je, &c., side by side, one being his predecessor's.

The young boy is taken from his parents and brought up by the priests, particular care being taken to instil firmly into his young mind, as into those of all Incarnations, his divine origin and mission.[1] At the age of eighteen, which is no more than seventeen and sometimes only sixteen by European reckoning, the Precious Protector is entitled to assume the temporal, as well as the spiritual, sovereignty over Tibet. His spiritual rule covers also La-dakh, Sikkim, and Bhutan on the Indo-Tibetan border, the whole of Mongolia, parts of China and Chinese Turkistan (Sinkiang), the Buriat country in eastern Siberia, and the Kalmucks in European Russia.

Ge-dün Trup-pa has his tomb in Ta-shi Lhün-po, the monastery that he founded. Those of the second, third, and fourth appear to be unknown. None is in the Potala

[1] For a fuller account of the method of choosing, the reader is referred to Ekai Kawaguchi's *Three Years in Tibet* (Theosophical Publishing Society, London), pp. 420–23, and to my *Tibet Past and Present*, pp. 50–54.

until that of the Great Fifth, who founded it on its present lines; and none in the Potala is so magnificent as his. The sixth is not there, as he died at a distance.

It is cold, this vast palace in winter-time. I found the water in the large bowls that find place on the steps of the tombs to be frozen from top to bottom, even at midday. At the bases of these mausolea, stand priceless old specimens of cloisonné and porcelain, the offerings of bygone Emperors of China.

At the foot of the eighth I noticed one of enamel, worked on metal, with representations of English houses and scenery, and English people dressed in the clothes of a hundred and fifty years ago. It had a Chinese mark on the base and was evidently a piece of work done for the East India Company. At the foot of the ninth, ranking proudly among the old porcelain and enamel, was an ordinary little looking-glass. It was prized as a thing of beauty, and had been kept there for many years past.

The anniversaries of the passing of the other Inmost Protectors are not kept on the scale of the Great Fifth. I can remember that of the ninth when I was in Lhasa. Musical instruments were played, and sacred butter-lamps were lighted in the Temple and the Potala.

The present Dalai Lama was born in 1875 of poor parents in Per-chö-de, a village in the province of Tak-po. The signs and portents were regarded as so conclusive that the Tibetans refused to submit his name to the arbitrament of China's golden urn. To the earnest seekers there appeared, among other signs, a vision of him in the 'Heavenly Lake' where the *la* of each Dalai Lama dwells.[1]

He came into his full twofold power when nineteen years of age. The Regency had been held by the Head Lama, himself a high Incarnation, of the great Ten-gye-ling monastery in Lhasa. This Lama was convicted of using witchcraft in an attempt to kill the Precious Sovereign by inserting a slip of paper, inscribed with an evil incantation, into the sole of his boot. All admitted that

[1] For the story of his choosing, see *Tibet Past and Present*, p. 53.

the foul crime of witchcraft had been committed against the person of his Holiness—for whenever he wore those boots, he unaccountably fell ill—but there were many who respected the Ten-gye-ling Regent and deemed him incapable of such an offence. These preferred to attribute the witchcraft to two brothers of the Regent, one of whom was his Prime Minister. However that may be, the Council of Ministers and the State Oracle, Ne-chung, were for punishment.

At the time of the Great Prayer in Lhasa verses appear suddenly in the minds of the women who draw water for the festival. It is believed that these are inspired by a goddess, who takes shape as one of them, and starts the verse on its round through the city. The verses are therefore prophetic. One such appeared some months before the Regent's fall:

> As a mouth the pond [1] is working,
> And the fish [2] lie at the bottom;
> So this year the yellow gander [3]
> May be driven to his ending.

Secretly and shudderingly men repeated this verse to each other, while the labouring women, as is their wont, sang it openly as they passed down the streets of Lhasa. For it is one of the oracular verses, and it is their privilege to sing these. Thus does public opinion express itself in a city devoid of newspapers.

The Regent, shut up in a small house in the grounds of the monastery, died from his punishment. There were many who not only deemed him innocent, but held his administrative ability in high respect. His own monastery was unflinchingly loyal to its head, and made use of every opportunity to rebel against the Dalai Lama and his government. Finally, it joined the Chinese in 1910 during Tibet's struggle for independence; and, two years later, when the Chinese were expelled from Lhasa, Ten-gye-ling

[1] The Ne-chung Oracle, which prophesied against the Ten-gye-ling Regent.
[2] The Councillors of State who are said to have moved them to the prophecy.
[3] The Ten-gye-ling Regent, who was a lama of the Yellow Hat sect.

was disendowed, the heavy stone buildings battered, and the monks expelled.

This universal belief that high lamas of the Virtuous Way, those who followed Tsong-ka-pa's purer faith, used witchcraft in an attempt to murder their divine Head, shows how deeply Pönism is ingrained even among the Yellow Hats of the Reformation. But, indeed, the old religion still lives in much of the new ritual and other forms of expression. All that can be said is that among the beliefs and practices of the unreformed school, the Red Hats, the Pönist element is even stronger.

His Holiness is somewhat below the average Tibetan height, and has the habitual stoop of one who spends most of his life seated cross-legged. His prominent eyes are of a dark brown shade. They are watery, and this is regarded as one of the signs of Buddhahood, as are his large, well-set ears. His eyebrows rise sharply towards his temples. His face is slightly pitted with smallpox, and is somewhat severe in repose; but, when he spoke, a quick, deprecatory smile would flash out, revealing the strong, white teeth. His courtesy and frankness, his shrewd, inquiring mind, willing to give out as well as to take in, made my long conversations with him an unvarying pleasure. Of these I had at least seventy or eighty, spread over two years in Darjeeling and one year in Lhasa, and always we two alone in his room. Indeed for me a most instructive experience, for inner secrets of Tibetan religion and politics were laid bare by the only authority who could venture to do this without fear of being called to task by his compatriots.

He is physically and morally courageous; quick-tempered and impulsive, but cheerful and kindly. Says the Tibetan proverb:

Though a lama may flare up,
He does not hold his anger.

So it is with the Dalai Lama. Withal, he is a shrewd judge of character, quick to understand, and quick to act on his decisions. To all these qualities he adds a will of iron and untiring industry.

'Ten-gye-ling was disendowed, the heavy stone buildings battered, the monks expelled.' Potala in the background.

Housetops in Lhasa. The gilt pagoda roofs are those of the Temple

In one respect he differs from all his predecessors, even from the 'Great Fifth'. He has exercised the temporal power throughout his reign. 'For the first five or six years,' the All-Knowing[1] frankly admitted to me, 'I felt greatly my lack of experience as to the governing of a country, though I could see that several changes were needed. However, within ten years I was able to bring order into the administration.' He has always been keenly interested in government and politics.

The Precious Sovereign has, indeed, been brought up in a hard school, but his shrewdness and strength of will have enabled him to surmount the lack of training and to carry through. His frail bark capsized for a time on the stormy sea of foreign politics; but later on was righted and resumed its precarious course.

One of his early tutors—a Buriat, known to the world as Dorjieff—received two posts in his household. To some he was known as 'The Abbot of the Innermost Essence', for he was a Professor of Metaphysics; to others as 'The Work Washing Abbot'. In the latter capacity it was his duty to prepare water scented with saffron flowers, and to sprinkle this, a little on the person of the Dalai Lama, but more on the walls of his room, on the altar, and on the holy books, as a purification.

His combined salary for these duties amounted to no more than one hundred and forty pounds yearly. But his influence was great, for to his store of knowledge he added strong driving power, with which he pushed the interests of his own Russia at the Dalai Lama's Court. This occasioned a collision with Great Britain, who, in 1904, dispatched to Lhasa a military expedition that drove the God-King into exile in Mongolia, and impelled him to visit Peking. The Chinese Emperor issued a proclamation dismissing him, but this the Tibetans treated with ignominy.

The British expedition and the treaty which resulted from it drew the relationship between Britain and Tibet

[1] *Kün-kyen* (ཀུན་མཁྱེན).

much closer. The Chinese were alarmed and endeavoured again to subjugate Tibet. The Dalai Lama reached Lhasa in 1909 after a five years' absence, and the Chinese advance rode in a few months later. His Holiness had, perforce, to flee again, this time to India, where over two years were spent, mostly in Darjeeling. It was not until 1912 that the Chinese troops were expelled, and he became again master in his own house, with friendly feelings towards Britain. When the world war broke out in 1914, he offered soldiers to fight on the British side.

PART TWO
HOW IT RULES

XIII

THE POWER OF THE MONASTERIES

Little by little Buddhism in its modified form has spread in Tibet, and, as the country stands now, its power is planted wide and deep. The monasteries are large, the monks innumerable. It is an ordinary event in a Tibetan family for a little daughter to leave the house and enter a nunnery; and one son at least, while still young, is likely to go off and take the vows of monkhood. Among the laity it is wellnigh impossible in this feudal land for a man of low birth to rise to a high position; but a monk, however humble his parentage, may attain to almost any eminence.

By reason of their sanctity the leading priests have great influence. Each Incarnation owes his headship of the monastery solely to his sanctity; but the others, having worked their way up through all stages of the Establishment, are necessarily men of ability. They have yet another source of strength. For the greater part of them have neither wife, nor children, nor property to consider, and can therefore adopt a bolder course of action than the nobles or other laymen. The Abbots of the different colleges in Dre-pung, Se-ra, and Gan-den have special influence through their voices in the powerful National Assembly, for they live on the very hub of Religion's Wheel. And, though their influence has been curtailed of late years because the Dalai Lama summons the Assembly less often in these days, and has also the backing of the army recently created, this simply means that the highest powers are—for the present—being concentrated more and more in the Head of the Church.

While riding along the road from Lhasa to the Drepung Monastery one morning, I met over two thousand of the monks on their way to deliver a fiery ultimatum at the Dalai Lama's Palace in the Jewel Park. The atmosphere was tense, but they passed me quietly, making way for me on the road. However, in the Jewel Park the troops stationed at Lhasa had to be called out to oppose them. The citizens of Lhasa, especially the merchants, were greatly alarmed, and sent their valuables by night out of the city for concealment in the villages around. Shortly afterwards between five and six thousand monks in this monastery broke into open rebellion, which was quelled only by bringing some three thousand troops of the regular army to Lhasa, and laying siege to the monastery.

When charged with offences against the criminal law, monks are tried by monks according to the religious code. But for a murder, large robbery, or other heinous crime, the monk is beaten, expelled from the monastery, and handed over to the secular authorities. In ordinary cases, where a monk is on one side and a layman on the other, justice is apt to be strained in favour of the monk.

During the 'Great Prayer'[1] festival in Lhasa, lasting for three weeks in February and March, and during that of 'The Offerings of the Assembly'[2] lasting for ten days in March or April, the magistracy and police of Lhasa lose their power. It is transferred to two powerfully-built monks of Dre-pung, who carry heavy iron staffs as their insignia of office and appoint their own police. In the times of the Regencies these monk-magistrates[3] used to present yearly to the Regent a sum equalling five to seven hundred pounds out of the profits made from the heavy fines that they exacted from the unfortunate inhabitants.

The capital is crowded during these festivals, and street affrays are common. After one such affray that occurred, when the young Dalai Lama was inexperienced in the art of government, the She-ngo let off the guilty parties lightly, reserving their heaviest fines for those who were least to blame. These latter waited until the Dalai went

[1] *Mön-lam Chem-po* (སྨོན་ལམ་ཆེན་པོ་). [2] *Tson-chö* (ཚོགས་མཆོད་).

[3] *She-ngo* (ཞལ་ངོ་)

Altar in Assembly Hall, Shi-de Monastery, Lhasa. To left, the Abbot's seat with his dress arranged on it

'Two powerfully-built monks'

to the Jewel Park, his palace outside Lhasa, and there attracted his attention by making repeated obeisances outside one of his windows. They were thus enabled to present a petition, as a result of which the monk-magistrates were fined and warned. Their power has since been much reduced,[1] though not perhaps their net profits, for His Holiness accepts no money from them.

Some priests rule districts. One such is Cham-do, two months' journey east of Lhasa, which is governed by a high Incarnate Lama of the Yellow Hats, known as the 'Pa-pa La' of Cham-do. The Grand Lama at Sa-kya, descendant of former rulers of Tibet, as well as His Holiness the Pan-chen Rim-po-che, especially the latter, hold still more important fiefs. But all these are subordinate to the central government at Lhasa, though some would like to be independent.

High officials and other laymen make a practice of giving presents, mainly of tea or money, to the large monasteries. Such gifts serve both spiritual and secular ends. Spiritual merit is laid up by the donor to be included in the count after death. This is, or should be, his chief motive, but he wishes also to secure the favour of the priesthood in worldly troubles. An influential monastery will always help its lay supporter.

The present Dalai Lama, while reducing the power of the priests and increasing his own, has increased also that of secular officialdom. He maintains that the priests' proper concern is with the affairs of religion, and that by directing their untrained minds on State affairs, they do but oppress the people.

One day a party of monks from Lower Se-ra, one of the three colleges in the Se-ra Monastery, betook themselves to Chu-shu, a village two days' journey from Lhasa, to realize some debts. The peasants not paying up quickly, the monks seized a large amount of their property and carried it off. The peasants petitioned the Council, who

[1] *Tibet Past and Present*, p. 141, contains an account of the Dalai Lama's ingenuity in removing these troublesome exactions.

referred the matter to the Dalai Lama. His Holiness summoned all three abbots of the monastery and kept them standing in his ante-room for two days, to bring them down to a proper appreciation of their own unworthiness. When he admitted them, the Abbot of Lower Se-ra was fined heavily, and all three were warned that, if such a thing occurred again, they would be dismissed from their posts.

Monks in the personal employ of the Dalai Lama, who win the approval of His Holiness, exercise great influence, for it is known that they have the ear of the Sovereign. Among such are his secretaries and their chief, and his librarian. His chief butler and his chief valet can, if they hold his confidence, exercise a large measure of power owing to the intimacy of their posts: their rank is equal to that of a colonel in the army, commanding five hundred soldiers, for much depends on their faithfulness.

Monasteries in and near Lhasa, especially 'The Three Seats', have in times past received large presents from the Chinese Government. The interest on such money is used mainly on the 'Great Prayer' and the 'Offerings of the Assembly'. Forty to sixty thousand monks crowd into Lhasa, and to each one attending the ceremonies is given:

(*a*) Tea and soup three times a day.

(*b*) A daily gift of a coin[1] worth between a halfpenny and three farthings to each monk from one of the lesser monasteries, and of double[2] this amount to each one from the Great Three. The coin, however, is handed out at such an early hour each morning that many do not trouble to come for it.

The food and money thus distributed are earned from the interest on that part of the Chinese contribution which has been stored in the La-brang Treasury in Lhasa. Other grants have been made in the Emperor's name to the monasteries themselves, and the interest on these they spend as they like. The money that the Treasury lends is mainly in copper coins, bulky and heavy though they be. Interest is charged at the rate of fourteen per cent.

[1] *Ka.* [2] *Kar-ma-nga.*

Young stag in the Jewel Park

Wild sheep (burrhel) in the Jewel Park

Wild ass (kyang) in the Jewel Park

In former times the Chinese Government realized the need of attracting the powerful monasteries to their side, and thus were enabled to gain influence in Tibetan affairs. But, later on, the heavy hand of the would-be strong man took the place of diplomatic generosity, and then China's power declined. As long as she maintains the independence that she won in 1912, Tibet does not expect fresh presents of this kind. Yet the apparent loss is real gain, for no longer are they liable to that expensive and irritating exaction, the necessity of giving free transport and supplies to Chinese officials and followers on their lengthy journeys in Tibet.

Priests who stray from the appointed path, whether individually or in the mass, are not countenanced by the laity. Discussing rebellious monasteries, a young friend of mine who belonged to the powerful Sha-tra[1] family, quoted to me a saying of his famous ancestor. This was he, who, though but a layman, was made Regent of Tibet, in preference to the six high priests that turn by turn hold the post. This Regent's verdict was that when a monastery rebelled there was no need to fight it, adding, 'Shut the monks up in their monastery with their lice, and they will soon find life unendurable'. No food to be bought in the neighbouring town or villages; no fresh clothes to be obtained from relatives or friends; no bathing excursions to rivers or ponds; and in the monastery everywhere—lice.

My young friend used to speak to me freely of the failings of the monks, but when in the presence of a lama he was always very respectful. Though his family was as high as any in the land, he would not sit down in the presence of the lama, an Incarnation, who governed the large Ta-lung Monastery, when the latter called on me. However, he more or less took charge of the interviews, and gave the holy man a hint as to when he should rise and take his departure.

Great indeed is the power of the priesthood among

[1] Pronounced like the English word *shutter*.

these people, who have all the religious devotion of nomads and all the conservatism of those that live among mountains. To them religion is everything. If that be seriously harmed, their country is but a profitless ruin. For their histories teach them, and they themselves believe, that when the religion is not supported the State decays through foreign wars and internal quarrels.[1] In Lhasa itself the lamas may be restricted, chiefly by their own Head, but in the wide expanses there is little to hold them. For they constitute the third Member of the Divine Triad, the Buddha, the Law, and the Priesthood.

[1] Tep-ter Ngön-po, vol. iii, fol. 2.

XIV

PRIESTS AS CIVIL AND MILITARY OFFICERS

NOT only do the priests influence the State through their monasteries, but they themselves serve also as government officials in civil, and even in military, employ. The regular civil service of the Central Government numbers three hundred and fifty members, of whom half are laymen[1] and half ecclesiastics.[2] The latter are usually picked when boys from the large monasteries near Lhasa and are trained in the Ecclesiastical School there. They are mostly of humble birth. Intelligent, pushing, resourceful, and not greatly hampered by family ties, some of the ablest administrators in the country are found among them. As in the monasteries, so also here, those recruited from the lowest social ranks can and do rise to the highest positions.

When I was in Lhasa, about forty out of the one hundred and seventy-five priest-officials were men of good family, that is to say, of the status of a trung-kor. The remainder were sons of peasants and the like, who had shown proficiency in letters when at Se-ra, Dre-pung, or Gan-den. From time to time the order comes to these three monasteries to send up the names of boys suitable for training. The lads are taken to the 'Nest of Letters'[3]—as the Ecclesiastical Court, where the three Grand Secretaries meet and work, is termed—without their own wishes or those of their parents being particularly consulted. The Grand Secretaries accept some and reject others. The boys must not only be clever, but must be free from serious physical fault or disfigurement. Anything clearly wrong with eye or limb, hardness of hearing, a hare-lip,

[1] Known as *Trung-kor* (དྲུང་འཁོར་).   [2] Known as *Tse-trung* (རྩེ་དྲུང་).

[3] *Yik-tsang.*

and so forth, will be a bar to employment. The governor of one of the districts which I visited north of Lhasa had a young son in the monkhood. One of his lower eyelids drooped just a little, so that the red of the eye showed, and that was sufficient to bar him from employment as a tse-trung. Those who are accepted are sent to the Peak School.[1] This, as its name implies, is in the Potala and is under the control of a 'Great Teacher',[2] himself an ecclesiastical official of high rank. The boys enter the school, which contains twenty to thirty boys, at ages varying from fourteen to twenty, and pass through it in three or four years. Their rate of passage depends not only on their own ability, but on the gifts which their parents are able to make to the Grand Secretaries. Examinations are held twice a year, and the candidate gains the rank of tse-trung either on New Year's Day (February) or on the twenty-fifth day of the tenth month (November–December). The latter brings the anniversary of Tsong-ka-pa's death; the former stands out as the leading date in the Tibetan calendar.

The priest-official performs various duties. He is often to be found in charge of an important district, and here you will find another official, probably a layman, as his colleague, for it is only a lesser district that is held by a single dzong-pön. One may be known as the Eastern, the other as the Western Dzong-pön. This does not mean a division of the district between them, but simply that their quarters in the dzong lie east and west of each other. Indeed, there is no division of work; they are expected to act jointly in all matters, the idea being that the government can use each as a check on the other. During my interviews with dzong-pöns, thus working in pairs, one would speak while the other would content himself with a few words from time to time, indicating that he concurred with his colleague. Later on, he might do the speaking, when the roles would be reversed. I never found the smallest sign of disagreement between them;

[1] *Tse Lap-tra.*

[2] *Ge-gen Chem-mo.*

Village children, Chumbi valley

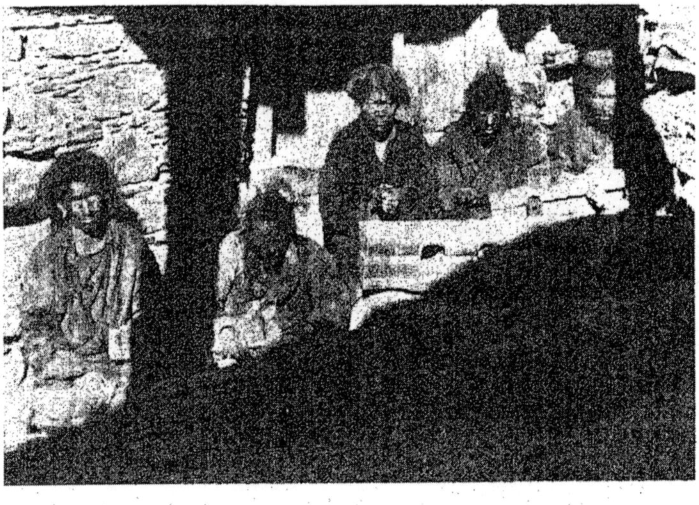

Convicts in the stocks in the prison below the Potala

the government being watchful, they cannot afford to quarrel.

In many posts tse-trung and trung-kor work together. Thus, the two police magistrates of Lhasa town are both laymen; of the three for the outskirts below the Potala, two are laymen and one is a priest.

There are three treasuries at the capital. The 'Lama's House'[1] in the city is worked by two priests and a layman. The Tre-de in the Potala is the Dalai Lama's private treasury; two priests and a layman manage it. The third is also in the Potala and is known as 'The Treasury of the Sons of Heaven'.[2]

The La-brang is inside the city. To it are remitted large amounts of the revenue due to the government. This arrives not only in the form of money, but also in butter, tea, gold from the mines, and other goods, for money is scarce in Tibet and revenue is mostly paid in kind. The landlords and tenantry pay a great deal of their dues in grain, but this is stored in the various dzongs and other government granaries throughout the country, to be used or sold as occasion may require. In the La-brang are also kept precious stones and other properties of the State. Another of its functions is to lend out money to those who are in a position to provide two substantial sureties. The rate of interest is 14 per cent.

The Tre-de has its own sources of revenue reserved for it in the government schedules. With the La-brang it shares the advantage of having landed estates of its own. The grain due to it is stored on the estates; the cash, butter, oil, &c. come to the Treasury. And the meat also, for meat in the dry cold of Tibet, if killed at the beginning of winter, keeps good for two or three years. Another source of income arises in the offerings of pilgrims to His Holiness, and by the relatives of those who have lately died. The latter type of gift, usually a large one, is known as 'The Support for Frying'. The meaning of this curious name is that, as barley by frying is rendered fit for use,

1 *La-brang*, pronounced *Lab-rang*.

2 *Nam-se Ken-dzö.*

being eaten, so the deceased by the Dalai Lama's power will be rendered fit for further good work and saved from going to hell.

In the Treasury of the Sons of Heaven are stored rare silks and the like, as well as gold, silver, corals, turquoises, diamonds, and other precious stones. The silver in it is let out to wealthy persons, who each produce two landed proprietors as sureties. The rate of interest is only 10 per cent. yearly, as the security is first-class. It deals with a few large sums instead of many small ones. The value of its contents is very large, because the storing has continued for several hundreds of years, and it is not used for current expenditure, but is maintained as a reserve against war or other expensive calamity. It is usual for a priest and a layman, working jointly and controlled by the Lord Chamberlain, to manage the Treasury of the Sons of Heaven.

So it is with other branches of the administration. Of the 'Barley Flour Takers', who hold the government stores of grain, meat, oil, and silver, one is priest, the other layman. They receive no salary, and have to meet authorized indents whether the goods are in store or not. It is an unpopular post, for they are always put to loss, but when they have served their term of three years, they find their reward in some profitable appointment.

Two out of the three officials, who superintend the Temple buildings in Lhasa are secular, but the three who hold charge of the chapels in the Potala are all priests. The servants work under them, and it is their duty, whether in the Temple or in the Potala, to go round at least every evening, to see that all is in order, and to guard against burglary and fire.

The priest official has usually worked hard from boyhood and remains industrious throughout his official career. The Dalai Lama and his Government attached two officials to my mission in Lhasa. One was a layman who had worked as the governor of a district, the other was a priest, one of the Private Secretaries to His Holiness. The former, Ku-sho Ne-tö, was a most pleasant companion, full of worldly wisdom and humour, ready for the duty that called him, but just as ready for ease and joviality when circumstances allowed. With the Secretary, a widely read and able officer, it was work first and last. Any arrangement that he organized was complete down to the last button. His duties with my party were considerable and continuous, but he found time to take up also special matters, for which his experience as a Secretary to the Dalai Lama fitted him. He worked hard, and had always done so. Beyond a day or two now and then when he had been ill, he had taken no holiday for twenty-five years.

There are four Grand Secretaries in the central government and these control the tse-trung establishment. They suggest the appointments and transfers among them. Suppose, for instance, a priest has to be sent to Shi-ga-tse, to hold joint charge with the lay governor of that district, which, though the residence of the Pan-chen Lama, is—perhaps for that very reason—under the direct control of Lhasa. The Grand Secretaries send up through the Prime Minister to the Dalai Lama the names of two officials, indicating their own preference among these two. His Holiness will appoint one of the two, if satisfied; if not, he will call for fresh names. He does not substitute the name of his own choice, but continues calling for other names until he gets it.

Serious disputes among monks, subsidies to monasteries, and many other branches of monastic government fall within their province. During the time that I spent in the Chumbi Valley, two of the monasteries failed to receive their annual subsidies of barley, but an application to the Grand Secretaries put matters right.

Whenever proclamations, orders, and the like, bearing the Dalai Lama's own seal, are issued, these are sent to their destinations through the Court of the Grand Secretaries. This has its own seal, a square red one; and a red seal in Tibet is a very high distinction, for even the Supreme Council[1] has to use a black one. Seals, no less

[1] *Ka-sha.*

than clothes, boots, and hats, are under firm and definite rule.

Such are a few out of the varied duties of this Court. The yearly pay of each Grand Secretary is no more than thirty-five pounds a year. But throughout Tibet the salaries of officials are minute. They recoup themselves by presents from interested parties. As long as they keep within the well-understood rules that govern such presents, one cannot blame them, for it is a recognized part of their remuneration, and they need a living wage. Some observe the rules, others do not; certainly one cannot praise the system. The Tibetan word for 'bribe' hits the mark; it is *pak-suk*, which means literally 'secret push'.

The monk-officials, as the Dalai Lama used to tell me, join the regular monks in speaking their opinions with greater freedom than do their lay colleagues. The Yellow Hats are especially independent; they rear no families. The Red Hats sometimes do, and know that they must be careful in a land where the whole family may be punished for the fault of a single member.

The head of all the priest-officials is he who holds the post of Lord Chamberlain in the Dalai Lama's household. Appeals and other matters, important and unimportant, fall to his lot. As Lord Chamberlain he is necessarily in charge of the parks round Lhasa. Though, like all his race, he is fond of flowers, he confided to me that he knew nothing whatever about trees. He was regarded as a good doctor, for he was, and had been for many years, the Dalai Lama's physician. Being in close attendance on His Holiness, he could not count on much sleep, as his master rose early and went to bed late.

Riding one day on the outskirts of Lhasa I passed a priest-official who had been appointed from among the Living Buddhas. 'It is unfitting,' remarked my Tibetan companion, 'but he was made a tse-trung, because there are very few in his family.' It is rare in Tibet for religion to give way to family convenience or the needs of the Government.

The Lord Chamberlain

A recent ruler of Sikkim—the reformer to whom allusion has already been made—was a Living Buddha. Most of his co-religionists held it wrong that he should defile the religion and himself by taking up the worldly duties of kingship. When he died young, that was one of the reasons ascribed, and many refused to count his name among those who ruled over this little State.

Ku-sho Ne-tö quitted his post with me in Lhasa on appointment to command one of the regiments in eastern Tibet. Though this spelt promotion, he viewed the prospect with strong dislike. 'I am thirty-six years of age', he explained to me, 'and that is rather old to learn military work. I have done some fighting in eastern Tibet, but have had no military training.' To Colonel Kennedy he said, 'If the Dalai Lama told me to go to Hell, I would go there gladly', speaking with perfect sincerity in the exaltation of religious fervour. Buddhist hells are not for ever and the Dalai Lama will put all things right for the faithful; meanwhile his orders must be carried out, however hard they be. Does not the proverb say?

> If told to strike a rock, strike!
> If told to go to Hell, go!

Ne-tö hoped for a few months' holiday at his home in Gyang-tse, where he might also gain some ideas from the detachment of Indian troops stationed there. His successor with me was a young lay officer of the Sha-tra family, who had started his career as a simple monk in the Se-ra Monastery. He had subsequently become a tse-trung and had held one of the 'Barley Flour Taker' posts for the full term of three years. His brother, a Colonel in the Dalai Lama's Bodyguard, died at this time, and young 'Corner Sha-tra'—so called because he took away his share of the family wealth and lived apart—succeeded him. Such a transfer from priestly to secular officialdom is uncommon, but I met with cases from time to time.

The tse-trungs, as well as the trung-kors, have their

yearly feasting each autumn in Lhasa.[1] That is a matter of pleasure, but the 'Presence Tea'[2] which the priest-officials stationed in Lhasa are expected to attend each afternoon at the Jewel Park, the Dalai Lama's country seat, is a matter of duty. It was instituted by the fifth Dalai Lama, who is, indeed, responsible for the whole order of priestly officialdom. From the Grand Secretaries downwards all are due at this compulsory tea. His Holiness does not attend; his 'room-stoppers' i.e. orderlies, join with the secretaries in taking charge. The ceremony lasts for about half an hour, and no talking is permitted. Should a tse-trung fail to appear one day, nothing is said; if for two days, his absence is remarked; and if for three consecutive days, he receives a reprimand. The Presence Tea is, in effect, a kind of roll call arranged to secure that the Lhasan priest-officials shall remain at work, and not go away on pleasure or on business of their own. And the giving of tea is an auspicious omen; just as in a house the servants should be entertained periodically by their master, in order to maintain and increase the household's prosperity.

Various indeed are the secular duties, both civil and military, in which one finds the priests exercising their wide capacity. Among others may be quoted the efficient head of the little Arsenal in its cold, narrow valley a few miles beyond the Se-ra Monastery. And the wise old gentleman, who holds the title of 'Little Abbot' and has for many years been stationed at Gyang-tse, dealing with the foreign interests that have grown up there during recent years.

No post was of greater importance than that held by the commander-in-chief of the forces in eastern Tibet. His every effort had to be directed towards holding in check the Chinese troops stationed on that side under ambitious generals, who hoped always for the opportunity to advance and seize Lhasa. During my last years in Tibet this post was held by a priest, a member of the Council of State. In 1917, the Chinese Commander thought he saw

[1] See *The People of Tibet*, p. 229.

[2] *Trung Cha.*

his opportunity when the Tibetan soldiers were engaged in their New Year festivities. He accordingly attacked, though a truce had been arranged, but his priestly opponent out-generalled and defeated him, capturing a territory twice the size of England and one that commanded the main avenues of approach from China to Lhasa.

A very prominent priest was the Dalai Lama's Chief Secretary, thin, sharp-featured, and unflinchingly loyal, who took up unpopular and dangerous duties which even the Prime Minister was afraid to tackle. When told that five thousand angry monks were threatening his life, his only reply was, 'What can they do? Let them dance as they will'.

XV

A DEITY AS KING

DURING the minority of each Dalai Lama a Regent takes charge of the Government. In this land of priests it is natural that even the deputy of the God-King should belong to the priestly order, and so it has always been, except for one instance. The four *Lings* of Lhasa are smallish monasteries, but have long held an exclusive and privileged position; though now one of them, the proud Ten-gye-ling, having fought openly on the side of the Chinese against their own country, has been devastated and closed. With these four are associated Re-ting and Mu-ru, two of the leading monasteries in central Tibet. The high priest of one of these six was normally chosen as Regent.

It may seem strange that the 'Three Seats' should not figure in this scene, but, in effect, they do. For the heads of these favoured six have always been high Incarnations, and all Incarnations of necessity attend Dre-pung, Se-ra, or Gan-den during a large part of their boyhood. These consequently have keen interest in the appointment of a Regent, and may be trusted to support one of their own pupils. It rests with the National Assembly, so largely under the influence of the Three Seats, to make the choice.

When none of these proved acceptable, the appointment sometimes fell on the 'Enthroned of Gan-den',[1] the highest of all lamas who are not Incarnations. To this eminence any monk can rise. It is a contest of industry and piety, backed by an able brain. Those who are wealthy, those who are of the highest nobility, have no start or privilege in the race. 'Anybody', a high Tibetan priest declared to me, 'of any nationality, whether Tibetan, Mongol, British, Chinese or other, can become the Enthroned of Gan-den, if he has the necessary qualifications.'[2]

[1] *Gan-den Ti-pa.*

[2] *Yön-ten* (ཡོན་ཏན).

From others one heard the popular saying:

> The power to mount? It is your own.
> There is no seal on Gan-den's Throne.

Regarded on account of his learning with immense respect, the Enthroned is occasionally chosen to fill the breach, much though he may dislike the pollution of his holy courses with worldly affairs. Failing him, the choice may fall on the young Dalai Lama's teacher[1] in spiritual and philosophical subjects.

Once only has the post of Regent been given to a layman. This one exception arose in the distinguished house of Sha-tra about ninety years ago. The head of the family was in high repute, for he had defeated a Dogra invasion in western Tibet. And the Gan-den monastery, to which he had given large presents of tea and money, supported his candidature. He compiled the code of laws,[2] which is chiefly used nowadays by Tibetan officialdom in its legal work. Since the days of Sang-gye Gyatso he is of all the Regents probably the most distinguished. From the hour of his appointment he dressed and lived as a priest, shaving his head, and renouncing wine and married life. Yet, as he did not come from the charmed circle, he can only be known as *De-si*, marking his inferiority to the Incarnations, each of whom was ranked as 'King of Tibet'.[3]

The present Dalai Lama appoints one 'Chief Minister' over the others. He, too, though a layman, is nowadays ranked as King of Tibet, and therefore, when the time comes, the then 'king' may resolve to continue in the post, if the modern army that has been recruited during the last twenty years, supports him. But the priesthood can hardly be expected to acquiesce in such a break-away from the established custom.

A Regent was always liable to be heckled by the Assembly that made him, and might perhaps unmake him.

[1] *Yong-dzin*, the 'All Holding'. [2] *She-che Chuk-sum* (ཞལ་ཆེ་བཅུ་གསུམ་).

[3] *Pö Gyal-po*.

But how different it is with the Dalai Lama! He is not a pope, but a god. Holding the twofold power, ecclesiastical and secular, Chen-re-zi's earthly Incarnation can reward or punish in this life, can draw up or let down in the next. His subjects, indeed, being nomads, are congenitally liable to outbursts, but there can be no sustained rebellion to the authority of a true Dalai Lama, so long as the Tibetan faith holds firm.

His spiritual sovereignty is no light charge, the strength of the priesthood being what it is. He must control the large monasteries, not excepting Se-ra and Dre-pung; he must preserve order during the religious festivals, when fifty thousand monks, many of them turbulent, are camped in and around Lhasa. This is for those in authority the most anxious time of the whole year.

Anything may provoke an outbreak. During the Great Prayer festival, when I was in Lhasa, the relations between the army and the monks, the new style and the old, were dangerously inflamed. And apart from this obvious danger, there was a Chinese merchant at Lhasa, who did not and could not pay his many debts. The Dalai Lama feared a disturbance here also, and once this commenced it might easily be extended. His Holiness and I discussed this matter during one of our *tête-à-tête* conversations in the private sitting-room in his country palace.

'When thousands are collected', he said, 'it is difficult to determine afterwards who started the fight. So I am not allowing the creditors to realize their debts in full, as there is not enough to go round. He owes many people money, to myself also a little (about £1,800). I think we should each lower our rate of interest, so that it will be the same for all. It is of no use killing the cow that gives the milk, as our saying goes. The meat will not last long. It is better to continue taking the milk.'

For the stern task of maintaining order he had his small army newly trained, but he was loth to use it. He preferred to rely on restraining the monks through their own heads. He made the latter understand that they would be

Picnic tent of a wealthy merchant in a park near Lhasa

Soldiers of the Dalai Lama's body-guard

punished, and that the monasteries themselves would be bound to suffer if a serious outbreak occurred.

I had suggested that, as he had now some six thousand trained soldiers at his call, it must be easier than before to keep the large monasteries in order.

'But still more,' the Dalai Lama replied, 'by choosing their Abbots and other leaders carefully, choosing men on whom I can depend.'

Such are the special steps which His Holiness takes to prevent monkish outbreaks. When he succeeded to his twofold throne he found that the Abbots and other high priests were fond of interfering in the secular administration, for the Tibetan is a born politician. That tendency he has steadily restrained, confining the priests more to their religious duties and occasionally dismissing the lazy ones. At the same time he increased the knowledge of religion among the priests; he increased also the ritual, the ceremonies, and the spectacles, which serve to magnify the priesthood and to attract a people that are still unspoilt by the theatres and cinemas of Europe. Owing to his general policy, backed by his little army, the control of a turbulent priesthood has been better during his reign than for a long time past.

In the exercise of his secular authority the Dalai Lama spends several hours daily. All cases of importance, civil, revenue, and administrative, are referred to him. When I was in Lhasa, disputes regarding land—which are always deemed to require especial care—came before him once a week, fifteen to twenty such cases on the average. Even an application by a tenant for the reduction of his rent has sometimes to be submitted to him.

He deals out even-handed justice. One of the days on which I visited the Prime Minister, I found him sorely depressed. He had stood surety for a merchant; the latter had defaulted, and accordingly the Presence had passed a decree against him for twelve hundred *do-tse*,[1] which he was required to pay off at the rate of one hundred *do-tse*

[1] One *do-tse* equals about five pounds sterling.

yearly. When called on for his statement on the case, the Premier had replied somewhat irritably, and this had done him no good.

During the early years of the Precious Sovereign's rule there were certain checks on his power. His subordinates would keep him in ignorance of what was happening. But now he has improved his system of private intelligence and various persons are encouraged to write to him direct. Another check lay in the rule that members of a Dalai Lama's family, e.g. his brother or nephew, should not hold public posts. But the present Prime Minister, appointed some years after I left Lhasa, is his own brother's son.

It is held to be unfitting that the Incarnation of Chen-re-zi, the Lord of Mercy, should immerse himself in criminal cases and the harsh code of punishment that Tibet attaches to these. So the Prime Minister takes the responsibility. Notwithstanding, a large number of the murder cases—and of these there are a great many in Tibet—have to be referred to the Dalai Lama for decision. Capital punishment is hardly ever inflicted, and then only for a very serious crime against the religion.

In cases of great importance, e.g. a dispute as to landed property involving a large area, or a case between persons of high rank, a petition is submitted in the names of His Holiness, the Prime Minister, and the Council. This is termed 'Placing the Names of the King and Ministers'.[1]

When a judge has decided unjustly, or the Council has wavered long over its decision, the aggrieved party will sometimes have the courage to submit an appeal direct to the Dalai Lama when in residence at his country seat or on his way thither. The law prohibits all such direct appeals, and the petitioner is therefore immediately thrown into prison. But he may, later on, expect a favourable decision.

Within the limits of his sparsely populated kingdom the Dalai Lama of Tibet is perhaps the most autocratic ruler in the world to-day. During former periods the National Assembly has often exercised preponderating in-

[1] *Gyal-lön tsen-kö.*

'The Lake of the Upper Pastures'

fluence in State affairs. But this cannot assemble until His Holiness bids it come, and only those may attend whose names are written on the Arrow List[1] that is appended to the summons. Of late years the call has gone out less frequently, and the Arrow List does not circulate to the full assembly,[2] at which some four hundred members may attend, but only to a committee[3] of the higher members, a body that is smaller and more easily managed.

The great monasteries are consulted still on important political matters, but do not exercise such influence as aforetime. Their chance, and that of the National Assembly, will come when inexorable time brings round another Regency. Meanwhile the real consultation is between the Precious Sovereign and his Ministers, and the real decision rests with the former. His word ranks immeasurably above all others in the estimation of his faithful subjects; and his army, though still small, is larger and more highly trained than before.

Not only in Tibet but also in Mongolia the Dalai Lama has great power in religious matters, and has hitherto been able in some degree to influence secular affairs. For in these lands religion and politics are inextricably interwoven.

As the result of his double charge, the religious and the secular—including also in the former those services and periods of meditation which occupy him for several hours daily—the Grand Lama's work is heavy, even excessive. He rises before six in the morning and is still working at midnight with but scant intervals for recreation. It is well that he is a quick worker, for the variety of duties that he shoulders is overwhelming.

In parts of Tibet, especially those which aspire to independence of Lhasa, there is constant criticism of the Dalai Lama's government, and, among intimate friends, of the Lama himself. Ta-shi Lhün-po is a case in point, for the central government has deemed it necessary to reduce the privileges of this administration, which in secular

[1] *Da-to.* [2] *Tson-du Gyan-dzom.*

[3] *Tson-du Hrak-dü* or *Tson-du Dü-pa.* These two are not quite the same.

affairs is subordinate to Lhasa. Bhutan has often had to fight for her independence, and in the leading history of Bhutan the 'Great Fifth Dalai Lama' and his government receive but little respect.

The standing of the Pan-chen Rim-po-che, as compared with that of the Dalai Lama from a religious point of view, is often discussed in books written by Europeans. Historically, as we know, Ta-shi Lhün-po was founded by the first in the line of Dalai Lamas. It is, however, argued that as the Pan-chen is the Incarnation of Ö-pa-me and the Dalai of Chen-re-zi, and as the former is the spiritual father of the latter, therefore the Pan-chen must be the higher. Other Tibetans say that the Pan-chen is the Religious Body[1] of the Buddha; while the Dalai is the Handle Body,[2] which the sufferer can hold, and so be drawn upwards.

Yet even though Chen-re-zi be but the spiritual son, he is, nevertheless, the patron deity of Tibet. The early kings, whose memories are universally revered, ruled over the entire country from Lhasa, and were regarded as Incarnations of Chen-re-zi. There is nothing in Ta-shi Lhün-po quite so holy as the Temple in Lhasa. 'The Place of the Gods'[3] is above all other places in name, in fame, in sanctity; and its Grand Lama sits above all others.

What the Pan-chen loses in other ways he gains in love. His worldly preoccupations, though not absent, are far less than those of the Dalai Lama, and his time for spiritual work is proportionately greater. Gifted, as he is, with a disposition of singular sweetness and charm, few heads of religion can be more beloved by their people. When he returned safely home after his journey to India, men and women wept for joy. A few years after I left Tibet he fled from the country owing to disagreements between his entourage and that of the Dalai Lama. There are very many in Tibet who mourn his long absence in China.

Tibetans always regard worldly affairs as something of

[1] *Chö-ku.* [2] *Lung-ku.* [3] Lhasa.

Dalai Lama's state chair on the march

a defilement, when compared with the purity of a religious career. So it befalls that some criticize the Dalai Lama for taking up the secular administration and for embarking on foreign travel to China and India, lands where Buddhism does not hold sway. As the secular head, he was felt to be taking part in the wars against the British and Chinese. These entailed the loss of many lives, a great sin for a Buddhist, and he, the Incarnation of the God of Mercy, was touched by this sin. Others criticized him for the treatment meted out to the Ten-gye-ling Regent, to whose death they attributed the subsequent troubles in Tibet. Of course such sentiments are never expressed except in secret—as Tibetans say 'between true friends'. All these maintain that His Holiness should devote himself entirely to religious affairs, avoiding the pollutions of the world.

The opposite party, especially those in Lhasa, uphold his actions. They say that had he not fled to Mongolia and China in 1904, when the British troops captured Lhasa, their country would have come under the British Empire. Had he not fled to India, when the Chinese troops invaded and held Lhasa, these would have captured him also, and demanded the surrender of his country. As for his secular work, they appreciate it highly, affirming that if he did not rule, calamities would arise as in China after the death of the Empress Dowager. The punishment of the Ten-gye-ling Regent they attribute to others.

It is no doubt a sin for a lama to take a share in destroying life. But the fighting with the Chinese was for the sake of the religion, which the Chinese tried to destroy. What says the inspired couplet?

> For the Buddha faced by foemen
> His disciples don their armour.

At the end of 1912 Yuan Shih Kai, the President of the Chinese Republic, endeavouring to excuse the Chinese invasion, sent a telegram to the Dalai Lama. In it he apologized for the actions of the Chinese troops, and announced that he had restored the Dalai Lama to his former rank. The reply of His Holiness, also by telegram, was that he had not asked the Chinese Government for any rank, and that he intended to exercise both ecclesiastical and secular rule in Tibet.

Educated Tibetans realize that not only did His Holiness defend the Faith, but by his strong attitude resulting in the expulsion of the Chinese troops, he gained independence for his country. 'Greater even than the Great Fifth', say the people of Lhasa. Many Tibetans, in fact, resent all criticism on the Divine Ruler. It is a shock to their inmost feelings: according to their own expression, 'it splits the heart'.

Though he directs the secular government, the Dalai Lama is devout in all religious observances, spending several hours daily on these. Morning, midday, and evening, each has its appointed curriculum of praise, invocation, reading, meditation. And throughout the day, whether he be engaged on religious or secular duties, any one may make his offering and implore his intervention to save the soul of a relative lately deceased.

His omniscience is not openly questioned, even by those of the highest position or by those in close attendance on him. It may be that disasters have happened and His Holiness has issued no timely warning. But people are wicked, and often unable to hear the truth.

Often, as you ride along a Tibetan valley, will you see an invocation to the Dalai or Pan-chen Lama traced out with light-coloured stones on the hillside high above you. And as pilgrims pass along the Sacred Way round the city of Lhasa and cross the road that leads to the Jewel Park, where His Holiness usually dwells, they will not forget to face towards it and prostrate themselves reverently in the deep dust of this dry land. Great, indeed, is his power in his own dominions, and great the reverence in which he is held by his people.

The Dalai Lama on his throne in the Jewel Park Palace

SOURCES

I. WRITTEN SOURCES

THE sources of this work are both written and oral. The former are derived from Chinese, Tibetan, and European writings.

A. CHINESE WRITTEN SOURCES

During the lifetime of each Emperor of China it was the practice for events to be recorded at the time of their occurrence by the official historians. After the fall of the dynasty these records were collected, and from them a history was compiled. If the dynasty was a long one, the history of the earlier years might be written during its continuance.

The great Tang Dynasty of China (A.D. 618–908) was commemorated by two histories, the Old and the New. The former was begun by Wei Ching in 110 books, comprising the years 618–741. It was subsequently supplemented and finally compiled by a commission, being completed in 200 books. When the dynasty began to decline, those charged with the collection of material neglected their duties, and the deficiencies had to be supplied from miscellaneous sources. During the Sung Dynasty (A.D. 970–1127), about the middle of the eleventh century, a fresh commission was appointed to remodel the work. As a result the New Tang History was written in 255 books. These two, the old and the new, circulated together until the middle of the eighteenth century, when the Emperor Chienlung arranged for them to be combined, the one being appended to the other as a running commentary in small type, and a note made of any discrepancy. The result was a collection of 260 books, of which the 256th and 257th are devoted to the Tibet of that period.[1]

[1] 'The Early History of Tibet. From Chinese Sources.' By S. W. Bushell, M.D., Physician to H.B.M. Legation, Peking (*Journal of the Royal Asiatic Society*, London, 1880, pp. 435–541).

The work of Chinese historians is held in high repute, and in many respects this reputation is well deserved. But it may be doubted whether they are at their best in writing about Tibet, a country whose inhabitants, differing so greatly from their own, they professedly despised, and still despise, regarding them as troublesome savages. And yet Europeans, who are well acquainted with both, testify that in many respects the Tibetan upper classes are the more civilized of the two.[1] This lack of sympathy and comprehension does to some extent warp the Chinese accounts in dealing with Tibetan affairs. For instance, the Tang history relates frequent, indeed almost continuous, invasions of China by Tibetan troops, ending in almost every case with the decisive defeat of the attackers. Yet, if this were really true, the invasions would not have continued so insistently, and would not have pushed in so far as they did. We know, too, from other sources, that Tibet conquered a large part of China at this time.

Even during the lifetime of the present Dalai Lama the Chinese Representative in Lhasa was regarded by the Tibetans as sending such untrue reports to his government in Peking, that the Chinese Emperor was known to the people of Lhasa as 'The Bag of Lies'.[2] When the information from their own authorities in Tibet is on so low a level, it is natural that in certain fields of inquiry the Chinese should sometimes stray from the path of truth.

Again, the references in Chinese histories to Tibet deal mainly with politics, geography, flora, fauna, &c., and do not appear to concern themselves greatly with the development of the Tibetan form of Buddhism, a religion with which the majority of the Chinese feel but little sympathy.

Still, the historical sense is so well developed among the Chinese, and the percentage of impartiality in most fields of inquiry is so high, that considerable value attaches to

[1] *Travels in Eastern Tibet*, by Eric Teichman, pp. 121, 122 (Cambridge University Press).

[2] *Tibet Past and Present*, p. 139.

Chinese records of Tibetan events. Only some discount on the above lines, and for national self-esteem, must be made.

'A Geographical, Ethnographical and Historical Sketch, derived from Chinese sources' was published by Rockhill in the *Journal of the Royal Asiatic Society*, London, in the issues of January 1921 and April 1921. Among the numerous Chinese works that he consulted Rockhill paid especial attention to the 'Topographical Description of Central Tibet',[1] written in 1792 by Ma Shao-yün and Mei Hsi-sheng. We do not, however, glean from these extracts much about either the old or the new religion of Tibet.

B. TIBETAN WRITTEN SOURCES

The oldest Tibetan documents, hitherto discovered, are the inscriptions on two of the stone pillars in Lhasa, and the writings unearthed by Sir Aurel Stein in Sinkiang. The former do not throw much light on the religion; neither do the latter, so far as they have been translated hitherto.

It would be a mistake to imagine, as some have imagined, that the Tibetans are a primitive folk on the borders of vacant savagery, devoid of all culture. Not only have they translated into Tibetan numerous Buddhist works from India, commencing in the eighth century A.D., and revising them again and again with meticulous care; but they have also their own indigenous literature. So voluminous has this become that in the inscription on a stone slab in Lhasa, erected at the close of the eighteenth century to commemorate the Chinese defeat of the Gurkhas, the Emperor rebukes the Tibetans, telling them that they have taken the pen in exchange for the sword:

> The people of central Tibet, abandoning military pursuits, devote themselves solely to literature. Thus they have become like a body bereft of vigour.

Among the great variety of books written were a number

[1] *Wei Ts'ang t'u chih.*

of historical works, many of these being biographies of saints. During the last three hundred years at least, Tibet has adopted the Chinese practice by which materials are collected during a ruler's lifetime and published after his death, thus forming a history of each reign. Beginning with the reign of the fifth Dalai Lama, all important governmental records, i.e. those of the different *dzongs* &c., are stored by the government, mostly in the Head Office of Accounts[1] in Lhasa. In the government treasury, known as *La-brang*[2], are kept detailed registers of the revenue and expenditure of the different districts. These are packed in large chests. In the *Tsi-kang* also these are kept in chests, some of them being in the main room, in which the Heads of the Treasury[3] and their clerks work. When in Lhasa, I visited this room, but was at the time unaware that it housed ancient records in addition to the modern documents that hung from the pillars.

Apart from these records the Dalai Lama is said to write notes—when he is a minor, his tutor[4] performs this obligation—of important events at the time of their occurrence, dictating them, maybe, to an official. The papers on which these notes are written are rolled up into bundles, and are transcribed ten or twenty years later into books, wooden block prints being made. Occurrences throughout the whole of Tibet are recorded.

Besides the above, men of learning have, for the last six or seven centuries at least, compiled their own general histories of Tibet. They put these together from a study of the earlier books, and partly also from the stories[5] of former times. The authors compared existing works, taking what they considered to be proved, and rejecting what they thought incorrect.

Such a history would often be entitled 'The Royal Lineage'[6] or 'The Coming of the Religion',[7] but whatever

[1] *Tsi-kang.*
[2] See p. 177.
[3] *Tsi-pön.*
[4] *Yong-dzin.*
[5] *Drung.*
[6] *Gyal-rap* (རྒྱལ་རབས་).
[7] *Chö-jung* (ཆོས་འབྱུང་).

Finance Office (*Tsi-kang*) Lhasa

The Financial Secretary is seated, his clerks on the left, candidates for Government service standing behind him, and their teacher on the extreme right

be the name, it is, according to our standards, a history of Buddhism in Tibet. For the secular events, though they may involve the fall of a kingdom or a dynasty, are of comparatively small moment to the Tibetan writer of history.

One defect of these works from a historical point of view is that they do not, as a rule, discriminate between history and legend. But this can be to some extent discounted, for the mingling of the two proceeds mainly along recognized lines. Especially is this so when eulogizing distinguished priests. For instance, they acquire at an early age vast stores of knowledge, deep spiritual and occult perception, and the power of working miracles. In the same way the Chinese histories and descriptions of Tibet tell of miraculous animals, e.g. in the *Hsin T'ang shu* a camel that can travel a thousand *li* in a day. And in the *I shih* 'a bird which flies. It resembles a dog in shape. . . . There is also a kind of black donkey swifter than the *suan-i*. In a day it can go a thousand *li*, and it can cope with a tiger'.[1]

Another limitation must be admitted. Tibetans, as a race, are artistic, but somewhat lacking in arithmetic, a trait that one sees clearly through their school days and on throughout their lives. This national characteristic leads the historians to a shakiness of dates, for these are apt to be lightly regarded. But fortunately this arithmetical weakness is not universal. In the Blue Treasury of Records, which will receive detailed mention later, there are numerous and careful computations.

Certainly, when allowance has been made for these two defects—the love of legend, and the dislike of working out dates—much has been removed; but enough is left to depict, sometimes faintly, sometimes more strongly, the religious life in the passing years and centuries. For the books give much valuable information that has the merit of real accuracy. Tibetans are well schooled to exactitude, as is evidenced by their accurate translations of the Indian Buddhist works. 'Books in Tibet', as the learned Secretary

[1] *Journal of the Royal Asiatic Society*, London, April 1891, p. 280.

of the Dalai Lama informed me, 'are regarded as sacred, because books brought to Tibet the religion of the Buddha, and it would be considered as sacrilege to write anything untrue in them. Moreover, the knowledge that others will see and read them makes the authors careful.'

Another side-light that illustrates the respect paid to books came to my notice, when I stayed in the great monasteries at Re-ting and Ta-lung—which formerly held almost sovereign sway in Tibet—between Lhasa and the Tengri Nor. In one of the halls in Ta-lung was a mass of books, piled up against two of the walls to a height of twenty-five feet, in three or four layers, one behind the other. There were ten to twelve thousand volumes in all, each in its massive wooden cover, some of the covers being plain, others carved and inscribed with handsome gilt lettering. The books themselves, many of which were written in gold letters, were those that had been saved from a disastrous fire that had devastated the great building several hundred years earlier. Consequently, they were not put to further work, but rest in peace against the lofty walls.

In Re-ting Monastery it was just the same. I was told that in such an event it is wrong to replace the burnt ones and complete the set. A fresh set must be prepared. The old ones receive, as it were, their wound pensions, and do no further work.

In addition to the histories and biographies there is a curious class of documents, the so-called 'treasures'.[1] These are prophecies that are believed to have been written by some of the very highest lamas and concealed in such a way that they are discovered when the religion stands in need of them. The one in my possession is attributed to Padma Sambhava, the Indian teacher, who, more than any other, laid the first foundation of Tibetan Buddhism. It is a copy of the actual prophecy; the copyist certifies it as correct, affirming that 'there are no more mistakes in it

[1] གཏེར་མ་

Re-ting Monastery, general view

The temple, Re-ting Monastery

than there are horns on a hare'. But in such documents the references to events are too vague to be of practical use in historical research.

On the secular side, the Tibetan Government hold in storage masses of records, both in Lhasa and in the provinces. They have ample material to prepare a full administrative history of their country, should they so desire. When the late Prime Minister, Sha-tra, came to India to attend the tripartite Conference between Tibet, China, and Great Britain, he brought several mule loads of original documents in addition to historical works, to support the claim of his government to various disputed territories. Copies of treaties, old and new, for the last eleven hundred years; orders issued to tribes even as far as Koko Nor; registers showing numbers and pay of soldiers to be furnished by different states and provinces; registers of monasteries and houses, including one 'of houses on the sunny side' of a valley; lists of fire-places and door-steps, each fire-place and door-step connoting one family; bonds of allegiance; regulations; registers of cases tried and punishments imposed; lists of appointments, titles, and ranks; registers of taxes, of incomes, and of expenditure in the dzongs and other governmental offices. These enabled him to show how each territory had been administered for many hundreds of years past.

It was a deep source of pleasure to me that I was able to gain the friendship of Their Holinesses the Dalai Lama, and the Pan-chen Lama, and of the leading members of the Tibetan Government. As one result of this friendship I received from the two Grand Lamas and others a collection of valuable books. Those that the Dalai Lama gave me, from the archives in Lhasa under his personal control, were printed off their wooden blocks with exceptional clearness; and a few, even clearer, were in manuscript.

Relevant portions of the leading histories so received have been translated for me by Mr. Negi Amar Chand, Mr. David Macdonald—who speaks and writes Tibetan more easily than English—and Rai Bahadur Nor-bhu Dhon-dup. A great deal has been done by Mr. Tse-ring Pün-tso, and most of all by that tower of learning, the late Kazi Da-wa Sam-trup, to whom I allude later on. It is only after very careful consideration that I have modified any of their translations.

I will now deal, as briefly as possible, with the religious histories on which I have relied.

First I would mention the work written by Pu-tön Rim-po-che. Pu-tön was born about A.D. 1290. It is said that he was so ugly that his mother used to hide him from the neighbours. One day a distinguished lama, passing by, asked that he might be called, and predicted a great future for him. Thereafter he came to be known as Pu-tön, i.e. 'The Boy who was Shown'. If there was such a prediction, it was certainly justified, for his name has always been, and still is, a household word for erudition. For instance, in the pages of the Blue Treasury, written one hundred and twelve years after Pu-tön's death in 1364, he is mentioned with great respect. And no wonder, for we know that he compiled or helped to compile the Kan-gyur, the Tibetan Canon, and the Ten-gyur, the Commentaries, which number altogether some three hundred and thirty volumes and combine to form the central authority in the sacred literature of Tibetan Buddhism. He was abbot of the Sha-lu Monastery near Shi-ga-tse, and, in addition to his history, is said to have composed works on logic, astrology, and medicine.

The date of his history appears to have been A.D. 1323, for it is recorded at the end of it as follows:

> This History of Buddhism, called *The Treasury of the Precious Scriptures*, has been written by Pu-tön of Tro-pu, who was born from the rays of the speech of the great and learned men of science.
>
> The religion of the Buddha has prospered for the last three thousand four hundred and fifty-five years. This history was written in the water-male-dog year when the author was thirty-three years of age.

The title at the commencement of the book runs thus:

The Treasury of Sacred Writings, giving clearly a History of the Buddhist Faith.

I have two copies of this work. The Dalai Lama gave me one; the Pan-chen Rim-po-che gave me the other. The copy from the Dalai Lama is on thick, good paper, and very clearly printed. The blocks from which the two are printed are different, the Dalai Lama's page of actual print—apart from margins—being twenty inches by three, the Pan-chen's nineteen by two and a half. The latter has six lines to each page, the former usually seven. The whole page in the Dalai's copy is twenty-three and three-quarters inches by four; in the Pan-chen's twenty-two and a half by three and three-quarters. In the Dalai Lama's copy there are two hundred and forty-four folios, i.e. four hundred and eighty-eight pages, for each is printed on both sides.

Pu-tön's history has a very high reputation in Tibet. I have made considerable use of it for the earlier period of Tibetan Buddhism.

The Tibetan history from which I have quoted most of all is the Tep-ter Ngön-po, *The Blue Treasury of Records*. Shramana Ekai Kawaguchi, the Japanese priest who spent three years in Tibet, including a prolonged period studying in the Se-ra Monastery, told me that he considered it the best of all the Tibetan histories. The late Sarat Chandra Das, who made a long study of Tibetan—mostly in Darjeeling, but for a year also in Tibet—wrote as follows:

> Among the ancient records the Debther-Ngonpo and the Chho Jung (Pu-tön's) are by far the most correct. Their authors appear to have been less influenced by love of the marvellous, or the appetite for wonders, which marks all early oriental writings, and to have collected their materials in an exemplary spirit of sober investigation. The Debther-Ngonpo and the Chho Jung are therefore unique and rare ancient historical records of Tibet.[1]

Mr. Tada, who had been studying in the Se-ra Monastery for eight years when I met him in Lhasa, classed

[1] *Journal of the Asiatic Society of Bengal*, 1881–7, p. 212.

Taranatha Chö-jung with Tep-ter Ngön-po and Pu-tön's Chö-jung as the best. These three gentlemen, two Japanese and one Bengali, were by their nature, training, and environment well fitted to express an opinion on this unexplored issue. My own observations entirely confirm this opinion, especially as regards the Blue Treasury (*Tep-ter Ngön-po*) for reasons which will appear presently.

The author of the Blue Treasury was named, 'Translator Gö, the Glorious Young Man'.[1] To be recognized as a Translator in Tibet was a very high honour, given only to one of exceptional intellect.[2] An entry in the eleventh volume, apparently by a commentator or publisher, refers to him as 'The Great Translator, the All-Knowing'.[3] We may infer distinction from the last epithet, for it is used of the highest in Tibet. Moreover, publishers' puffs are not prominent in that country; they would bring neither money nor fame. Like most Tibetans who have risen from below by their own ability, he was a priest. This we know, not only because he held the name of Translator, but because he speaks of his spiritual teacher (*guru*), and the course of religious instruction in the 'Heart's Drop' doctrine, that, as disciple from guru, he learned from him.[4]

It is fortunate that the date of this valuable work can be fixed. From time to time throughout his many volumes the historian gives a clear calculation based on his own date, and the latter always works out to about A.D. 1476. In his second volume we read,

> From the time of Song-tsen Gam-po's birth in the Earth Bull year to this Fire Monkey year in which this writing was done is eight hundred and forty-eight years.[5]

Csoma De Körös, the well-known Hungarian scholar, calculating from the 'White Lapis Lazuli',[6] a well-known work written by Sang-gye Gya-tso, the Tibetan Regent,

[1] འགོས་ལོ་ཙཱ་བ་གཞོན་ནུ་དཔལ་

[2] Tep-ter Ngön-po, vol. viii, fol. 104.

[3] Idem, vol. xi, fol. 41.

[4] Idem, vol. iv, fol. 45.

[5] Idem, vol. ii, fol. 2.

[6] *Bai-durya Kar-po* (དཀར་པོ་).

in A.D. 1686, dates Song-tsen's birth at A.D. 627.[1] This would put the date of the history at 1474 (for in a reckoning of this kind Tibetans count both years), but the historian states over and over again that his year was that of the Fire-Monkey; and the latter fell in 1476. In other words, the Blue Treasury considers Song-tsen to have been born in 629.

In another place[2] he gives the date of his work, the Fire-Monkey year, as four hundred and sixty-five years after the birth of Mar-pa in a Water-Mouse year. This puts Mar-pa's birth in A.D. 1012, and we know that this year, or one very near to it, was his birth year. As each Tibetan cycle runs for sixty years, the Fire-Monkey year next to 1476 would be either 1416 or 1536, and neither of these is possible.

Again, the Blue Treasury links his own date with that of Pak-mo-tru, saying, 'It is three hundred and sixty-seven years, i.e. A.D. 1110, since the birth of Dro-gön Rim-po-che (i.e. Pak-mo-tru, not Dro-gön Pak-pa) to the present Fire-Monkey year'.[3] The Bai-durya puts Pak-mo-tru's birth at 1108. Here, too, he adopts a date just two years before that given by the Blue Treasury.

Finally, the historian records that the Kashmiri pandit, Sakya Sri, dated a certain event in his career in Tibet as 'one thousand seven hundred and fifty years two months and a half and a forenoon since the Parinirvana of the Lord Buddha'. The Buddhists of Ceylon fix the Buddha's death in 544 B.C., and this puts the pandit at A.D. 1206. We know from the Bai-durya Kar-po that the pandit came to Tibet from about 1202. And the Blue Treasury tells us that he stayed ten years in Tibet; i.e. from 1202 to 1212. So here we are on firm ground. The Blue Treasury also states that since this event (in 1206) 'it is four cycles of sixty plus thirty years to this Fire-Monkey year'.[4] This dates the completion of the history exactly at A.D. 1476.

[1] Csoma's Tibetan Grammar, p. 181.
[2] Tep-ter Ngön-po, vol. viii, fol. 7.
[3] Idem, vol. viii, fol. 84.
[4] Idem, vol. xv, fol. 1.

On these grounds we may be fairly sure that the Tep-ter Ngön-po was finished in 1476. I have taken some pains to establish its date, for it is an outstanding history, and trustworthy dates in Tibetan chronicles are precious.

The object of the historian in writing this long and careful work was to compile a comprehensive outline portraying the history of Buddhism in Tibet. At the end of the tenth volume, which deals with the 'Wheel of Time' doctrines, there is a note by a commentator or publisher. It runs as follows:

> Thus this brief account has been put down to fulfil what was promised before, but whatever is omitted in this book, owing to the lack of previous records bearing on this particular school of teaching, may be filled up for the benefit of the Church and Faith by others who can do so correctly. The All-Knowing Translator, Gŏ, himself expressed this hope. . . . Seeing that the printing of this work in accordance with the wishes of the historian was indispensably necessary for the perpetuation of the religious history, it was done at the command of Ta-shi Tar-gye Lek-paï Gyal-po,[1] the Ruler of the Southern Line.[2]

His material Gö took, as did others, from existing histories. For instance, when writing about a celebrated translator in his volume on the doctrine of 'The Great Symbol',[3] he notes that his information was extracted from another history by 'Power Wealth Young Man'.[4] Again, when compiling an account of Kamalasila's doctrine called 'The Alleviation of Misery', he says: 'I have extracted all these details from the account written by Nyang-ben-po Dharma Siddhi, who was a personal disciple.[5]

The Blue Treasury does not deal chronologically with Tibetan events as a whole, but, except for the first two volumes, takes each doctrine or school of Tibetan Buddhism and follows it through. The first three folios of vol. i are dedicated to invocation; towards the end of the third

[1] བཀྲ་ཤིས་དར་རྒྱས་ ལེགས་པའི་ རྒྱལ་པོ

[2] Tep-ter Ngön-po, vol. x, fol. 40.

[3] Idem, vol. xi, fol. 16.

[4] དབང་ཕྱུག་གཞོན་ནུ

[5] Tep-ter Ngön-po, vol. xii, fol. 49.

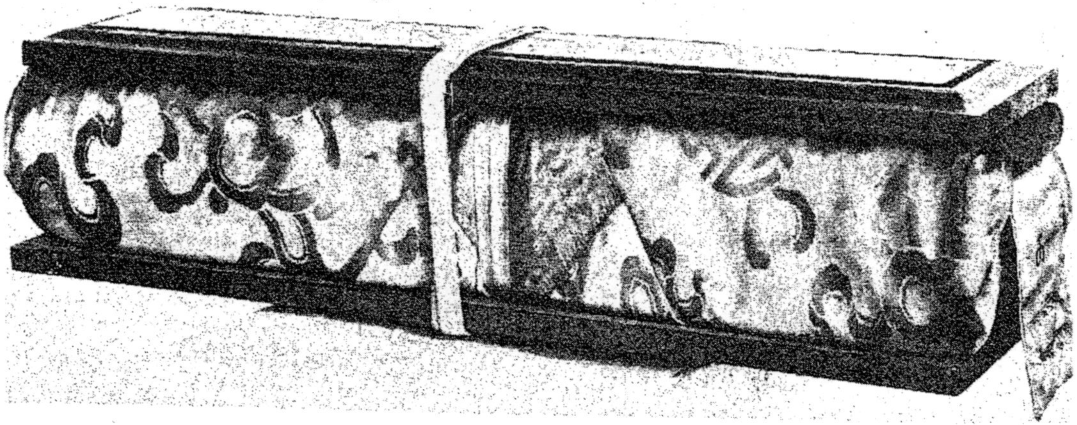

Tibetan book in silk cover with title at one end, encased in boards. In title letter ཆ, being sixth in Tibetan alphabet, denotes Vol. VI

folio the history commences with a synopsis of the Buddha's pedigree. The birth and life of the Buddha, as well as a few events in Indian Buddhist history after the Buddha's entry into nirvana, are touched on but briefly, the historian saying that he has not at his disposal records sufficiently authentic and complete to warrant a fuller account. The remainder of vol. i treats of the coming of Buddhism to Tibet and its vicissitudes up to the time of its suppression by Lang Dar-ma. Vol. ii narrates the early years of the Buddhist revival. It was not till then that the different schools began in earnest. Vol. iii, therefore, deals with the early Tantrik schools, iv with the later Tantras, and so on.[1]

Gö brings his work down almost to his own date. When narrating the lives of the successive leaders of the Kar-ma-pa sect, he does not stop until he has reached his own contemporary 'Self-Produced All-Knowing King of Religion', who is the high-priest of a monastery. Of him he writes with restrained appreciation. 'He is very remarkable, and is performing the appropriate duties of his holy career in the best possible manner'.[2]

Any one who reads this history cannot fail to be struck by the writer's carefulness and sobriety. He recounts plenty of miracles, but the Tibetan, while looking on a miracle as wonderful, does not regard it as unlikely. Gö abounds in dates, calculating these from near and far, and using the Tibetan calendar to check them. Throughout his long narrative, he keeps telling us the year, Wood-Female-Bull, Earth-Male-Dragon and so on, in which events occurred. Sometimes also he details how many years elapsed between two distant dates. Thus he finds that it is two hundred and seventy-one years from the birth of King Song-tsen Gam-po to the Earth-Female-Sheep year in which the apostate king Lang Dar-ma ascended the throne. Two years later, in the Iron-Female-Bird, he suppressed Buddhism, and was assassinated. He adds, 'In

[1] For a brief summary of the contents of each volume of this history, see Appendix.

[2] Tep-ter Ngön-po, vol. viii, fol. 50.

Nel-pa's religious history it is said that the holy religion was suppressed in the Earth-Female-Sheep, but that is two years too early.'[1] Throughout his work he calculates and checks by the calendar.

He does not lightly accept previous histories, but checks them by original, trustworthy documents. Thus, discussing the age at which Re-chung, Mi-la Re-pa's famous disciple, died, he writes:

> In the initiatory line of the life-prolonging art which Re-chung had obtained from a saintly lady in India, named Ma-chik Trup-gyal, it is said that Re-chung died at the age of eighty-two, but a more accurate calculation, based on the account of Re-chung's nearest disciples, shows that the correct figure is seventy-eight.[2]

In another place he notices the discrepancy between two biographies as to the time during which a certain Hierarch ruled in the Ta-lung monastery, and gives his own version.[3]

Undoubtedly the author of 'The Blue Treasury of Records' is an exceptionally careful historian. He shows that, though the ordinary Tibetan would not allow himself to be bound too closely to time in the routine of his daily life—for, indeed, clocks and watches are, even nowadays, comparative rarities in this country—yet a light regard for dates is not necessarily a characteristic of the serious Tibetan annalist. I could easily multiply instances of his carefulness, but this chapter promises to be unduly long.

My friend, 'Great Minister'[4] Sha-tra, the wise old statesman who died in 1919, gave me one of my copies of this valuable work. The print, however, is often indistinct, and so the Dalai Lama gave me another copy from the same blocks, and it is on the whole clear. That it is not quite so distinct as the numerous other volumes that he sent me is due, as His Holiness explains in his letter, to the blocks being old. Great also is the gratitude that I feel towards the late Kazi Da-wa Sam-trup, that learned scholar in the Tibetan religion and literature—the two

[1] Tep-ter Ngön-po, vol. i, fol. 25.
[2] Idem, vol. viii, fol. 17.
[3] Idem, vol. viii, fol. 104.
[4] Lön-chen.

are inextricably intertwined. He translated for me a very large portion of the Blue Treasury and other histories with scholarly discernment. And through long hours of instruction, untouched by a single dull moment, he taught me to understand some of the salient features in this complicated religion.

The next Tibetan history for mention is that which is usually known as 'The Clear Mirror of the Royal Line' (*Gyal-rap Sal-waï Me-long*). In my copy the title is Gyal-rap Chö-jung Sal-waï Me-long,[1] i.e. 'The Clear Mirror of the Royal Line and of the Coming of the Religion'. Its date is later than that of the Blue Treasury, for on its seventeenth folio it says with reference to a certain period, 'If you wish to know the full details of China and Hor look in Tep-ter,' which latter is perhaps the Tep-ter Ngön-po. Rockhill believes this *Gyal-rap* to be of comparatively modern origin and to have been compiled under Chinese influence.[2]

The author's own account, given as usual at the end of his work, is as follows:

> This condensed history of the Religious Kings has been compiled carefully by the Sceptre Holder, Sö-nam Gyal-tsen, at the urgent request of the highly revered Rin-chen Pal. It is free from all mistakes.[3]

Then follows a prayer, and a brief statement that Chen-re-zi leads all living creatures along the path of deliverance, and that the kings of Tibet, beginning with Song-tsen Gam-po, and their ministers diffused the religion of the Buddha in Tibet. The writer states that the Buddha did not himself visit Tibet at any time, but the rays of his speech filled the country. He continues:

> This history was compiled by Sö-nam Gyal-tsen of Sa-kya in the noble Sam-ye monastery in the earth-male-dragon year.[4]
>
> Glory.

[1] རྒྱལ་རབས་ཆོས་འབྱུང་གསལ་བའི་མེ་ལོང་

[2] *Notes on the Ethnology of Tibet*, London, 1895, p. 671.

[3] Fol. 141.

[4] Fol. 142.

'Fortunate Flag of Victory'[1] does not deal with the whole course of Tibetan Buddhism, but, after recounting the miraculous life of the Buddha, concentrates on the time of the early kings, to whom Tibetans, both in books and conversation, refer with affectionate pride as 'The Religious Kings'. He concludes shortly after the assassination of King Lang Dar-ma in A.D. 900. His work inclines more to mythology, and stands on a much lower level of historical value than Pu-tön or the Blue Treasury.

My copy is beautifully written by hand in the *u-me*, i.e. semi-printed type of script, not in the cursive writing, known as *kyuk*. It contains one hundred and forty-two folios, these being slightly smaller than those of the Blue Treasury and the copy of Pu-tön which the Pan-chen Rim-po-che gave me. It was presented to me by the Dalai Lama, and, like other books that I received from him, whether printed or written, is on good paper and very clear.

We come now to a brief history ascribed, as are many other works, to that leading figure, the fifth Dalai Lama, who reigned during the seventeenth century. This is not his diary, which runs to six long volumes, but a history of Tibet, both religious and secular, in one volume of one hundred and thirteen folios (i.e. two hundred and twenty-five pages). The lengthy title runs, *The Record of the Sayings of the Chief Ones among the Powerful and Exalted Kings and Ministers in the Land of Snow, the melodious Songs of the Queen, the Feast of Pleasure for the Youths of the Perfected Age*. It is held in high reputation by leading Tibetans, owing partly to its distinguished authorship. Sha-tra was one of many who relied on its secular side, when engaged in diplomatic intercourse. We may abbreviate the title and call it the *Feast of Pleasure*.

The last page, as usual, tells us of the authorship. We read that the author was Nga-wang Lob-sang Gya-tso.[2] The date is given as 'the first day of the first half of a

[1] The English equivalent of the name 'Sö-nam Gyal-tsen'.

[2] The fifth Dalai Lama.

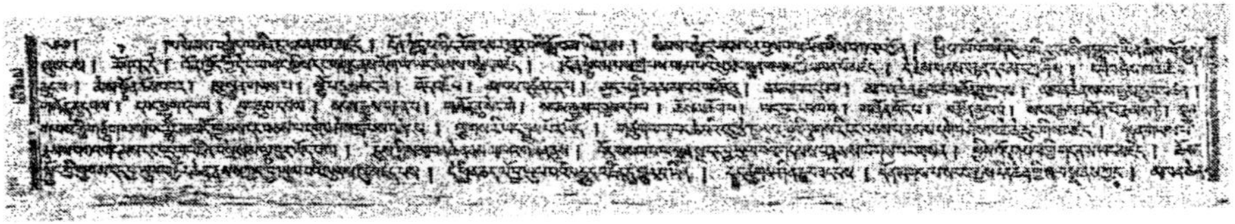

A page of block print from the Blue Treasury

Words are not spaced; the vertical lines show, more or less, the ends of sentences

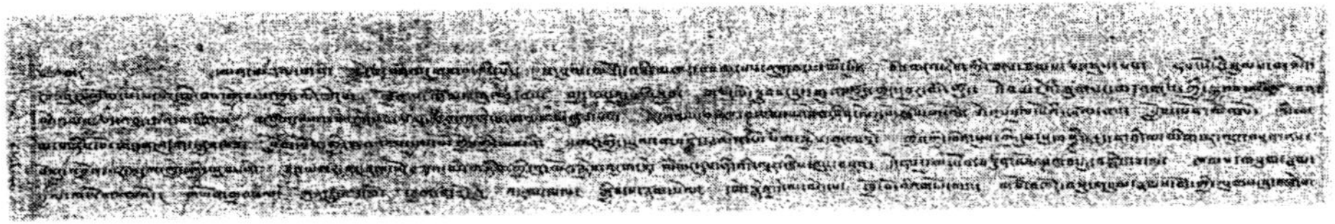

A page of manuscript from the Gyal-rap Chö-jung Sal-waï Me-long

The cursive character used in ordinary correspondence is again different

month in the Water-Female-Sheep year. Reckoning from the date of the birth of the Buddha in the Iron-Monkey year, this was written at the end of two thousand six hundred and three years[1] in the Joyous Palace,[2] the navel of the world.

May Virtue Increase!'

The date therefore is shortly after the fifth Dalai Lama obtained the secular sovereignty over Tibet, an event which may be placed in 1642.[3] It deals with events down to the time of the Dalai Lamas.

Among the biographies, the first that calls for notice is the highly interesting and informative autobiography of Mi-la Re-pa, 'Cotton-clad Mi-la'. His life and achievements are described in the seventh chapter. It is sufficient to note here that he was born about the middle of the eleventh century of the Christian era, and died eighty-three years later, after attaining Buddhahood in a single lifetime. This attainment was the more remarkable in that his earlier life had been one of sinfulness.

Mi-la dictates his autobiography to Re-chung, one of his two chief disciples. Re-chung had joined the Master, when the latter was advanced in years, after the wicked days and the early penances were past. He therefore seeks full details from the beginning, and the account is carried on to the time of Mi-la's nirvana, with a brief mention also of his disciples' subsequent lives.

There have been several versions or editions of this autobiography in Tibet, and it would appear that those now available were written a considerable time after the saint's death.

I have two in my collection, made from separate blocks, for the pages do not tally, though the words, at any rate in the beginning and end, are almost the same. The copy, that the Pan-chen Lama gave me, is on rough paper, indistinct and often smudged. It runs to one hundred and twenty-one folios. So I obtained one from the Dalai Lama. In his letter he describes his copy as 'from the old block',

[1] A.D. 1643. [2] *Gan-den Po-trang* [3] See Chapter X.

but the paper is good, and the print on the whole is clear. It totals one hundred and sixteen folios. At the end of both copies the author says that he has 'seen several histories of the Revered One'. I will quote his words *verbatim*:

> This is the history of the Revered Mi-la Re-pa, the Holy One of the ascetics (*Nal-jor*), Rich in Power (*Wang-chuk*), the deliverance and the guide to all knowledge. And with it is the Book of Songs. I have seen several[1] histories of the Revered One, just as they were spoken by the mouth of the Master, who is no common[2] Master. Yet I, the ascetic, who roam about the corpse-grounds,[3] clad in ornaments of human bones,[4] have composed this writing and finished it on the eighth day of the waxing moon[5] in the middle month of autumn in the year of Pur-pu,[6] in the wilderness of the great pilgrimage, where mother-goddesses and sky-goers (*kan-dro*) collect, at the fence of Lap-chi Kang.[7] This writing is accurate and complete. May it bring vast benefit and happiness to the religion and to the beings, until the Round of Existence be emptied.
>
> Blessing.

It will be noticed that the year of composition is mentioned, but not the cycle. On this question of date all that can be safely said is that there are but few obsolete words in the book.

Ge-dün Trup-pa's Biography.[8] This narrates in sixty-three folios the life of the first in the line of Dalai Lamas. It was written at Ta-shi Lhün-po in 1494, i.e. twenty-one years after Ge-dün Trup-pa's death. The book evidently belongs to some series, for it is numbered volume v. My copy, given to me by the Dalai Lama, is very clearly printed.

The title runs thus: *The Rosary of Gems which tells the*

[1] དུ་མ་ Might also be translated 'many'.

[2] ཐུན་མོང་

[3] The places where human corpses are cut up and given to the vultures, the ordinary method by which the dead are disposed of in this ice-bound country, where space is plentiful, but fuel for cremation is scarce, and digging difficult.

[4] To remind himself of the transience and vanity of worldly existence.

[5] The eighth day of each month is an auspicious day, and therefore it is well to finish a work upon it.

[6] i.e. the Earth-Monkey year.

[7] A snow mountain near Mount Everest.

[8] Chapter VIII.

Wonderful and Excellent History of the All-knowing Lord Ge-dün Trup-pa Pal Zang-po.

The concluding page tells us:

At the earnest request of Lama Kün-ga De-le Rin-chen Gyal-tsen Pal Zang-po, who is born with a spiritual treasury full of knowledge and prophecy, and on the repeated pressure of many Doctors of Divinity,[1] this Rosary of Gems, a very wonderful history of the noble Lama,[2] the sole benefactor of all living creatures, has been written by a Ge-long[3] of the Buddha, named 'Peak of Divine Wisdom'.[4] Having bowed to the Lama's feet and remembered his kindness, this Ge-long has written this history in the History Temple[5] with the high royal banner of the House of Great Happiness,[6] which is victorious in all directions, and appertains to the noble monastery of Ta-shi Lhün-po. The history has been finished on the morning of the twenty-fifth day of the first month—the anniversary of the great miracles[7]—in the Wood-Male-Tiger year, known as the All Joyous. This year is the next after the completion of two thousand three hundred and twenty-seven years according to the unusual method of reckoning. According to the common[8] method of reckoning, it is the next year after the completion of three thousand six hundred and twenty-six years,[9] it being understood that the Buddha's doctrine will last for five thousand years.

Sö-nam Gya-tso, the third Dalai Lama, lived from about 1541 to 1586. His biographer consulted various authorities before setting out his narrative, which is

[1] *Ge-she.*

[2] i.e. Ge-dün Trup-pa.

[3] i.e. a fully ordained monk.

[4] *Ye-she Tse-mo.*

[5] *Nam-tar Lha-kang.* It keeps the history of Ta-shi Lhün-po and the Pan-chen Lamas.

[6] The residence of the Pan-chen Lama, now known as the 'Palace of Great Happiness' (*De-chen Po-trang*). It is possible that it was not then known as a Palace. One cannot help noticing that the author uses the words 'victorious in all directions', which are invariably applied to the Central Government's Gan-den Palace as the attribute of sovereignty.

[7] When the Buddha displayed miracles and defeated the six Tirthika teachers who opposed his doctrine.

[8] ཐུན་མོང་

[9] Pu-tön's history can be dated at A.D. 1321. It is said in it that Buddhism had prospered for 3,455 years. The figure here, being 3,626, seems to indicate that this biography was completed in 1492, i.e. 19 years after Ge-dün Trup-pa's death.

marked volume viii in the same way as Ge-dün Trup-pa's is marked volume v. He writes:

This history of Sö-nam Gya-tso Pal Zang-po, the All-knowing Deliverer of the Chinese, Tibetans, and Hor-pas,[1] called *The Ocean Chariot of Real Attainment*, has been compiled from the notes collected by Lama Trin-le Gya-tso of Trong-me in accordance with his admonition. The following books were also consulted as a basis for the compilation.

The history entitled *The Carriage of the Happy Ones, copied by the King of the Gods*. This was written by the Incarnate Lama Pal-den Lo-trö Zang-po of Trang-ka before the Iron-Horse year.

The history in verse composed by the same author, when Sö-nam Gya-tso had passed his fifteenth year.

The road-book,[2] both in prose and poetry, written by Sö-nam Ye-she Wang-po and brought to Do-kam.[3]

A full history written by Translator[4] Pal-jor Gya-tso of Kar-nak.

The history written by Rab-jam-pa[5] Ge-lek Lhün-trup.

Other works.

I have used the above as a basis, but the dates and other information set out by him of Trang-ka are the most accurate. The years and dates given by the others are wrong; such is my conclusion after a detailed investigation.

I have considered also what I have heard from many holy teachers of the religion,[6] such as the Revered Dor-je Chang Chem-po Kön-tön Chö-kyi Gyal-po Pal-jor Lhün-trup and others. I have heard, too, from Lama Jam-pal Dor-je, the Interpreter and Translator of Zhang-kar, and others; and I have had reliable accounts from many learned Abbots. I, the writer of this account, am named Nga-wang Lob-zang Gya-tso Jik-me Ko-cha Tup-ten Lang-tso. The language, except the verses, can be easily understood by all. The book has been compiled from the above sources and completed at the

[1] Primarily the word Hor-pa denotes the nomad tribes of graziers, some of whom live to the north of the Tengri Nor, others in eastern and north-eastern Tibet, Sinkiang, &c. But it is sometimes also applied to the Mongols.

[2] ལམ་ཡིག་ [3] i.e. Am-do and Kam. [4] Lo-tsa-wa.

[5] A high rank among the Ge-she (Doctors of Divinity).

[6] ཡོངས་འཛིན་ The word is used nowadays for the chief spiritual instructors of the young Dalai and Pan-chen Lamas.

Joyous Palace[1] on a date of the third Conqueror in the House of Scales[2] in the Fire-Male-Dog year.[3]

All is Glory.

On a few points I have consulted a *Religious History of Mongolia*[4] in Tibetan by one Jik-me Nam-ka,[5] published and translated into German by Dr. Georg Huth.[6] His Tibetan text is out of print, but I was able to find a copy of it in the British Museum. The work is modern, having been completed in A.D. 1819.

The history of Bhutan, entitled *The Religious History of the South*[7] appears to be worthy of a high place among Tibetan histories. My copy was given me by the late king of Bhutan, a strong, far-seeing administrator of his turbulent domain, kindly to those who did not disobey him, and humorous always. If he chose you for friendship, he was your friend indeed. How well I remember him, surrounded by his retinue, walking with them, barefooted, his sturdy frame well set in the rough country clothes! And, never failing, the courteous word, yet straight to the point.

But to return to the history. It is a block print, numbering one hundred and fifty-one folios, i.e. three hundred and one pages. The paper is excellent, as indeed it should be, for the paper from Bhutan is adjudged the best throughout central Tibet. The print is remarkably clear.

The history tells us that it 'was commenced in the king's palace at Pung-tang,[8] in the presence of the image of "The Great Precious Mother who is at the Feet" with offerings of buttered bread and good tea'. It was begun in the Iron-Pig year, was written 'bit by bit' and was 'finished on the anniversary of the birth of the Buddha, i.e. on the fifteenth day of the month of Sa-ya in the Earth-Female-Hare year'. It thus took twenty-eight years to

[1] *Gan-den Po-trang.* [2] Sign of the Zodiac. [3] This passage is not clear.

[4] Hor Chö-jung (ཧོར་ཆོས་འབྱུང་). [5] འཇིགས་མེད་ནམ་མཁའ་

[6] Strassburg (Karl J. Trübner), 1896. [7] *Lho-i Chö-jung.*

[8] Usually known as Bum-thang. It has long been the capital of the chief that ruled eastern Bhutan and now rules the whole kingdom.

write. In addition to the ordinary narrative it deals with the arts and crafts of the country, the laws, &c.

This history passes rapidly to the seventeenth century, when the first Shap-trung Rim-po-che established his sway over Bhutan. It stands above the average of Tibetan histories, but deals almost entirely with the affairs of Bhutan, rather than with the central current of Tibetan events. The inhabitants of Bhutan are, indeed, in the broad sense Tibetans, and this is a good history, well deserving of publication on its own account, but to include much of it here would overload this book. I have therefore taken from it only when it joins the main stream of Tibetan happenings.

Another local history, the *Nyang Chö-jung*, concerns itself with the 'Valley of Taste' (*Nyang*) and surrounding district. About half-way down this valley Gyang-tse, the third among Tibetan towns, spreads itself round the incurving angle of a plain. And where the Nyang flows into the broad Tsang-po, the main artery of southern Tibet, Shi-ga-tse, second only to Lhasa itself, stands like a sentinel at the gate of the Pan-chen Lama's great monastery, only half a mile or so away. This little work—of which, with some difficulty, I obtained a copy, as so many of my friends recommended it—does not contain much history of general interest, but is rather a guide to this Nyang valley, showing how the different monasteries were built and the visions, miracles, and legends of the saints who lived there. Among many others it mentions Ne-sar Monastery, and confirms—as I heard when I visited Ne-sar in 1915—that it was built by the great king, Song-tsen Gam-po, being older even than Sam-ye itself. There are brief descriptions, too, of the different kinds of people and goods. We learn that excise laws were introduced to govern the sale of beer. On the whole, one may say that there is much of legend, but something also of practical matter, both religious and secular.

There are other such local histories in Tibet. Of these I have a few, e.g. two of Sikkim, others of the successive

'Gyang-tse spreads itself round the in-curving angle of the plain'

Grand Lamas (Pan-chen) of Ta-shi Lhün-po, and so on, but they have not been translated into English, except one of the two that tell the chronicles of Sikkim. Of general histories there is no end; they are being written still. One, little more than a pamphlet, was written by the late Prime Minister Sho-kang, who gave it to me when I was in Lhasa in 1921. It is taken from the Ma-ni Ka-bum, the Gye-rap Sal-waï Me-long, and a third history, called the Tep-ter Chi-lu. Strictly speaking, it is an historical essay written to establish Tibet's claim to political independence.

Another in my possession is by one Den-je, an ex-clerk in the Nar-tang Monastery near Ta-shi Lhün-po. He wrote it at the request of his nephew and terms it *The Abridged Essence of Secular and Religious Histories.*

No doubt the best histories are those that were compiled nearer to the events that they describe. In any case, when their mountain of books gradually finds competent translators, an increasing mass of material will become available to the western world for writing a full history of Tibet, especially on the religious side. But great care will be necessary in discounting legends. Care will also be required in reconciling the dates given by different writers, and even by the same writer on different pages. Tibetan figures demand the closest scrutiny. As for myself, I have in this book utilized only a small fraction of my translations, in order to avoid over-taxing the patience of my readers.

C. EUROPEAN WRITTEN SOURCES

The first European known to have made contact with Tibetan influence was the Flemish friar, William de Rubruquis, who visited Karakoram, the capital of Mongolia, in A.D. 1253. There he found monks conducting religious services, as Tibetan monks did and do in Tibet to-day. This was during the reign of Mangu, two or three years before the great Khubilai ascended the throne. Particulars of this valuable journey are published by the Hakluyt Society.

About A.D. 1277 Marco Polo appears to have come to the border between Tibet and Szechwan, but gives little information.

Between 1624 and 1721, Jesuit missionaries visited Tibet. Antonio de Andrade lived for a time in western Tibet, Stephen Cacella and John Cabral in Bhutan and Shi-ga-tse. John Grueber and Albert d'Orville paid a brief visit to Lhasa in 1661, but do not give much information. Hippolyte Desideri lived in Lhasa and elsewhere in central Tibet from 1716–21, and such writings of his as have been made public furnish much first-hand information of high value.

The original data left by these travellers have been summarized in English by C. Wessels, S.J., in his volume *Early Jesuit Travellers in Central Asia 1603–1721.*[1] For Grueber we have also the book of Father Athanase Kircher, *China Illustrata*, in a translation, *La Chine Illustrée*, published at Amsterdam in 1670. Kircher was Grueber's official editor, but there were many disagreements between the two, and Grueber was by no means satisfied with the result. Some of Desideri's writings have been rescued from unmerited obscurity by Professor Carlo Puini in *Il Tibet* (*Geografia*, *Storia*, *Religione*, *Costumi*) *secondo la Relazione del Viaggio del P. Ippolito Desideri* (*1715–1721*), published at Rome in 1904.

During the years 1708 to 1711 and again from 1716 to 1733, Capuchin missionaries lived humbly and worked on a starvation diet at Lhasa. First-hand accounts of their experiences can be read in A. A. Georgi's *Alphabetum Tibetanum Missionum Apostolicarum commodo editum. Romae, 1762.* Also in Klaproth's *Breve Notizia del Regno del Thibet, dal frà Francesco Orazio della Penna de Billi. 1730.* in the *Nouveau Journal Asiatique*, Tome xiv (Paris, 1834).

The accounts of Bogle's Mission through Bhutan to the Pan-chen Lama in 1774, and of Manning's journey to Lhasa in 1811, are available in Markham's book.[2]

[1] The Hague, Martinus Nijhoff, 1924.

[2] *Narratives of the Mission of George Bogle to Tibet, and of the journey of*

A street in Lhasa

Turner's Mission through Bhutan to the Pan-chen Lama in 1783 is fully described in his own narrative.[1] It was in 1846 that Huc and Gabet, the two French Lazarist Fathers, made their notable journey to Lhasa from the north, and on through eastern Tibet to Szechwan. M. Huc's vivid narration has been translated into English.[2] Beyond this point it is unnecessary to continue the list.

II. ORAL SOURCES

A residence of some nineteen years among Tibetans enabled me to have intimate detailed conversations with all classes from the Grand Lamas downwards. During the last twelve of these years as the diplomatic representative of the Indian Government, in an atmosphere of growing friendliness, I was brought into close touch with the cultured classes. And this was especially the case during the two and a quarter years that the Dalai Lama and his Government spent on the Indo-Tibetan frontier, the eleven months of my companionship with the Tibetan Prime Minister and his Staff in Tibet and Simla in connexion with the Sino-Tibetan Conference of 1913–14, and, most of all, during the eleven months that I lived in Lhasa itself, the heart of things Tibetan.

No doubt, leisure for studies such as these was difficult to obtain, for the very growth of friendliness increased not only the pleasure but the volume of daily work. And in addition to the time which the intricacy of Tibetan affairs rightly claimed, Bhutan was constantly seeking my advice in her own administrative problems. Finally, until the last two years of my incumbency Sikkim was under my

Thomas Manning to Lhasa, by Clements R. Markham (London, Trübner & Co., 1879).

[1] *An account of an embassy to the Court of the Teshoo Lama in Tibet*, by Captain Samuel Turner. (Printed by W. Bulmer & Co., Cleveland Row, St. James; and sold by Messrs. G. & W. Nicol, Booksellers to His Majesty, Pall Mall, London, 1800.)

[2] *Travels in Tartary, Thibet, and China*, by M. Huc. Translated from the French by W. Hazlitt, Reprint Edition (Chicago, The Open Court Publishing Company. London Agents: Kegan, Paul, Trench, Trübner & Co., 1898).

direct administration; and, even when its young ruler took over the government of his State, he consulted me often in matters of difficulty.

It is true that this work, in its varied aspects, unfolded an ever-widening vision of Tibetan hearts and minds, but my main opportunity for study lay in the fact that there were very few British, or others of white races, in Tibet and Sikkim, and none in Bhutan, during all the years that I travelled and lived in those territories. For over a year I saw no white man, save one; for a year and a half no white woman. This kind of life was, no doubt, to me a limitation, but it had, at any rate, this advantage, that, the ordinary social distractions being absent, such leisure as I obtained could be largely devoted to the delights of Oriental research in the company of Oriental friends. Always and everywhere was an inflow of sights and sounds challenging comprehension; always and everywhere kind friends were near at hand to help the understanding. Conversations were often *tête-à-tête*; third parties were sometimes present, interpreters never.

I write but briefly of these oral sources of information. But in actual fact they helped me to understand, as nothing else could, the old histories and biographies, the poems and legends, and to trace their developments in the Tibet that I saw around me. To me the advantage has been incalculable, and I am beyond measure grateful to my friends, Tibetans, Bhutanese, and Sikkimese, from whom it is derived.

APPENDIX

See *Sources*, p. 205.

A brief Summary showing the length and contents of each volume of 'The Blue Treasury of Records'.

Volume.	*Title of Volume.*	*Number of folios.*
1	The Root of History. The first period when the religion flourished.	28
2	The later period when the religion flourished.	17
3	The first period of the translation of the Secret Formulae (Tantras).	46
4	The new Tantras, 'The Road and the Fruit', and their adherents.	13
5	The Tree of Worship, the Sole Ornament of the the World. Index of temples, &c.	38
6	The period of Ngok, the Translator, and his followers, and of the coming of the Madhyamika and Maitreya doctrines to Tibet.	10
7	The period during which the Tantrik doctrines were explained.	20
8	The period of Mar-pa, the Prince of Translators, and his successors, the so-called Ka-gyü-pas.	142
9	The period of Ko-trak-pa and Nigu.[1]	13
10	The period of the Wheel of Time (Kala Chakra) Tantra and its teachings.	41
11	The period of the Great Symbol (Mahamudra).	16
12	The period of Kamala Shila and his doctrine, called 'The Alleviation of Misery'.	50
13	The period of Ka-rak and the doctrine called 'The Object of Cutting'.[2]	12
14	The doctrines relating to The Great Compassionate One (Chen-re-zi), and the Sublime Rosary (Vajramala) doctrines.	25
15	A summary showing how the Holy Religion came, and how the sect known as Sarvastivadins came.	14

[1] Ko-trak-pa was a well-known lama, and Nigu was Naropa's wife.

[2] This is one of the only, perhaps the only, Buddhist school, which originated in Tibet and thence spread to India. It appears to involve living in awe-inspiring places, renouncing all attachment to one's body, and thereby obtaining freedom from one's Ego or individuality.

INDEX

TIBET
Statute Miles
50 0 50 100 150 200
MONGOLIA
CHINESE TURKISTAN
SINKIANG
TAKLA MAKAN DESERT
PAMIRS
AFGHANISTAN
KASHMIR
LADAKH
LAHUL
PANJAB
CHANG TANG
TIBET
NAGCHUKA
TSANG
Lhasa
Shigatse
AMDO
GOLOK
SZECHWAN
YUNNAN
NEPAL
BHUTAN
ASSAM
BURMA
UNITED PROVINCES
BIHAR
BENGAL
INDIA
CHINA
KANSU
TSAIDAM
Kokoshili
Tang La Mts
Delhi
Agra
Simla
Lahore
Srinagar
Katmandu
Mt Everest
Chamdo
Batang
Chengtu
Lanchowfu
Khotan
Kashgar
Yarkand
Gartok
Darjeeling